AMERICA'S DARK THEOLOGIAN

America's Dark Theologian

The Religious Imagination of Stephen King

Douglas E. Cowan

NEW YORK UNIVERSITY PRESS
New York

NEW YORK UNIVERSITY PRESS
New York
www.nyupress.org

References to Internet websites (URLs) were accurate at the time of writing. Neither the author nor New York University Press is responsible for URLs that may have expired or changed since the manuscript was prepared.

Library of Congress Cataloging-in-Publication Data
Names: Cowan, Douglas E., author.
Title: America's dark theologian : the religious imagination of Stephen King /
Douglas E. Cowan.
Description: New York : NYU Press, 2018. | Includes bibliographical references and index.
Identifiers: LCCN 2017037991 | ISBN 9781479894734 (cl : alk. paper)
Subjects: LCSH: King, Stephen, 1947– —Criticism and interpretation. |
Religion in literature. | Theology in literature.
Classification: LCC PS3561.I483 Z6289 2018 | DDC 813/.54—dc23
LC record available at https://lccn.loc.gov/2017037991

New York University Press books are printed on acid-free paper, and their binding materials are chosen for strength and durability. We strive to use environmentally responsible suppliers and materials to the greatest extent possible in publishing our books.

Manufactured in the United States of America

10 9 8 7 6 5 4 3 2 1

Also available as an ebook

This one's for Gary, who taught me that everything's grist for our mill.

CONTENTS

Imagine you're in an airport boarding lounge, or the waiting room at virtually any train station or bus terminal in the Western world. Maybe you commute to work or school by subway. It doesn't matter. Look around. Somewhere in there, among hundreds of fellow travelers, lurks the shade of a tall, lanky man in a Red Sox gimme cap. Maybe they brought him with them, or bought him at a newsstand after swiping through the turnstile. Maybe they downloaded him, seemingly out of thin air, and he's hiding on an iPad or a Kobo. He may even be lying open in someone's lap, real words on a real page. However he appears, though, chances are he's there. Somewhere.

Stephen King.

America's dark theologian.

For more than four decades, in more than sixty novels, ten collections of short stories, and half a dozen nonfiction works, King has been one of popular culture's most constant and consistent literary companions. His books have sold hundreds of millions of copies and been translated into dozens of languages. Drawn in by his storyworlds, millions of fans avidly await each release, entranced in ways they might not even understand, yet eager to see what the acknowledged master of modern horror has to offer. Whenever a new Stephen King novel hit the shelves, the mother of a friend of mine always bought two copies: a first-edition hardcover "for keeping," the spine never cracked, the dust jacket kept in mint condition, and a softcover reading copy, carried everywhere and read to tatters. Today, a signed first edition of any of King's early works easily commands thousands of dollars on the used book market. A matched, signed, and uncut set of *The Dark Tower* novels can be yours on eBay for a little more than $30,000—about what many people pay for their first new car.

Countless more people are familiar with King's work as it's been adapted for film and television, whether that means for the big screen by A-list directors (Stanley Kubrick's *The Shining* or Brian De Palma's *Carrie*) or serialized for broadcast on B-list networks (TNT's *Nightmares and Dreamscapes*). Many of King's novels and short stories have been filmed for the straight-to-DVD market, while others have seen world-wide release and won entertainment culture's highest awards. Maybe you've seen *The Green Mile* or *Misery* or *Under the Dome*. Maybe you've read a few of his novels or a collection or two of his short fiction. Maybe you think you know Stephen King.

Think again.

One afternoon, as King tells us in the author's notes to *The Bazaar of Bad Dreams*, his wife, novelist Tabitha King, sent him to the store for "batteries and a non-stick frypan." Seems a simple enough task, but one that apparently also required "a few other absolute necessities (cinnamon buns and potato chips)." While weighing the merits of low-sodium ridged over kettle-cooked, King was approached by an elderly woman. "She was a Florida snowbird archetype," he writes, "about eighty, permed to perfection, and as darkly tanned as a cordovan shoe."[1]

"'I know you,' she said. 'You're Stephen King. You write those scary stories. That's all right, some people like them, but not me. I like uplifting stories, like that *Shawshank Redemption*.'" Looking down from his towering height, King told her, "I wrote that too." We can only imagine the woman's eyes narrowing ever so slightly as she replied, "No, you didn't," and then continued down the aisle, primly ensconced in her motorized cart.[2]

The elderly woman's disbelief notwithstanding, the sheer range of King's writing is almost without precedent. To get a sense of his work, go to any large bookstore and see how many *different* titles he has on the shelves. Browse the publication dates and you'll realize that he has averaged more than a book a year, sometimes several in one year, since his breakout novel, *Carrie*, first appeared in 1974. Not only can few writers lay claim to such productive consistency, fewer still can do so while working in as many different subtypes of genre fiction. While he may be best known for his "scary stories," *The Eyes of the Dragon* and *The Dark Tower* series, which King himself regards as his *magnum opus*, are solidly in the realm of epic fantasy. *Joyland* is a hard-boiled *noir* crime tale, while the Bill Hodges novels—*Mr. Mercedes*, *Finders Keepers*, and *End of Watch*—are more at home as murder mysteries.

In terms of critical attention, however, King's prodigious output has often worked against him. Tony magazines and newspapers often take a certain delight in damning King with faint praise, scorning his work as boarding lounge fiction and deriding it as escapism paddling about at the shallow end of the literary pool. "I don't really think of King as a bad writer," begins the *Guardian*'s Alastair Harper. "As my girlfriend is always reminding me, his portrayals of small-town America are sometimes brilliant."[3] In 2003, when King received the National Book Foundation's Medal of Distinguished Contribution to American Letters, an outraged Harold Bloom condemned the decision in no uncertain terms. Writing in the *Boston Globe*, the so-called dean of American literary critics declared it "extraordinary, another low in the shocking process of dumbing down our cultural life."[4] Describing King as "an immensely inadequate writer," though Bloom thought even that was "perhaps too kind," he concluded that the only reason that explained the foundation's decision was "the commercial value" of King's books.[5] Bloom admits that King's novels and short story collections sell "in the millions," but complains that they "do little more for humanity than keep the publishing world afloat."[6] Four years later, when Bloom edited an anthology of essays on King's work, he concluded that rather than as a writer "King will be remembered as a sociological phenomenon."[7] Which is to say, he will be known for the fact that millions of people loved his books and found something meaningful in them.

As much as anything, these debates disclose the often petty and manufactured distinctions between genre fiction and "serious literature," suggesting almost nonsensically that readers who embrace one cannot enjoy the other. By ignoring or rejecting writers such as Stephen King, critics reinforce these arbitrary notions of taste, of *distinction*, as the French sociologist Pierre Bourdieu put it, of highbrow versus lowbrow art.[8]

For his part, King accepts the reality of "being dismissed by the more intellectual critics as a hack," though he points out that "the intellectual's definition of a hack seems to be 'an artist whose work is appreciated by too many people.'"[9] Indeed, few such reviewers pause to ask *why* we find King haunting airports, train stations, and bus terminals around the world. Fewer still seem to realize that many of King's readers seek their escape in his sinister storyworlds precisely because of the plain, unremarkable, yet profoundly disturbing "us" he presents. Reflected there in his dark mirror, we see shades of ourselves.

This book explores the storyworlds of Stephen King, and shows how his novels and short stories continually confront the answers we have been given about questions of ultimate meaning, questions we often think of as "religious." It makes the case that, whether we are talking about sacred narrative or genre fiction, the *stories we tell* play an indispensable role in the ongoing human quest to understand our place in the universe.

No book on popular culture can, or should, be considered the complete guide to anything. Certainly not an *anything* as expansive and varied as the work of Stephen King. Rather, explorations of literature, film, art, and television succeed or fail precisely to the degree that they open audiences up to *possibility*, to the myriad questions of human being that popular culture continually prompts us to ask. Possibility does not depend on the answers we get, however, since questions are ultimately more interesting, more revealing, and more enduring than answers. Because while answers change—"No, Your Holiness, the earth actually revolves around the sun"—the questions remain largely the same: Who are we? Where do we come from? Where do we go when we're gone?

Like much of popular culture, though, genre fiction has often been dismissed as unworthy of scholarly attention. "Popular," however, must never be mistaken for "unimportant." Those ensconced in the ivory tower often argue themselves silly over a broken bit of pottery from an early hominin kitchen site—a shard that may or may not have been from the bowl where the family spat its olive pits—but they ignore the midden of popular culture that is all around us and can tell us so much about who we are and who we aspire to be.[10] In answer to the question "Why study religion?" my alma mater's website reads, "Religion has inspired great works of art and literature." This is certainly true, but what about other kinds of art and literature? What about those that take us in a different direction? That is, what can *popular* culture tell us about religious beliefs, practices, and imaginings? As it happens, quite a lot.

Whether we're talking about the nature of death and what lies beyond, or the religious rituals that invest our lives with meaning; whether we're watching varieties of faith experience unfold in his storyworlds, or wondering about the nature of the universe itself; whether we see ourselves reflected in his fiction, or see in it those around us—King's work constantly invites his readers to consider their place in the grand scheme of things. This is part of what it means to read Stephen King religiously.

And, however loathe some intellectuals may be to admit it, masses of people *do* read King's work. They are moved by it. They are changed by it. They eagerly await whatever he has coming next. This is because, above all, King believes in the power of narrative, the ability of a well-told story to affect people at the most profound levels. He sees "stories as a great thing, something which not only enhances lives but actually saves them."[11] "Nor am I speaking metaphorically," he continues. "Good writing—good *stories*—are imagination's firing pin, and the purpose of the imagination, I believe, is to offer us solace and shelter from situations and life-passages which would otherwise prove unendurable."[12]

This book takes Stephen King, America's dark theologian, at his word.

* * *

As always, there are a number of people to thank for their contributions to this book. No author works entirely alone, however much it may feel that way at times. Though there are more people to salute than I can include here by name, I'd like to single out a few.

My gratitude goes first to my editor at New York University Press, Jennifer Hammer. We met a long time ago and have always wanted "to do something together." For a variety of reasons, it's taken fifteen years, but I could not be more pleased that this book wound up in her careful hands. It is all the better for that. I would also like to thank the three external reviewers for the time and careful attention they gave the book's initial draft. Time is often a scholar's most precious resource, and I want to acknowledge the willingness of colleagues to spend some of theirs with my work. It's always a bit daunting to await the evaluation of colleagues, but it never fails to be rewarding. I would like to acknowledge my friend David Annable, who graciously allowed me to use the anecdote about his late mother, Stephen King's "number-one fan" in southern Ontario. There is also my own Constant Reader, my wife, Joie. She's not a horror fan; her tastes run more to murder mysteries, the dark Scandinavian ones that I don't understand. Despite that, as she has with each of my other books, she read the initial drafts and offered her usual helpful, if occasionally critical ("This part doesn't make any sense") commentary.

More than that, she read some of Stephen King's books, notably the Bill Hodges trilogy, and pointed out where they fit with the notion of reading horror religiously—and, more importantly, where they didn't.

Lastly, I want to thank Gary Ebersole, historian, scholar of religion, consummate gentleman. At some point in Stephen King's literary history, an acquisitions editor at Doubleday pulled a manuscript titled *Carrie* off the slush pile and launched a career that, more than four decades later, shows no signs of slowing down. That is, at some point, someone gave King a break. And we all need that occasionally. What we do with the break is up to us, but we still need it. My break came when Gary pulled my application off the slush pile of CVs and resumés, and hired me for my first job out of graduate school. During the years I spent working with him at the University of Missouri–Kansas City, he taught me many things—nearly all of which I still carry with me into the classroom and pass on to my own students. Among the most important of these insights was, "Everything is grist for our mill." Nothing is insignificant, except in the ways we choose to look at it. Many people may find Stephen King's work interesting, but I hope this book demonstrates why it is also important. It is grist for the mill of our religious imagination.

Introduction

You know the place. Every small town has one. The place your parents warned you about, where you're never supposed to go. The abandoned mill out by the rail bridge. The mental hospital up on the hill, now silent and shuttered. The last house on the left at the end of the block. In our town, it was the old Walker place out on Marsden Road.

And, of course, we went. It was the summer of 1984, the last time I slept a whole night through.

The Walker place had been deserted long before any of us were born. As far back as we could remember, there were two signs hung on the gate with baling wire. One said, "For Sale," the other, "Keep Out." Mom said it was because old man Walker had been crazy, and dug wells all over the place, and we could fall in and die. "You'd be like one of them milk-carton kids," she said, lighting up another Marlboro. I don't know. Maybe that was it. Maybe it was something else. By the end of school that year, though, when we all got out of grade seven, we knew: We were going to the old Walker place.

The day we rode out there was like any other summer day. We all met up at the school and started out. Jerry was on his new ten-speed, the one his parents got him from Happy's for passing seventh grade. I'd saved all winter and just put new tires on my BMX. Knobbies, for better traction. Kelsey had borrowed her brother's bike. I always wondered if he knew.

As always, we talked about what we thought happened. "Baby sacr'fice," Jerry said, laughing like he knew everything. He always talked like he knew everything. "Nah," I said, "it's just murder. Mom says old man Walker killed his whole family one night. Said he went crazy 'cause they were taking his farm."

"No!" Jerry insisted, "he didn't *kill* them, he sacr'ficed them. That's how he got to keep the farm so long. He made a deal with the Devil, that's what Matt's dad says." Matt's a PK, a preacher's kid. We don't go to his church—most of us are Catholic—but we let him hang around sometimes. He wasn't there that day, though.

1

"You're so full of shit," Kelsey said, leaning on the handlebars of her bike when we stopped for a rest. She was the oldest, by a few months, and the tallest, and the smartest.

I miss her.

From the gravel shoulder off Marsden Road, it looked like any other abandoned farm. There were enough of them around. Yard overgrown with weeds and volunteer wheat, an old disc harrow rusting by the side of the drive shed. The sort of thing photographers from the city came and took pictures of, to document something our parents called "the crisis."

Others had been here before us. Older kids mostly, come out here to drink or smoke, maybe do other things. They'd left their mark, painting their courage on the derelict walls with spray cans. *Bobby Maxwell was here* on one side of the garage. *Fuk you, Jason* on the other, with what might have been a drawing of a bloody machete. We'd all seen the movies. "See," Jerry said, pointing at an upside-down star painted in red on the sagging boards of the porch, "that's a Satan symbol." Kelsey just curled her lip and cupped her hands around her eyes, trying to see in through the grimy glass of the front window.

The creepiest, though, was right over the door. A single word.

Don't.

We thought the door would be locked, but it wasn't. Mark pushed and it swung inward on rusty, squealing hinges. He went in first. Mark never said much, but he was the strongest and he always went in first. We watched as he took a few steps into the narrow foyer. "It's fine," he said. We crowded in behind him. The light was dim and the air smelled of mold and damp and bird shit. Some furniture was still there, but it was all falling apart too.

"Jesus," Jerry said, "wouldja look at this place?" We moved along into the living room, our flashlights cutting through the dust, but not really giving us much light. I smacked mine on my palm and wished I'd thought to look for fresh batteries. I heard a creak and turned my head as Kelsey started up the stairs to the second floor. I was just about to warn her, when Mark spoke again, this time louder.

"Who shut the door?" he asked.

* * *

Throughout history, we have embedded the most powerful products of our imagination in narrative. When things come to us in the form of a legend, a parable, a fable, or even a local ghost story, we remember them more easily and pass them on more eagerly to friends and family. This is true not only of scary stories, but also of religious myths, the tales of faith in which we are often most deeply invested. Indeed, rather than seemingly endless lists of rules, directives, and prohibitions, religious belief has evolved principally through shared storytelling. At some point, one ancient Mesopotamian said to another, "Hey, tell us about Gilgamesh again," and our earliest recorded creation myth was passed around the campfire once more. Fifteen centuries later, the Greek poet Hesiod gathered the tales of the gods into his *Theogony*, one of our first attempts at a systematic cosmology. A thousand years after that, followers of a Nazarene peasant began weaving stories together that gradually became the Gospels of Jesus Christ. It seems that, as a species, we are addicted to narrative, and wherever our questions of deepest meaning began—a sudden awareness of the *difference* of death, an existential *dread* roused by the sheer weight of the stars—we have always couched our answers, the certainty of our religious imaginings, in story.[1]

For more than twenty-five years, Cedar Creek's Trinity Church has mounted a massive, Christian-themed alternative to the traditional Halloween haunted house. Using its version of the "old Walker place out on Marsden Road," this fundamentalist congregation southeast of Austin, Texas, presents its vision of the relationship between humankind and the divine, between the seen and the unseen orders of reality.[2] As long lines of visitors tour the house, culturally relevant vignettes tell a series of short stories. A young man suffering with AIDS refuses to repent of his "homosexual lifestyle" and accept Jesus as his savior. When he dies, a pair of cackling demons drag him away. Bleeding to death after taking RU-486, the so-called morning-after pill, a young girl screams, "Jesus save me!" moments before she dies. Suddenly, an angel appears in the room, imperiously warding off the Devil's minions come to claim her soul. Over the years, tens, perhaps hundreds, of thousands of people have witnessed the Hell House performance. In doing so, they have experienced the stories through which Trinity Church answers questions of meaning and significance, or, as Douglas Adams put it, questions of life, the universe, and everything. Not everyone agrees with their answers, but that isn't the point. It's the questions that matter.

Week in and week out, sermons without number lay the consequences of sin before the Christian faithful. What makes Hell House different is *story*. These devout believers present their theology, their god-talk, through imagination and performance, every part of which says to visitors, "under the right set of circumstances, this could happen" to you, so choose wisely.[3] Indeed, a regular contributor to Trinity's annual production claims that he doesn't really understand much about theology. He just "knows the Bible is true," that "Jesus died for my sins," and that the stories presented in Hell House are God's way of reaching out to the lost.[4] Because the notion of "theology" has become mystified over time, however, as though only certain people are qualified to do it, this man doesn't realize just how much theology, how much god-talk, is actually happening in these few words. However complex Christian fundamentalists want to make it appear, their theology, which is nothing more or less than their understanding of how the seen and the unseen orders of reality relate to each other, is not much more complicated than he describes. Making no apologies for their religious beliefs, members of the Trinity Hell House team don't pretend to explore issues in depth or to present alternative viewpoints. That's not the object of the exercise. For them, their Hell House storytelling leads only and always to what they consider The Answer.

Not so with the work of Stephen King.

As "America's dark theologian," for more than four decades King has raised the same questions of meaning and existence in his horror fiction. His work only rarely offers anything like a solid answer, though. "I didn't want to write about answers," he tells his readers in *Just after Sunset*, "I wanted to write about questions."[5] From short fiction such as "Children of the Corn" and "N." to "That Feeling, You Can Only Say What It Is in French," from novels such as *The Stand*, *It*, and *Pet Sematary* to *Insomnia*, *Desperation*, and *Duma Key*, his storyworlds continually probe the same issues the good people of Trinity Church claim to have settled. It is this questioning through story that places his work alongside religion in the long history of human inquiry and imagination. More often than not, King's "scary stories" contest religious certainties and challenge the limited ways we grapple with our place in the unknowable and the unseen. "Each answer remains in force as an answer," wrote philosopher Martin Heidegger in "The Origins of the Work of Art," "only as long as it is rooted in questioning."[6] An answer is an answer only so long as we continue to ask the questions. For Stephen King, when it comes to issues of ultimate meaning, "only fiction can approach answers to those questions. Only *through* fiction can we think about the unthinkable, and perhaps obtain some kind of closure."[7] Indeed, as writer Gordie La-Chance says in King's novella "The Body," "*the only two useful artforms are religion and stories.*"[8]

In this respect, like that of myriad other horror writers, King's work is not that different from stories that have become classics of religious mythology.[9] Forerunner legends, ghost stories, spooky tales, and the like all offer their own form of "god-talk." They invite us to consider the questions that matter most, but they do so outside the bounds of formal religious institutions. "A good horror story," King writes in *Danse Macabre*, which still stands as one of the most useful histories of the genre, "is one that functions on a symbolic level, using fictional (and sometimes supernatural) events to help us understand our own deepest fears."[10]

Scholars from a variety of disciplines argue that the human experience of religion began with fear, particularly our awareness of death.[11] Others have noted that religious mythology worldwide is replete with both monsters and monstrosity, the vocabulary we use to give voice to our fears.[12] More than any other genre, with the possible exception of science fiction, this connection makes the horror story religion's conceptual and cultural sibling, often asking the same questions as religion while challenging religion's answers to them.

Considering such works as *Carrie*, *The Dead Zone*, *The Shining*, and *Under the Dome*, this book asks what the novels and short fiction of one of the acknowledged masters of modern horror can tell us about the religious imagination. "Some of horror's current popularity," King told interviewers and audiences early in his career, "has to do with the failure of religion."[13] His comment, though, begs the question, failure at *what*? Failure *to do* what? King describes himself as a "fallen-away Methodist" and his wife, Tabitha, as "a fallen-away Catholic." They are a modern man and woman for whom the answers provided by their respective churches no longer hold much significance. All of which is to say, yes, for millions of people like Stephen and Tabitha King, religion *has* failed to provide meaningful answers—sometimes spectacularly so. But the *questions* have not disappeared. The fears and anxieties, the profound ambivalence with which we regard the world—these remain. The existential crises haunting humankind since our minds first developed the capacity to wonder about life are not resolved simply because many of us now realize that children's stories about a talking snake or a boat carrying two kinds of everything are not sufficient for adults.

Who are we? is not answered with a catalog of social roles or a recitation of scriptural pieties. *How did we get here?* might be explained in strict biological terms, but to avoid existentialist despair we crave something more than that. *What is the purpose of our existence, the meaning of life?* Because we are both self- and other-centered, because we have strong instincts both for self-preservation and for the protection of the group, we wonder at the heart of it all, *Do we matter?*

Although, by cultural convention and social dominance, we have tended to label these kinds of questions *religious*, they are not. For millennia, they have been both relegated to and co-opted by that part of our life experience we call "religion," but they are not religious questions per se. Instead, we should more appropriately consider them *human questions*, wonderings and inquiries universal to our species, and to which horror writers such as Stephen King return over and over. They belong to us as a function of our humanity, not our participation in this belief system or that. Put simply, questions of meaning and purpose, suffering and justice, existence and extinction, even truth and beauty—these are all *properly human questions*.

As we will see, storytelling in popular culture is not only a fitting way to consider key questions and concepts ordinarily associated with "religion," it is often a more useful and more elegant way to engage these topics. Reviewers and critics commonly hold up *The Stand* as King's most obvious (or even his singular) "religious" novel, or they point out in passing that *Carrie* features a fundamentalist Christian as a principal character. What they rarely note, however, and what no one has considered in any serious way, is the depth to which religious imagery, themes, characters, contexts, and problems inform the range of King's horror fiction. In fact, a great many of his novels and short stories not only treat these topics in compelling and sophisticated ways, but also place religious questions center-stage in his many and varied storyworlds.

Fair Warning: Religion and the Scary Story

This book, it should be noted, is not about "horror *as* religion," and King himself proposes no particular "dark theology," no unified vision of the relationship between the seen and the unseen order. Nowhere does he suggest, "This is how it is" or "how it should be," as though diligent readers could piece together a systematic theology from scattered fragments of his novels and short stories. King's horror fiction contains no counterpart, for instance, to the Cthulhu mythos that legions of H. P. Lovecraft's fans have assembled in the decades since his death.[14] Although Stephen King's storyworlds, thematic approaches, and plotlines live with each other in a kind of loose connection—most notably through the Castle Rock novels and what I call the Derry cycle—they invite no equivalent attempt to create a coherent or consistent theology. Rather, his novels and short stories continually confront the answers we have been given and often hold to as gospel.

Neither is this "horror *in place of religion*," as though, as many critics argue, scary stories somehow function as stealth arguments for secularization.[15] Certainly, few of King's overtly religious characters come off well, but his myriad dark wonderings are not meant to reflect the end of religious belief as we know it. Indeed, quite the opposite. Rather than secularization, horror stories regularly reveal "an overwhelming *ambivalence* toward the religious traditions, beliefs, practices, and mythistories by which we are confronted, in which we are often still deeply invested, which we are distinctly unwilling to relinquish, and which we just as often only minimally understand."[16] Though his characters and plotlines regularly comment on recognizable religious belief, King's stories consistently question the limited and provincial ways we understand the unseen order and our relationship to it.

Our society is, for all practical purposes, religiously illiterate. For many of us, if we know anything about religion at all, it tends to be that razor-thin slice of the religious spectrum we call our own—and then, perhaps not even that very well. "The paradox is this," writes religious studies scholar Stephen Prothero: "Americans are both deeply religious and profoundly ignorant about religion. They are Protestants who can't name the four Gospels, Catholics who can't name the seven sacraments, and Jews who can't name the five books of Moses."[17]

This phenomenon does not suggest that Americans are not devout, that tens of millions do not remain deeply committed to religious faith as a bedrock principle in both their personal lives and larger society. Indeed, according to the Pew Research Center, slightly more than half of Americans say that religion is "very important" in their lives, and this number rises to nearly 80 percent when we include those who respond that religion is "somewhat important" to them. While "the share of U.S. adults who say they believe in God" has declined slightly in recent years, Pew researchers point out that this number is "still remarkably high by comparison with other advanced industrial countries."[18] As we will see, many of these believers regularly haunt the pages of King's storyworlds.

Yet Prothero is not wrong. Devotion to one's faith does not necessarily equate to a depth of knowledge about it or an ability to recognize when that faith is being represented. And, if he's right, and we know so little about our own religions, how much less do we know about the faith traditions of others? Put differently, more often than not we reduce "religion" to what we most readily and easily recognize as religion, and are comfortable accepting as religion. Churches, mosques, and temples we understand. Confronted with the frantic abandon of the Hindu festival of Holi, however, or the profound silence of a Zen Buddhist *sesshin*, how many United Methodists, Roman Catholics, or Sunni Muslims would see there a faith as deep as the one they proclaim? Religiously speaking, then, and this is King's point throughout his work, we barely know where we are, let alone understand where we came from, how we got here, or where we're going.

As we will see throughout this book, although King regularly uses religious themes and routinely thrusts religious characters onto his storyworld stage, these are only partially intended as commentary. That he detests fundamentalism is clear. Jerry Falwell, for example, he considers "a monster."[19] But that doesn't mean that he doesn't believe in the phenomenon of religious fundamentalism, or the power of single-minded zealotry. His storyworlds are *about* religion in that they consistently call into question the incomplete, insular, and self-congratulatory ways we so often imagine the unseen order and our place in it. Over and over, he suggests that things may be vastly different than we suppose. Put differently, Stephen King's novels and short stories are horror fiction written *alongside* religion, and emerge from the same place in the human imagination.

For this book, we will stay with the works for which King is most commonly albeit incompletely known: the "scary stories" so disliked by the elderly woman in the Sarasota supermarket. We will focus on his horror fiction, rather than epic fantasy such as *The Eyes of the Dragon* or his magisterial *Dark Tower* series, or his ventures into the crime procedural.[20] We will also concentrate on his literary works, rather than the various and uneven ways filmmakers and television producers have adapted his novels and short fiction for both the big screen and the small. If fear is the genesis of the human religious imagination, a "subject for which tales of the fantastic were made," then King's horror fiction invites us into storyworlds that cut closest to the bones of faith.[21] His work in other genres may certainly include scenes that frighten the audience in order to advance the narrative, but King's scary stories are written explicitly to frighten his Constant Reader. "In the former, fear is a side-effect; in the latter, it is the object of the exercise."[22] Because of this, the dark theologian's god-talk is read most clearly through the lens of his horror fiction.

Something's Coming: The Road Ahead

One of the most obvious yet least acknowledged aspects of religious belief and experience is that what we *know* about reality pales almost to insignificance when compared to what we *don't*. No matter how dogmatically religious believers declare the truth of their convictions, theology of any kind remains contingent and conjectural. The first two chapters of this book begin our journey of "thinking religiously" about King's scary stories. We will grapple with what we think religion means, and with what we fear it might suggest. Because, at the end of the day, "reality is a mystery," as the tormented N. tells his therapist in the short story of the same name. "There are places where the cloth gets ragged and reality is thin."[23]

What presses in on those thin spots, what peeks through the cracks in the world, endlessly intrigues Stephen King, just as it has our ancestors going back hundreds if not thousands of generations. Are human beings the product—or perhaps the by-product—of some ancient alien planetfall (*Dreamcatcher*; *The Tommyknockers*; *Under the Dome*)? Does this crack in the world lead to some other, unimaginable dimension (*From a Buick 8*; "Mile 81")? Or is our world little more than a fragile globe of seeming sanity, surrounded by monstrous and malevolent gods ("N."; *Revival*)? And, however it happens, when those cracks in the world are forced open, what looks back at us from beyond? What tries to push its way through? And how do we react when it succeeds?

If the religious imagination claims to describe the framework of reality, King's writing constantly pokes at whatever structure we erect, asking, among other things, How do you know? Where is your evidence? What if you're wrong? Hidden among these is the question of where the human religious experience, our overwhelming sense that *this is not all there is*, originates. In this respect, between the seen and the unseen orders, few spots are thinner than the moment of death. Faced with the inevitable prospect of a world in which we are *not*, how can we do anything but ask, What comes next?

Death is the great and certain mystery. It is the primal experience, the *ur*-fear from which so much of our religious imaginings have evolved and toward which so much of religious belief is directed. What we think about death informs how we think about reality. This is one reason, as King writes in *Just after Sunset*, that "the subject of the afterlife . . . has always been fertile soil for writers who are comfortable with the fantastic."[24] As the dark theologian, King returns again and again to the question that has haunted hominins since they first realized there was something inescapably *different* when one of their small clan stopped moving. At their most basic level, after all, religions are ritualized conjectures for answering our questions about death, allaying our fears when it happens, and preparing us for it when the dark rider appears on our own horizon. Horror fiction treads this same path, asking its questions and telling its stories alongside religious myth.

Beginning with the experience of death, chapters 3 and 4 consider not only the origins of religious belief—ghost stories as god-talk—but the ways we pass those beliefs on to our children. That is, how do we go about becoming religious? How we become believers, learn about our faith, and maintain those beliefs in the face of both option and opposition is the problem of *religious socialization*. Equally important, though, are the lasting effects of this process, the various ways that socialization shapes events that occur even decades later. Once again, these are not stories that settle the issue. They're not intended as comfort food for the faithful. Rather, they continually remind us of our hunger for answers.

However we acquire them, our religious beliefs come to life through ritual: from the simple act of lighting a candle to the complexity of a Buddhist sand mandala, from the solemnity of High Mass to the riot of Kumbh Mela. Through ritual we embody the great questions of existence. We place them in cosmic context, while grounding them in the circumstances of everyday life. We ritualize life events, locating them in meaningful relationship to both the seen and unseen orders. Through ritual we *realize* our beliefs, and for decades anthropologists and ritual studies scholars have pointed to *the ritual process* as one of the principal ways we make our deepest beliefs tangible. Chapters 5 and 6 explore King's approaches to these key questions of *religious experience*.

Finally, chapters 7 and 8 return to the big issues of meaning and existence. How we believe "God" acts tells us who (or what) we think "God" is. Picking up various threads of religious experience, King tugs at the question, What if "God" is not there, or what if "God" is there, but just doesn't give a damn? Which would be worse? What if "God" turned out to be unlike anything we could possibly imagine—or would even want to imagine? These are the questions of *theodicy* and *theology*, the justification of God as a function of the nature of God. Two of the most important topics in any system of religious belief, together they raise the central question beating at the heart of all horror fiction: Why is there evil? How do we explain suffering? Why are there monsters? And how do we survive?

"When we discuss monstrosity," King writes in *Danse Macabre*, "we are expressing our faith and belief in the norm and watching for the mutant. The writer of horror fiction is neither more nor less than an agent of the status quo."[25] Historically, religions have been the *sine qua nons* of normative agents, in part because they raise questions of normativity in cosmic terms: salvation is at stake, not simply difference; the universe hangs in the balance, not just whether one group triumphs over another. Religions continue, and continue to evolve, because we are rarely satisfied with the answers we get, and those we can imagine rarely survive for long.

Just so our scary stories.

1

America's Dark Theologian

Reading Stephen King Religiously

Few critical works that concentrate on Stephen King's horror fiction contain a separate index entry for "religion," none for "theology."[1] Tony Magistrale's *Landscape of Fear* is a rare exception, but even that relegates discussion of religion to a few pages, and Magistrale, who has written more about King than other scholars, concludes that "the religious dimension in King's work defies easy categorization."[2] This may be true, but merely pointing that out isn't very helpful. After a few passing comments, which include an almost obligatory nod to *The Stand* as "perhaps King's most religious book to date," on the one hand, Magistrale ends up avoiding the issue, content instead to regard "the real horrors in Stephen King's canon [as] sociopolitical in nature."[3] That is, in an analytic move that is common in pop culture critique, whatever looks like religion, or could be interpreted religiously, must mean something else. On the other hand, Magistrale suggests that the "fictional portrayal of organized religion in his books is an untempered reflection of King's own personal beliefs."[4] In this he's not entirely wrong, but his conclusion reflects a rather limited and parochial understanding of "religion." When he uses concepts such as "basic Christian principles" and "true religious sentiments," they become little more than superficial abstractions, empty placeholders in the broader conversation about religion in general and King's work in particular.[5] They suggest that religion in Stephen King is the exception, rather than the rule, and that his real questions lie elsewhere.

The reality is rather different. Indeed, religion as a social and cultural constant, and theology as a way of thinking about the nature of reality itself, are rarely absent from King's varied storyworlds.[6] Many different types of religious believers populate his stories. Some of them are bad people—*Carrie*'s mother, Margaret White, *Under the Dome*'s corrupt politician, Big Jim Rennie, or the unnamed woman in *Cell*, "the elderly crazy lady with a Bible and a beauty-shop perm" who attacks survivors of the Pulse as they flee Boston.[7] Others, such as *Desperation*'s David Carver and Johnny Marinville, *Under the Dome*'s Piper Libby, and even *The Dead Zone*'s Vera Smith, who struggles to maintain her faith in the face of her son's horrific accident, are more like the people we see around us every day. They're just trying to get by. Simply saying that there are "religious" characters in King's fiction, though, or that they are of a certain type doesn't begin to plumb the depths of what these storyworlds can tell us about the nature of religious belief and the power of the religious imagination at work. Indeed, phrases such as "basic Christian principles" and "true religious sentiments" are often little more than sly ways of saying "my (correct) religion" as opposed to "your (false or hypocritical) religion." When we oversimplify the vast and complex array of human religious beliefs and practices, "religion" often becomes "that which we clearly and unambiguously recognize *as* religion"—which, as Stephen Prothero points out, is often an indictment of people's religious illiteracy, rather than a comment on the poverty of our mythic imagination.[8]

Often regarded as one of King's most explicitly religious works, *The Stand* follows humankind's struggle to survive in the wake of a global pandemic, the Captain Trips virus. Although this is hardly a novel scenario, in King's hands one side in the war to reinvent society lines up behind God's champion, embodied in the elderly Mother Abagail, the other behind Randall Flagg, who is alternately imagined as the Antichrist or the Devil himself. Magistrale calls the book an "elaborate allegory embracing the ultimate conflict between the forces of good and evil in the world."[9] While many fans do read the book as a religious allegory, they do so because King makes these allegiances explicit. We see "religion" because he tells us that that's what we're supposed to see, and because he provides us with clear and easily identifiable religious markers.

Indeed, although it's written neither for Christians nor by an evangelical believer, *The Stand* can be read in a line of Christian apocalyptic fiction that stretches back more than a century.[10] The seemingly endless *Left Behind* series, written by televangelist Tim LaHaye and novelist Jerry Jenkins, is merely the genre's most recognizable entry. Since the late 1960s this kind of end-times storytelling has been buttressed by an evangelical cottage industry devoted to analyses of current events through the lens of what believers consider biblical prophecy. Rooted in nineteenth-century evangelicalism, though popularized by Hal Lindsey's 1970 bestseller *The Late Great Planet Earth*, the genre has spawned myriad imitations. These are stories told by believers for believers, however, and millions of Christians read them already convinced that God has divided history into a number of distinct periods, known among the faithful as "dispensations." Worldwide chaos heralds the last of these periods, which is marked by the rise of a charismatic, seemingly all-powerful world leader and savior, but concludes with the battle of Armageddon. In the end, as scripture foretells, God triumphs—something Christian readers both understand and expect. Certainly, *The Stand* can be read this way, but so what?

Mapping easily recognizable religious ideas onto King's story may satisfy our sense of the novel's allegorical importance, but it also blinkers us to the myriad other ways religion and theology permeate his work. Put differently, if we simply rely on the familiar, we are less likely to recognize the unfamiliar as "religious." We are less inclined to consider the possibility that what we typically think of as "religion" might encompass only a small fraction of human interaction with the divine, or that it might have other connotations altogether. Good and evil, for example, are neither explicitly religious concepts nor the proprietary domain of religion. Yet, when we use them as ways to limit whether something is religious or not, we exclude the many other ways King prods us to question the nature of what we call "religion" and its implications for our understanding of reality. Because, with both Stephen King and the human religious imagination, it's not about the answers we get.

It's all about the questions we continue to ask.

Although we often treat it this way, it is *not* the case that something called "religion" exists as a category separate and distinct from the rest of the social and cultural world. It's not that we know a story is "religious" simply because it contains readily available religious iconography or symbolism. There may be a priest or a church, someone may shout, "Oh God, save me!" in a moment of panic, but this kind of superficial equation is both too easy and too common.[11] It ignores a much deeper truth about the stories we tell—and the stories that stick in our minds and our culture. Both the stories we have labeled "religious" and the other fictional storyworlds we create emerge from the same place in our imagination. Both are manifestations of the human search for meaning, our ongoing need to question, and our constant dissatisfaction with whatever answers we find. It's important to remember that for many thousands of years, we have not answered our most basic existential questions with *facts*—because we have had so few and understood them so poorly—but with *stories*. Some of these, over time, have formed the basis of what we call "religion," while others have remained simply stories.

Much of King's horror fiction falls into the literary category that narratologists call the *unnatural narrative*: stories about things that couldn't possibly happen. Narratologist Jan Alber, for example, defines stories of this type according to "the various ways in which fictional narratives deviate from 'natural' cognitive frames, i.e., real-world understandings of time, space, and other human beings."[12] Put differently, they are "physically impossible scenarios and events, that is, impossible by the known laws governing the physical world."[13] Yet we constantly and continually entertain these stories as though they could and do happen. We respond to them as though they are happening.

When we're frightened by a horror story or a scary movie, we do not so much suspend our disbelief as we give in to belief in the story—both willingly and unwillingly. Drawing on cognitive and social neuroscience, literature scholar Brian Boyd points to the "emotional contagion" that is inherent in fictional narratives. Specifically, "mirror neurons fire when we perceive someone performing an action, as they would if we were performing it ourselves."[14] Often, horror culture is derided for its reliance on things that couldn't possibly happen. Why would anyone believe such stories, critics ask, or react as though they do believe? Forgotten here, though, is that as a species we have considerable experience with unnatural narratives. What is religion, after all, but an assembled case history of believing the unbelievable? From Jonah's three-day sojourn in the belly of a "great fish" to Muhammad's night ride across the Middle East on a flying horse, from a boat designed to repopulate the earth in the wake of a global extinction event to several thousand people fed from a couple of fish and a few loaves of bread—as a species, we believe the unbelievable on an astonishingly regular basis.

Stories such as these do not simply spice up our varied religious narratives, they constitute the very substance of what we have come to accept as "religion." That is, the *claim* that Moses met Yahweh on Mount Horeb when he encountered the burning bush, that Muhammad saw the angel Gibreel on Mount Hira, that Jonah emerged alive from the belly of the fish, or that Jesus performed miracles both *authorize* and *certify* their claims to divine authority. We believe because these stories are unbelievable, precisely because they are "violations of the ordinary."[15] As Boyd points out, "religion consists less of a coherent body of dogmas or explanatory systems than of these memorably surprising stories."[16]

Yet, no matter how people construct belief in the literal truth of such events, they can never be anything other than stories. Nor does the fact that billions of people believe that they represent both historical and theological reality change or diminish their power *as* story. Millions regard them as meaningless fiction, hundreds of millions more as true stories. But *stories* nonetheless.

A Brief Walk in the Maine Woods

One problem with the reception of genre fiction, especially of an author who writes as fluidly and prodigiously as Stephen King, is that novels such as *Pet Sematary* or *The Girl Who Loved Tom Gordon* can easily be read in a single evening. In the rush to find out what *happens*, though, we often miss *what* happens. We don't slow down enough to see what's *there*. As we will see, the central action in *Pet Sematary* is structured around the classic anthropological notion of the ritual process, and includes what we might call a mini-seminar on various religious conceptions of death and dying. *The Girl Who Loved Tom Gordon*, on the other hand, is a straightforward child-lost-in-the-wilderness story, solidly in the tradition of fairy tales such as "Red Riding Hood," "Snow White," and "Hansel and Gretel." In this short novel, however, through young Trisha McFarland's experience in the depth of the Maine forest, King explores one of humankind's earliest religious impulses: sympathetic magic, the belief that actions in the seen and unseen orders are connected, and a means by which hominins have for millennia controlled their fear of chaos and disruption.

Night approaches. What could be scarier than this, evoking narrative territory haunted by lean, hungry wolves, by witches in gingerbread houses, by shadows that come alive just as day departs? *The Girl Who*

Loved Tom Gordon needs little more than the simple coming of darkness to invoke the fear of being cut off from the community. Yet it is another path down which King explores our ambiguous, ambivalent relationship with the unseen order, offering another example of how deeply imbued his work is with god-talk. Like many of King's stories, this one begins with the most mundane of circumstances: a bitter divorce, confused children who have grown hostile and resentful, a day trip to the woods intended to smooth things over, and a moment's inattention.

With nothing more than her daypack and her little-girl grit, Trisha McFarland tries to find her way back to her mother and brother—indeed, to find her way back to anyone. Running from a swarm of wasps, she slips and falls down a rocky slope, tearing her clothes, bloodying her arm, and destroying her Gameboy. Even her blue rain poncho, which wasn't much to begin with, is now "torn and flapping in a way she would have considered comic under other circumstances."[17] As she sits by a small stream, assessing the damage, she has only one clear thought: Don't let me be truly alone. "Please, God," she said into the tiny dark space behind her eyelids, "don't let my Walkman be broken."[18] The Walkman's radio is her only link to the world beyond the forest. Without even its small voice in her earbuds she is truly, desperately *alone*. She presses the power button and the radio comes to life, the local Castle Rock station broadcasting an alert about a nine-year-old girl "missing and presumably lost in the woods west of TR-90 and the town of Motton."[19]

Foxhole prayers and desperate appeals to a dimly remembered deity are far more common than not. Sometimes we beg, sometimes we bargain. In King's novella "The Body," which was adapted as the classic coming-of-age film *Stand by Me*, as the night noises creep in on the boys' camp, twelve-year-old Vern Tessio is terrified that Ray Brouwer's ghost is coming for them out of the dark. "'Oh, God!' Vern screamed.... 'I promise I won't hawk no more dirty books out of Dahlie's Market! I promise I won't give my carrots to the dog no more!' I . . . I . . . I . . .' He floundered there, wanting to bribe God with everything but unable to think of anything good in the extremity of his fear."[20]

In these two children—Vern and Trisha—we see the double helix of our religious DNA: fear and hope. In his terror, Vern cries out, desperate to coerce God with the only currency he knows: renunciation of what he understands as sin, a willing return to the straight and narrow. Trisha offers no such false promises. She may be just as scared—indeed, dying in "the woods west of the TR-90" is for her a very real possibility—but she simply, desperately *hopes*, "Please, God, don't let my Walkman be broken." While not immediately apparent, Trisha's panicked plea is another opportunity to wonder whether there really is anything else out there—one of the quintessential questions that has exercised our imagination for thousands of years.

For Trisha, praying that her Walkman had not been damaged in the fall "had been easy because it had been unthinking," almost instinctual, though the instinct to pray does not mean there is Something There to pray *to*.[21] Even a nine-year-old girl knows that. Later, when she tries to pray, to really pray for rescue, she "discovered herself lost and without vocabulary. . . . She said the Our Father and it came out of her mouth sounding flat and uncomforting, about as useful as an electric can opener would have been out here."[22] Daughter of a "lapsed Catholic" and a father who "had never had anything to lapse from," Trisha has little if any religious socialization to fall back on. She may know the words to the Lord's Prayer, but she lacks their conceptual framework. They don't *mean* anything to her. "She couldn't remember ever discussing spiritual matters with her mother," King tells us, "but she had asked her father not a month ago if he believed in God."[23]

Her father, Larry, is a positively disposed agnostic, though he professes belief in something called the "Subaudible," a concept he compares to the dim, constant, and largely unregarded background noises of everyday life.[24] The compressor motor in your refrigerator, the stand-by hum of a dozen different electronic devices—white noise we appreciate only when it's no longer there. "I don't believe in any actual thinking God," he tells his daughter, "a God that records all of our sins in a big golden book and judges us when we die—I don't want to believe in a God who would deliberately create bad people and then deliberately send them to roast in a hell He created—but I believe there has to be *something*."[25] At this point, we know little about Trisha's father, except that he articulates our deeply embedded need to believe in something rather than nothing, in something greater than ourselves and to which we are somehow related. Put differently, in cosmological terms, since there *is* something rather than nothing, there must be some kind of existential meaning. For Larry, it's too much to imagine a meaningless something. His is a vague "spiritual-but-not-religious" conceptualization, which has become little more than a cliché, but which quickly shades into a kind of New Age positive thinking.

"Yeah, something," he continues. "Some kind of insensate force for the good. Insensate, do you know what that means?"[26] While we might be tempted to answer, "completely lacking in sense," that clearly isn't what Larry means. He means that there is *something there*, blindly, heedlessly, without meaning or larger purpose, apparently, that just makes most things come out alright in the end.

> I think there's a force that keeps drunken teenagers—*most* drunken teenagers—from crashing their cars when they're coming home from the senior prom or their first big rock concert. That keeps most planes from crashing even when something goes wrong. Not all, just most. . . . There's something that keeps most of us from dying in our sleep. No perfect, loving, all-seeing God, I don't think the evidence supports that, but a force.[27]

For Larry, because aircraft land safely and children wake up in the morning, there must be a reason—though his god-talk is no more precise than that. "The Subaudible," his daughter replies, though even she sees through her father's anemic argument from design, our propensity to link the appearance of order in the world with the existence of someone, or something, who controls that order. Like all such arguments, however, his insensate, subaudible force neatly sidesteps any question of drunken teenagers who *do* crash their cars, planes that *do* disappear, seemingly without a trace, and people who *do* die in their sleep for no apparent reason. Larry's belief comes nowhere close to satisfying his daughter. For Trisha, "it was like getting a letter you thought would be interesting and important, only when you opened it it was addressed to Dear Occupant."[28] As with the many varieties of god-talk King explores through his storyworlds, Larry's vague agnosticism leaves his daughter with far more questions than answers. In the end, the little girl lost "almost nine miles west of the area the searchers considered their highest priority," thinks to herself, "*I can't pray to the Subaudible. I just can't.*"[29]

What we see here—and we can only wonder what Larry thinks about the Subaudible, now that it's *his* daughter lost in the wilderness—is the shift from a vague confidence in *something out there* to one of the oldest forms of religious practice: sympathetic magic, the principle of "as above, so below." Coined by nineteenth-century anthropologist James Frazer, the term "sympathetic magic" describes a particular conception of the relationship between the seen and the unseen, in which "things act on each other at a distance through a secret sympathy, the impulse being transmitted from one to the other by means of what we may conceive as a kind of invisible ether."[30] Sympathetic magic operates on the principle of an intimate connection between the natural and the supernatural. Fertility rites, for example, theoretically ensure crop growth or healthy livestock by means of human sexual relations. In ceremonial magic and many forms of modern Paganism, the *hieros gamos*, the sacred marriage between the high priestess and her high priest, joins human sexual energy as a reflection and invocation of conjoined divine energies. As above, so below.

To combat her fears during the long, dark nights, as one of the "Fenway Faithful" Trisha listens to Red Sox games on her Walkman, always hoping for an appearance of her favorite player, closer Tom Gordon. When the Sox are down and it's late in the game, Gordon takes the mound to pitch for the save. Connected to the unseen order through her radio, Trisha tells herself that if Gordon saves, she will be saved.

"*If we win*," Trisha thinks, as Gordon walks his first opponent, "*if Tom gets the save*, I'll *be saved*."[31] Note that she doesn't think, "if *they* win," or "if *Tom* wins," but "*if* we *win*." She has linked herself emotionally, both to the man on the mound and to the Fenway Faithful gathered to watch. She is as involved as they, though with considerably more at stake. "This thought," writes King, "came to her suddenly—it was like a firework bursting in her head. . . . It also seemed irrefutable, as obvious as two-and-two-makes-four: if Tom Gordon got the save, *she* would get the save."[32]

In one sense, this is her way of managing the uncertainty of her situation, of coping with her entirely reasonable anxiety. Like those who have employed sympathetic magic for thousands of years, Trisha also realizes that there are dark forces aligned against her and her champion. She doesn't only mean the New York Yankees, but others who work their own form of sympathetic magic, and who may not have the interests of a lost little girl in mind. There are those who speak different words. When Yankee center fielder Bernie Williams steps to the plate, cautiously eyeing Tom Gordon sixty feet away, one of the announcers describes him as "always a dangerous hitter."[33] Williams takes the first pitch and "immediately ripped a single to center, sending Jeter to third."[34]

"'Why did you say that, Joe?' Trisha moaned. 'Oh, cripes, why did you have to *say* that?'"[35] It's no longer just about whether the Red Sox chalk up another win; for Trisha, her very life is at stake. If Gordon saves, she will be saved. If not . . .

As psychologist Stuart Vyse notes, "the superstitions of baseball players are legendary, as much a part of their peculiar subculture as rosin bags and chewing tobacco."[36] Indeed, of Baseball Hall of Famer Wade Boggs, Vyse writes, "Having eaten, Boggs begins a pregame ritual that takes five hours to complete that includes such eccentricities as ending his grounder drill by stepping on third, second, and first base, taking two steps in the first-base coaching box, and jogging to the dugout in exactly four strides."[37] Like Trisha in the woods, he attempts to manage the *uncertainty* that is a fundamental part of daily life.

With her beloved Sox "clinging to a one-run lead," the game continues, both in Fenway Park, where "the Fenway Faithful were getting to their feet like a church congregation about to sing a hymn," and hundreds of miles away in the forests of northern Maine, where a frightened young girl sits under a tree, wearing a tattered blue rain poncho, and listening on her Walkman.[38]

> "Don't you say it," Trisha whispered, her hands still pressing against the sides of her mouth, "don't you *dare* say it."
>
> But he did. "And the always dangerous Darryl Strawberry coming to the plate."
>
> That was it; game over; great Satan Joe Castiglione had opened his mouth and jinxed it. Why couldn't he just have given Strawberry's *name*? Why did he have to start in with that "always dangerous" horsepucky when any fool knew that only *made* them dangerous?[39]

Our pattern-seeking nature often leaves us profoundly uncomfortable with randomness and uncertainty. When Joe Castiglione, the Red Sox announcer, warns listeners of the dangerous Yankee hitters coming to the plate—Jeter, Williams, Strawberry—despite the fact that Trisha doesn't want to hear it, her interpretation of his words as an omen creates for her a meaningful connection with the events at the ballpark. We force explanations onto events and phenomena, rationalizations intended to lower our anxiety and increase our sense of control. When Gordon defeats Strawberry—at the time, one of the most intimidating hitters in the game—Trisha "cried in relief. She was lost but would be found. She was sure of it. Tom Gordon had gotten the save and so would she."[40] Not everyone in the storyworlds of Stephen King is so lucky.

Reading *Carrie* by Firelight

While many readers may not be familiar with *The Girl Who Loved Tom Gordon*, few who know Stephen King will not also know *Carrie*. Published in 1974, *Carrie* was King's breakout success as a novelist, the book that gave him the freedom to write what he loved for a living.[41] The outlines of the plot are simple: Carrie White is a plain, socially awkward teenager who is bullied in every area of her life and responds in the end with catastrophic violence. Dominated by a fundamentalist Christian mother at home, she is the butt of everyone's joke at school. She is also psychokinetic, a trait that emerges when she is particularly disturbed emotionally. When a monstrously cruel trick is played on her at the prom, Carrie reacts with singular fury, destroying most of the small town of Chamberlain, Maine, in the process.

What, then, is *Carrie* about?

One of the basic problems with this question is that as soon as we answer it, we tend to think we have *the answer*. We've solved the story's interpretive puzzle and can safely move on. But this isn't how storytelling and storyworlds work in our lives. How we perceive something and how we interpret it are as much functions of what we bring to the story as what it brings to us. A person who is not particularly bothered by clowns, for example, may not find *It* as frightening as does someone who suffers from *coulrophobia*. For me, when It assumes final form, a giant spider hunting the main characters through the sewers beneath the town of Derry, *arachnophobia* kicks my adrenal system into gear and pops the clutch on my fight-or-flight response. Spiders terrify me; clowns—not so much.

What a story *means*, then, emerges in the gap between the page and the reader, the imaginative space where readers write themselves into the story—whether they want to or not, whether they know it or not. So, with that in mind, what is *Carrie* about?

In the opening scene, Carrie experiences her first menses. For a sixteen-year-old, this is late but certainly not unprecedented. What happens for most young women over the course of a few years, however—the hormonal and physical changes signaling sexual attraction and availability, the social and cultural shifts that structure "proper" sexual relationships—Carrie goes through in just a few days. And each of these coming-of-age challenges is met with shock and ridicule from those around and closest to her. From the girls in the locker room, pelting her with sanitary napkins and squealing "*PER*-iod! *PER*-iod! *PER*-iod!"[42] to her mother, who throws her to the floor, screaming, "Get up, woman. Let's us get in and pray. Let's us pray to Jesus for our woman-weak, wicked, sinning souls,"[43] she cannot escape the torment. In this sense, is *Carrie* a horrific inversion of the coming-of-age story?

Jesuit scholar Edward Ingebretsen doesn't see it this way. He considers *Carrie* "a text in the apocalyptic tradition of [Cotton] Mather, in which a war between invisible and visible is rewritten as a private obsession and narcissism" and he sees its central character as the literary embodiment of "a communal narrative of self-hate."[44] Drawing from the wells of his own religious storyworlds, Ingebretsen locates *Carrie* in the long line of terrifying morality tales.

Is this what the story is about? Or, as King himself suggests, is it a chilling update of *High School Confidential*, driving home the brute reality that, for many students, navigating the various groups, cliques, and wastelands of senior high is a lonely, living hell? In this sense, *Carrie* is *Heathers* or *Mean Girls*, years before either appeared, and a quarter century before *The Craft* combined the trope with modern Paganism, or *Saved!* with evangelical Christianity. All the elements are there—the clannish nature of high school society, the cruelty and vindictiveness of teenagers—and each is a site of exclusion for Carrietta White. The perky cheerleaders in the locker room will never allow this "frog among swans" into their magic circle, the zone of popularity they create and enforce by excluding and belittling others.[45] Despite her devout religious beliefs, Carrie doesn't fit in at a church youth camp either, even though "she had fought Momma tooth and nail" to attend. Where she might have felt at home among friends, in the midst of fellow believers, "a thousand practical jokes had been played on ol' praying' Carrie."[46] Between her social exclusion at school and her religious confinement at home, she never imagined going to her senior prom, but that would become the site of her most profound and destructive marginalization.

Following on this interpretation, is *Carrie* King's horrific take on the venerable "Cinderella," as various other critics have suggested? While one reviewer all but dismisses the novel as "essentially the Cinderella story tricked up with telekinesis and bloody special effects,"[47] another labels it "a dark modernization of 'Cinderella,' with a bad mother, cruel siblings (peers), a prince (Tommy Rees), a godmother (Sue Snell), a ball, and a theme in which a persecuted victim recovers her female power."[48] Satisfied to pigeonhole King's work thus, literature scholar Linda Badley concludes that *Carrie* "is Cinderella in the body language of menstrual blood and raging hormones."[49] In *Stephen King's America*, on the other hand, Jonathan Davis describes *Carrie* as "the story of Cinderella-gone-bad; there is no Prince Charming to come back to fit the glass slipper onto her foot and take her away from a life of suppression."[50] While Davis clearly bases his interpretation on the saccharine Disney telling of the tale—the one with the happy ending—fantasy author Chelsea Quinn Yarbro at least acknowledges its much darker source.

"In the original versions of Cinderella," Yarbro writes, "when she is given the chance to be revenged upon her family, she has their noses and hands cut off. Carrie goes further than that; she wrecks the entire town in a display of psychokinesis that smacks of Jovian rage."[51] In her rush to link *Carrie* to a chain of myths, legends, and fairy tales, however, in effect to rehabilitate Carrie in the midst of her "Jovian rage," Quinn pushes the connection further than the story itself will bear. "It is the right of the Queen of the fairies to punish erring mortals," she continues, "and Carrie, being psychically gifted, reflects not only the beautiful and beneficent nature of fairy-folk, but their malignancy and caprice as well."[52] Though she admits that suggesting that King "deliberately set out to do a modern-day Cinderella story with a nasty end would be silly and misleading,"[53] even more misguided is Yarbro's own notion of Carrie as the Fairy Queen. Each of these critics' readings seems to imply that the fairy tale represents a kind of *ur*-text on which King based his story, and that this original both grounds all later tellings and confines them to the fairy tale tradition.

They are in fact linked, but not in nearly so neat a fashion.

If *Carrie* tells a Cinderella story, it is because both tales present us with similar questions and concerns. Sibling rivalry and issues of parental approval have antecedents going back to Cain and Abel, and likely far earlier than that. Despite superficial equivalence and similarity, it isn't that "Cinderella" (or its Grimm original, "Aschenputtel") leads to *Carrie*, but that *both* emerge from a much deeper well of human experience sunk deep in expectation, competition, and disappointment.[54] Thus, locating *Carrie* in the Cinderella storyline does not, in fact, simplify the problem of how it should be interpreted. Quite the opposite. It reminds us once again that the answers we get depend largely on the questions we ask. While this seems common sense, we often forget that what we take from a text is in many ways a product of what we bring to it.

Ask how *Carrie* reflects a *High School Confidential* experience and we'll get a certain answer. Ask how it's like a well-known fairy tale and we'll learn something different. Question the novel's meaning in the era of second-wave feminism, and we'll get yet another response. "If *The Stepford Wives* concerns itself with what men want from women," King writes in *Danse Macabre*, "then *Carrie* is largely about how women find their own channels of power, and what men fear about women and women's sexuality, . . . which is only to say that, writing the book in 1973 and only out of college three years, I was fully aware of what Women's Liberation implied for me and others of my sex."[55] Indeed, most of *Carrie*'s male characters, with the possible exception of Tommy Rees, are all but incidental to the plot. Far more obvious and more powerful are the ways women constrain and control other women. Read psychologically, *Carrie* aligns with how many critics have interpreted William Friedkin's classic horror film *The Exorcist* as a horrific menstruation fable, a young girl's seeming invasion of and betrayal by her own body.[56] In *The Exorcist*, religion becomes part of the solution; for *Carrie*, as we will discover, it lies at the heart of the problem. Interpreted psychosocially, suggested one early critic, *Carrie* can be read as "a feminist novel which confronts a young woman's psychic conflict when she attempts to live as a strong and autonomous individual in a culture that would prefer to see her as a passive and powerless piece of femininity."[57] Read today, *Carrie* might seem the quintessential anti-bullying parable, something of a horror fiction PSA on the dangers of pushing people too far.

What happens when we shift the lens yet again, reading King's novel in terms of the questions a scholar of religion might ask, or a theologian, or a religious believer? It's not that any of the foregoing interpretations are incorrect—though some may seem thinner than others—it's that they inevitably reflect the kind of questions we bring to the text. They become problematic only when they claim to have *the* answer to the question, the singular key to a story's particular lock. Indeed, as we will see, to read *Carrie* religiously, we look not so much to her but to her mother, a character King draws in more vivid detail than any other in the book—including, arguably, Carrie herself.

Dark Theologian: Horror Fiction as God-Talk

From *Carrie* to *Revival*, from "Children of the Corn" and "N." to "That Feeling, You Can Only Say What It Is in French," from *Pet Sematary* and *It* to *Desperation, Insomnia, Duma Key*, and dozens of others, Stephen King's storyworlds investigate precisely the same questions religious believers of all kinds ask—and claim to have answered. This is the mind of the dark theologian at work. Once again, though, this isn't to say that King proposes a "dark theology" of his own, as though throughout his canon a singular understanding of the world prevails. Instead, throughout his stories, he asks again and again questions that have come to be called "religious" but that are more appropriately called "human." It is in posing these questions that he does his theology. In proposing different answers, his scary stories participate in humankind's ongoing conversations about the nature of the divine.

What does it mean to "do theology," especially when we're talking about an author who makes no such explicit claim? Here's the trick: we all "do theology." Whether we are professional theologians, clerics, or laypersons—indeed, even if we are nonbelievers—the ways we talk about God, question God's nature and will, and even wonder about God's reality constitute our theology, our god-talk. Certainly we don't wonder about these questions all the time, and most of us don't engage them for a living. Indeed, for many of us they have little obvious effect on our lives. But ask people whether they believe in God, however well- or ill-defined the concept, and many of them will answer, "Yes, of course, don't you?"[58] A growing number, however, are beginning to express either their uncertainty about God's existence or their certainty that God does *not* exist. Thus, we all have a "logic of God," which is one way of defining theology, even if that logic insists that there is no God and that continued belief in a nonexistent deity can only do us further harm. We all *do* theology, even though we may not be aware of it, and theology is not the sole province of the religious believer. "I believe that Jesus died for my sins," one person says to another, "and the only way to heaven is through him." "Really," the other responds, "well, I believe that Jesus is only one prophet among many who have come to lead humankind to a higher spiritual plane," while someone else declares, "Jesus is just a fable. He never existed—and neither does heaven." Among the most basic of theological conversations, statements such as these are rudimentary, lacking both complexity and sophistication. While they may not be theoretically informed or elegantly phrased, each facet of this brief exchange is theological dialogue nonetheless. It is *god-talk*.

As King points out in "That Feeling, You Can Only Say What It Is in French," however, what we think about God, Allah, Buddha, Ishtar, Hanuman, or any of the other numberless deities that crowd our pantheons is rarely our own choice. Throughout history and around the world, what we believe is largely "the choice of those who had taught you what to believe."[59]

Unfortunately, the notion of being a theologian has become bound up with theology either as a profession or a vocation: the seminary professor or the parish clergy. For both, and it matters little what religion their particular god-talk serves, theology is often a loose synonym for "apologetics"—why *my* god is the *right* god. But what is a theologian, really, but someone who meditates in whatever fashion on the nature of reality? Whether the "ground" of that reality is Yahweh, Amaterasu, the Great Mother Goddess, or Yog-Sothoth, theologians explore the nooks and crannies between what we claim to understand and what we hope (or fear) might be the case. Through intellectual conjecture and active imagination, they question the dark, uneven spaces between the seen and the unseen orders of reality. In this, theology recapitulates cosmology. What we believe about the unseen order necessarily informs what we think about the world around us—and how a shift in one bodes a change in the other.

Take, for example, "The Man in the Black Suit," King's self-admitted homage to Nathaniel Hawthorne's classic tale "Young Goodman Brown."

The story's framework is simple enough: a year after the death of his brother, a young boy fishing in a local creek is confronted by a strange man wearing a black suit. The man, whose "eyes were the orangey-red of flames in a woodstove" and whose skin smelled of "burned matches," tempts the boy through fear, guilt, and grief.[60] In the end, the trickster himself is tricked and the world is rendered safe once again, if only for that moment.

Far more than a simple retelling of Hawthorne, though, "The Man in the Black Suit" marshals a number of religious themes that appear throughout the King canon. At the most basic level, we have hypocrisy, which is little more than the difference between people's claims to piety and their behavior in the world. More important is theodicy, our ongoing attempts to understand suffering in the context of belief in a loving God. Taken together, the gap between expectation and experience highlights the problem of pain in terms of human suffering and divine consent. There is religious socialization, how it is we learn what we're supposed to believe, and what sort of hold those beliefs maintain over us. Often, the strength of our faith is challenged precisely at the crossroads of what we've been taught to believe and what we know can't possibly be true. Finally, we see two of the ways humans have sought to influence events around them: talismanic protection, the power we vest in the physical objects of our faith, and substitutionary sacrifice, which throughout history has been one of religion's principal mechanisms for maintaining balance between the seen and the unseen orders. Whether implicitly or explicitly, each of these experiences invokes the kind of questions humans have asked since our ancestors first looked beyond the shadows and wondered what it was like outside the cave.

"She claimed she was done with church," recalls Gary, the nonagenarian narrator of "The Man in the Black Suit."[61] Gary is telling his tale in retrospect, many decades after the events. This is a story from his childhood, when he was growing up on a farm near the small community of Motton. A year earlier, Gary's brother had died from a bee sting—today we would recognize it as anaphylactic shock. This, though, is rural Maine in the early years of the twentieth century, a time and place where healthy young farm boys simply don't die from something as commonplace as bees. We learn as well that his mother was driven away from the local Methodist church by what so many well-meaning Christians often mistake for compassion. At least, we can only hope they mean well, since the alternative is a calculated *hypocrisy*, a kind of narcissistic cruelty that beggars imagination.

Still mourning her loss, Gary's mother is "comforted" by a variety of women in the local congregation, including The One Who Feels Your Pain. In this case, it's "Mama Sweet, the oldest lady in the Methodist Ladies' Aid."[62] Rather than sit quietly with her, perhaps holding her hand and simply sharing a young mother's grief at the death of a child, believers like this inevitably turn attention onto themselves. Heavy with sincerity, they assure us that they "know what it's like," that it's "happened to them," that they "understand what we're going through." For Mama Sweet, it was a "favorite uncle back in '73" who died the same way.[63] Suddenly, the tables are turned in the temple of compassion, and the one who needs comforting must become the comforter. It's as though we're being told we have no right to our own pain because someone else has suffered too. It's too much for Gary's mother, and she "clapped her hand over her ears, got up, and walked out of the church basement. She'd never been back since."[64]

Does "being done with church," however, mean "being done with God"? Or is the possible hypocrisy of one old woman in a rural congregation a minor reflection of a much larger, divine duplicity? Here, the question is *theodicy*, which, simply put, asks why a loving God would allow such needless and apparently abundant suffering. Arguably one of the greatest challenges to belief in any kind of divine order, this is the cry of Job from the midst of his own great loss, the heartache of a father who cannot save his daughter lost in the woods, the "Why me?" of a mother who will never taste honey the same way again. If God is so great, this question demands, then why is our pain so deep? Does God allow suffering for some purpose we cannot possibly fathom, otherwise known as the "God works in mysterious ways" defense? Or is God unable to prevent our suffering, even to the extent of a small breeze moving a tiny insect a few inches to the left? Certainly, if this is the case, it begs the question whether such a being is worthy of the job title. Or, instead of a god at all, is there simply a void, what *Under the Dome*'s Piper Libby calls "The Not-There," a universal lacuna we fill with little more than fear and hope?[65]

As with so much of horror culture, "The Man in the Black Suit" highlights the threatening presence of the Devil through the uncomfortable absence of God. Indeed, throughout the story God is nowhere to be found. The closest we come to a divine presence is Motton's little Methodist church, the one the narrator-as-a-young-boy eventually encourages his mother to embrace once again. Even in the closing moments of his long life, though, Gary wonders whether the Devil will come for him again, and whether God will be there when he does. As he lies in his bed, wearing "the ruined sand castle that is my body" and thinking about the man in the black suit, Gary know that "a man in his nineties should be well past the terrors of childhood."[66] That said, he feels "more and more strongly that escaping him was my luck—just *luck*, and not the intercession of the God I have worshipped and sung hymns to all my life."[67] At this level, King's dark theology speaks to us of uncertainty and ambivalence, the equivocal nature of our religious beliefs, and the need for their ongoing reinforcement.

"I was raised a perfectly conventional Methodist," Stephen King tells his Constant Reader, the imaginary person sitting with him in his study when he writes, though "I rejected organized religion and most of its hard and fast assertions long ago."[68] It's a bit of a rabbit hole to go looking for autobiographical clues in every story, but what Gary's mother endured at the hands of Mama Sweet is common enough among believers that any number of King's readers will see themselves in the story. Like many of his fellow horror writers, King gave up the institutional church, but did not give up the faith, that bundle of loosely wrapped but tightly held beliefs taught to him by the organization. Richard Matheson, James Herbert, Alan Ryan, V. C. Andrews—all were raised in religious, occasionally *very* religious, homes, and all retain some belief in the supernatural, some remnant of wonder connected to the teachings of their church.[69] To that extent, although none of them wants anything to do with the institution in which they were raised, their *religious socialization* as believers in some kind of unseen order lives on.

When the strange man first approaches Gary, leaving "not a single broken twig, crushed leaf, or trampled shoe-shape" in the slick, wet grass leading down to the stream, everything the boy learned in church becomes real in that moment.[70] Like many "the Devil came a-callin'" stories, this one takes place at a crossroads, the metaphorical point of decision in every person's life. In this case, it's a fork in Castle Stream, a place beyond which Gary has been sternly warned not to go. First, the

Devil plays the fear card, telling the young boy that his mother is dead, stung by a bee in their kitchen and making "the most wonderfully awful noises" as she died.[71] Then he ups the ante, adding guilt to the pot and suggesting that "it's almost a case of poetic justice, isn't it," since she is responsible for Dan's death. You see, he says, leaning in and speaking in a breath "foul beyond belief," "it was she who passed that fatal weakness on to your brother."[72]

The man in the black suit plays his final card. He offers to kill Gary, to murder him as an act of compassion. Death, he says, will spare him the sight of his dead mother, the unimaginable grief of his father, and long, dark, difficult days ahead. "I'll save you all that discomfort and unpleasantness," he says. "Also, you'll go to Heaven, think of that. Murdered souls *always* go to Heaven. So we'll both be serving God this afternoon, Gary. Won't that be nice?"[73]

What the Devil presents is a *choice*, a tactic that always gives him a measure of plausible deniability. We can almost see him spreading his hands in mock(ing) innocence, and saying with oily sincerity, "I didn't force you to eat the apple. I just pointed out how good it looked . . ." "Faust? That pretentious old fraud. I didn't make him do anything, least of all sell me his soul. All I did was make him the offer . . ." In this case, fear, guilt, and grief huddle together in the temptation to believe the lies. And this is the lens through which Gary's religious teachings focus the problem. "Tears streamed down my cheeks," he recalls. "I didn't want to believe him and knew from my church schooling that the devil is the father of lies, but I *did* believe him just the same."[74] However strong Gary's belief or how deep his faith, always hiding in the bushes or whispering on the wind is the question, *What if I'm wrong?*

The essence of temptation is not pressure, but choice: a fork in the stream, a crossroad separating one life from another. In the story, the young boy either resists temptation, however artlessly applied—we don't ever really believe that Gary's mother is dead—or buys his way out of the bargain by tempting the Devil in turn. Always voraciously hungry, the Devil is constantly "seeking whom he may devour" (1 Pet. 5:8). Reaching into his battered creel, Gary desperately offers him a substitute, a *sacrifice*: a freshly caught, nineteen-inch brook trout. "'Big fish!' the man in the black suit cried in a guttural, greedy voice. 'Oh, *biiig fiiiish!*'"[75] While the Devil is distracted by the morsel, which he stuffs into "a mouth that

opened wider than any human mouth ever could," the boy runs franti-
cally for home.[76] He has escaped, just barely, and only for the moment.

Meeting his father on the way, Gary pours out his tale of terror. Not
unreasonably, his father at first discounts the story as a dream: too much
summer sun beating down on a child's active imagination. Here, as with
every parent who has peered under a bed or opened a closet, reassuring their frightened child that no monster lurks in the dark, his is the
voice of *rationality*, the adult realist who will soon be confronted by that
which could not possibly be real.

A couple of hours later, when they go back to the stream to collect
the boy's fishing gear, almost as *talismanic protection* Gary insists on
taking with them the large family Bible. "I wanted to be prepared," he
tells us. "I'd set out just to bring my New Testament, which I had won
for memorizing the most psalms in the Thursday night Youth Fellowship competition . . . but the little red Testament didn't seem like enough
when you were maybe going to face the Devil himself, not even when
the words of Jesus were marked out in red ink."[77] His father notes the
Bible with "a look of mixed grief and sympathy," but lets him bring it
along.[78] Sometimes, heroes just need a good sword to feel brave. When
they reach the creek, "I stood where I was, holding the Bible stiffly out
at the ends of my arms like a willow-fork, my heart thumping wildly."[79]

Is that why the man in the black suit did not reappear, we wonder?
Was he frightened off by "the sword of the Spirit, which is the word of
God" (Eph. 6:17)? From the crosses we use to ward away vampires to
the holy water driving out demons, from the myriad lucky charms and
magical amulets, to blessed objects of all types, the technology of salvation has long played a significant role in the religious imagination. In
this case, it's not about the stories contained in "the old Bible, swelled
with family documents and pictures," it's about the book itself, the physical sign and symbol of a power we believe greater than the one that
threatens us.[80]

In the end, the man in the black suit does not return to the fork in
Castle Stream, but that doesn't mean he isn't still there. Until Gary's father saw the burnt grass where the man walked, the patch where he lay
now "dead and yellow in the shape of a man," until he smelled his son's
old wicker creel, now reeking of diabolical stench, the Devil had been a
fairy story. He was something the preacher told on Sundays to frighten

the children and the gullible. Now he knows better, and "he grabbed another quick glance over his shoulder, eyes wide, as if he had heard something move in the woods."[81]

We are all familiar with that feeling: heart beating hard, hair rising on the backs of our necks, breath coming quick and shallow. We know there's nothing there—in the closet, under the bed, in the woods—but shivers skitter down our spines nonetheless. When these ancient fears are triggered, rationality is poor defense, and, with Gary's father, we are only too glad to say, "Let's get the hell out of here."[82] In the light of day and the safety of the crowd, we may tell ourselves we don't believe in the Devil, in spooks and spirits, in the Boogeyman, or in any of the numberless monsters that haunt our imaginations. But, asks Stephen King, what happens when they show up?

The Fifth Business

Most of King's novels are what we might call "fifth-business" stories. The phrase comes from Canadian writer Robertson Davies's novel of the same name, a concept he created for the story and which he defines as characters or situations that, while neither hero nor villain, are essential for the movement of the plot.[83] Without them, there would be no story. We meet an old college friend in the street and our lives are changed forever. A misaddressed letter arrives in the post, and sets in motion an unfortunate chain of events. An angry email, which we meant for only one person, is mistakenly sent to the entire company—with predictably adverse results. At the beginning of his 2014 novel *Revival*, King describes the "fifth business" as something that fits none of life's normal categories, "the joker who pops out of the deck at odd intervals over the years, often during a moment of crisis."[84] Everything is normal, familiar, unremarkable until one thing changes: an invisible dome appears and cuts off a small Maine town (*Under the Dome*); a reclusive writer of genre fiction discovers an alien spacecraft buried for millennia on her property (*The Tommyknockers*); a strange, compelling figure arrives in town offering the one thing you think you need the most (*Needful Things*). A man in a black suit appears, a man who "was on fire inside, and his eyes were like the little isinglass portholes you sometimes see in stove doors."[85]

If we expected to meet the Devil every time we went fishing at the fork in Castle Stream, few of us would ever venture out. If we felt the need to carry a heavy family Bible on a routine trip to the market, we might just as well choose to stay at home. But we don't. A common misconception about god-talk and popular culture is that for something to be *about* religion it has to be about religion *explicitly* or *primarily*. The Devil comes a-callin' as a young boy dips his line in the water, for example.

Apart from the professionally, vocationally, or neurotically religious, however, the reality is that relatively few of us think explicitly or primarily about religion during the course of our daily lives. Far more conversations begin with whether we saw the latest summer blockbuster or reality TV episode than with running commentary on the pastor's Sunday sermon. Because for so many people in America religion occupies such an odd place—important, but marginal in the decision-making process; central, yet adjunct to most of our day-to-day activities—it tends to show up less in the daily round than at the crossroads. These are the fifth-business moments that Stephen King continues to poke and prod.

Not all of King's novels, short stories, or screenplays give the fifth business over to religion or the supernatural, but far more do than the casual reader might suppose. It's easy to get distracted by the pyrokinetics of Carrie White's final acts of vengeance, and miss the underlying forces that drove her to those dire straits. If we don't understand the concept of sympathetic magic, it's easy to dismiss *The Girl Who Loved Tom Gordon* as just another "little girl lost" tale. At the fork in Castle Stream, if we stop at the notion of the Devil as a liar, King's much more nuanced telling of the classic temptation narrative is easily swept away. In each of these stories, King points us toward the thin spots in the world, the places where the seen and the unseen orders rub up against each other, where the shadows gather and the monsters lurk, where all our fears are still alive.

2

Thin Spots

What Peeks through the Cracks in the World

"Children of the Corn" is among Stephen King's best-known short stories. Published first in *Penthouse* in 1977, it grew into a multipart film franchise that both deepened its mythological background and extended his initial vision of a mysterious religious cult planted deep in Midwest corn country. For King, the original was one of those stories "where things happen just because they happen."[1] Like *Desperation*, published nearly two decades later, "Children of the Corn" is based on a classic horror trope: wrong place, wrong time.

For Burt and Vicky Robeson, the place is Gatlin, Nebraska, the time is the twenty-first year of the Age of Favor, more than two decades after a sinister force blew in from the cornfields and changed the small town forever. Driving cross-country in a last-ditch attempt to save their marriage, they find themselves in a seemingly deserted rural community. But everything is not as it seems. Shortly after their arrival, a crowd of children attacks them and carries Vicky off into the cornfields, where she is murdered and hung in mock crucifixion, a sacrifice to the mysterious god known as "He Who Walks Behind the Rows." Not long after, when Burt is taken, we learn that he, too, "began to scream. But he did not scream long."[2] As King does with *Desperation*, in "Children of the Corn" he embeds a number of important religious themes that are easily missed if readers mistake the story for little more than *Lord of the Flies* meets *The Wicker Man*.

"What are we afraid of, as humans?" King asks. "Chaos. The outsider. We're afraid of change. We're afraid of disruptions, and that's what I'm interested in."[3] This is the *metataxis of horror*, one of the principal fulcra of the horror story: our deeply ingrained fear of a shift or reversal in the accepted order of the universe.[4] Almost more than anything else, we dread that the world is not as it appears. In "Children of the Corn" these disruptions appear in two ways: (a) an invasive change in the sacred order, one that renders old understandings of reality essentially meaningless, and (b) a new and more terrifying vision of the unseen order itself, one that calls into question everything we think we know—and why we think we know it.

Like William Golding's classic novel or William Nolan and George Johnson's dystopic *Logan's Run*, "Children of the Corn" can be read as a metaphor for something all children experience at one time or another: the desire to be free of adult control. When the Age of Favor dawned in Gatlin, when He Who Walks Behind the Rows first appeared and called the children to him, anyone over the age of nineteen was immediately offered as a sacrifice to this new god. First and foremost, this meant the two adults most symbolic of social authority, "the Blue Man and the False Minister"—the local police constable and the Baptist pastor. To read the story simply as an allegory of adolescent rebellion, though, avoids asking how King imagines this upheaval and what it implies about the religious imagination. He gives us no hint how or why things changed in the small Nebraska farming community, merely that "something had happened in 1964. Something to do with religion, and corn . . . and children."[5]

As Burt and Vicky approach Gatlin, we get our first hint that something might be wrong. A youthful preacher comes on the radio, his message fairly typical, but for one sentence. The one thing Stephen King changes. The fifth business. "The Lord has said there's many mansions in His house," we're told, "but there's no room for the fornicator. No room for the coveter."[6] Obnoxious, maybe, but not uncommon among American religious conservatives. "No room for the defiler of the corn. No room for the homasexshul."[7] Hang on a minute, what was that? Right there, in the middle of a fundamentalist Christian rant that could be heard almost anywhere in the Bible Belt, the first discordant note is dropped softly enough that readers anxious to get on with the story might miss it: "No room for the defiler of the corn." Indeed, Burt and Vicky are too caught up in their endless bickering to notice anything except how *young* the radio preacher sounds.

A few minutes later they pull up beside "a neat white church," a standard bit of municipal set decoration, and "the only place in town that looks as if there isn't ten years' dust on it."[8] "Look at the sermon board,"

Burt says to his wife, who will be dead in less than an hour. "She looked. Neatly pegged white letters under glass read: THE POWER AND GRACE OF HE WHO WALKS BEHIND THE ROWS. The date was July 24, 1976— the Sunday before. 'He Who Walks Behind the Rows,' Burt said, turning off the ignition. 'One of the nine thousand names of God only used in Nebraska, I guess.'"[9] Apprehensive, but not yet frightened, they enter the church, and "the first thing he noticed was a pile of wooden letters in the far corner, dusty and jumbled indifferently together," letters Burt realizes once spelled GRACE BAPTIST CHURCH.[10] "It wasn't the Grace Baptist Church anymore," he surmises. "So what kind of church was it? For some reason, that question caused a trickle of fear."[11] Venturing further into the sanctuary, he and Vicky find that various sections of the large pulpit Bible have been removed, cut out, mostly passages from the New Testament.

"The Old Testament was intact."[12]

Readers familiar with King's influences, those writers who inspired his own dark essays in theology, will sense here echoes of H. P. Lovecraft's classic story "The Shadow over Innsmouth" and the narrator's discovery there. As he tries to learn more about the mysterious New England town, the secretary of the local historical society assures him "that the rumors of devil-worship were partly justified by a peculiar secret cult that had gained force there and engulfed all the orthodox churches."[13] Like the fate that overtook the former Grace Baptist Church in Gatlin, the shadow that drew over Innsmouth is a devastating shift in the sacred order, a sea change in the relationship between humankind and its gods.

When Burt finally looks at the image of Christ hanging behind the pulpit, "the oddest thing was that this Christ had green hair . . . hair which on closer examination revealed itself to be a twining mass of early-summer corn."[14] Hardly the "gentle Jesus, meek and mild" that adorns so many Christian sanctuaries. There is nothing here of Warner Sallman's iconic imagery or the comforting stories we tell our children in Sunday school. Rather, this was "an Old Testament Christ, or a pagan Christ that might slaughter his sheep for sacrifice instead of leading them."[15]

Is this "He Who Walks Behind the Rows"?

As King says, "things happen just because they happen," and we learn nothing of this new god's origins, nothing of its cosmology.[16] In this, though, "He Who Walks Behind the Rows" exemplifies what William James called "the unseen order," remaining hidden, exposing himself only obliquely and infrequently. Just a few hours later, as Burt is deep in the cornfields and seized by "an ecstasy of superstitious terror," his few remaining moments of life reveal only that it was "something huge, bulking up to the sky . . . something green with terrible red eyes the size of footballs. Something that smelled like dried cornhusks years in some dark barn."[17] Whatever sinister vision He Who Walks Behind the Rows represents—even if only that of a local pagan deity—it has forced a change in how we perceive the cosmic order. It has redefined what we consider good and right and true in the world, and completely revised the statutes of our relationship with whatever lies beyond. However it came about, this is an entity powerful enough to supplant the old god, to rewrite the religious socialization of Gatlin's Baptist youth, and to turn them against all forms of adult authority: parental, legal, and ecclesial.

Unspoken here are issues to which Stephen King returns again and again. How fragile is the unseen order on which we think we depend? How solid is the rock of our salvation? That is, how long did Gatlin's Baptist solidarity last when He Who Walks Behind the Rows first appeared? More than that, how thin was the veneer of civilization, of religious and cultural socialization, that the children of the corn could so quickly braid their own beliefs with the new edicts of the corn god in what amounts to an orgy of human sacrifice? These are the certainties King calls into question, the supposed bedrock of faith and belief, indeed, the very definition of what we mean by "religion."

A Necessary Conversation: Mr. King, May I Present Dr. James?

As King points out in *Nightmares and Dreamscapes*, "I believe that there is an unseen world all around us."[18] Yet many of his storyworlds also highlight that what we actually know about the different orders of reality pales to insignificance when compared to what we don't. Just like poor Burt and Vicky Robeson, for millennia humankind has operated as though we do understand, and as though we can in some way influence the relationship between the seen and the unseen orders. It is this certainty that Stephen King relentlessly challenges. He recognizes that there may be "thin spots," places where different orders of reality bump up against one another—the cornfields of Gatlin, Nebraska, perhaps, or a peaceful river fork near Motton, Maine. No matter how dogmatically religious believers declare the truth of their convictions, theology of any kind remains fundamentally conjectural.

Besides whether it's "true" or not, when we think of "religion," we tend to ask three interrelated questions: what is it, what does it do, and what does that imply? Structural approaches tell us what religion *is*, often in terms of how we distinguish one faith tradition from another: statements of doctrine, belief, and ritual practice; daily life as a believer; the organizational form of religious community. All the mental content and physical behaviors people associate with "religion," either theirs or someone else's, serve as a kind of ready-reference guide, a template that helps us to quickly and easily identify (a) *that* something is "religious" (e.g., a group of elderly woman gathering to pray the rosary), and (b) *which* religion (e.g., Roman Catholic). The more attributes we can identify, the more fine-grained our identification. Functional understandings, on the other hand, consider what religion *does*, the social and psychological roles belief and practice play in our lives. Less concerned with the details of doctrine and ritual, functional approaches ask how this rite or that, this belief cluster or another, serves the needs of the community and in what ways. What happens when the Rosary Society gathers in prayer? What does it do for the participants and their community? In one sense, for functionalists the specific content of religious belief is largely irrelevant. If shared prayer or ritual serves to maintain a group bond, for example, then it matters little whether its object is the Virgin Mary, Kwan Yin, a pagan version of the Mother Goddess, or He Who Walks Behind the Rows.

Then there is the question of meaning: what "religion" implies. Whatever they are, whoever holds them, and however they change over time, religious belief and practice tell believers two important things about the world: how it works, and how it *ought* to work. Religion posits a world-state, a sense of the world-as-it-is. Perhaps it's a world filled with unbelievers, among whom the chosen people must walk as a beacon of light. Religion also imagines the world-as-it-should-be—perhaps cleansed of all who have not seen the light and who refuse to follow the true path. King notes over and over that a principal layer of horror fiction is allegory. What his novels and short stories *imply*, then, about questions and concerns that are often relegated to "religion" are as important as what these storyworlds *say* about religious belief, and the behavior of religious believers.

At their core, religious belief and practice contend that *this* is not all there is. However dogmatically put, however horrifically realized, religion conjectures the existence of an unseen order, domains of reality above, behind, and beyond our own. Our varied dialects of god-talk speculate—often in the most breathtaking and arrogant terms—on the nature of our relationship with that order.

What, then, is "religion"? Although dozens of different definitions are on offer, more than a century ago psychologist and philosopher William James gave us a particularly useful one, one that is a great help to us in understanding Stephen King as the dark theologian. Concerned to avoid many of the problems that to this day plague religious studies, in his 1902 Gifford Lectures James proposed a simple, elegant description, one narrow enough to exclude what is not religious, yet broad enough to include religious behavior we might not immediately recognize. In his third Gifford Lecture, he asserted that "*the life of religion . . . consists of the belief that there is an unseen order, and that our supreme good lies in harmonious adjustment thereto.*"[19] Particularly useful for exploring religion in popular culture, this definition obviates both the "supreme deity" problem and the good, moral, and decent fallacy.

Since throughout history far more gods and goddesses have filled our pantheons than exist now, acknowledging religion simply as the belief that there is a realm of existence apart from ours does not require that this "unseen order" be populated by any particular deity, let alone any of those currently in fashion. It could as easily be the "gentle Jesus" of Gatlin's Grace Baptist Church as the "grinning, vulpine"[20] Christ of He Who Walks Behind the Rows, the orthodox god of Lovecraft's Innsmouth or "a debased quasi-pagan thing imported from the East a century before."[21] As I have noted elsewhere,

> By refusing to limit religion to those traditions that hold to belief in a supreme being of one kind or another, [James] avoids the problem that marked many early attempts to establish a working definition and allows for a greatly expanded understanding of religious belief and practice. Moreover, it does not restrict religion to those groups that believe in a

socially approved supreme being or spiritual path, relegating all others to the murky and indistinct world of "cults," "sects," and "false religions."[22]

In terms of horror culture specifically, the most useful aspect of James's definition is that it avoids the *good, moral, and decent fallacy*, the widespread belief that religion is, by definition, a good thing, that it works for the world's benefit, and that if it doesn't it's not "really" religion. This fallacy most commonly appears after acts of religiously motivated hatred or violence, when other believers are quick to distance themselves, proclaiming loudly that the perpetrators do not represent the "true" faith—whatever that is. Islamist terrorists have "misinterpreted" the call of their prophet. Christian hate-mongers at Westboro Baptist Church have not "properly" understood the message of Christ. Buddhist fundamentalists in southern Sri Lanka have "abandoned" the Dharma. More than anything, the power of this fallacy blinds us to the simple fact that, as historian of religion J. Z. Smith points out, "Religion is not nice; it has been responsible for more death and suffering than any other human activity."[23] Goodness, morality, and decency may be the human values for which we strive, but they are neither necessary nor sufficient conditions for calling something "religious"—and they never have been.

Although the blurb for King's 2013 novel *Doctor Sleep*, the sequel to *The Shining*, presents the group known as the True Knot as a kind of shadowy cult haunting America's back roads and blue highways, there is little about them for many readers to appreciate as "religion"—until we consider William James. True Knot members are psychic vampires: they extend their lives not by draining their victims of blood but by "taking steam"—literally absorbing the life energy of other people. Children are most highly prized. Heightened during moments of extreme terror, when we sense that the veil between life and death is thinnest, "steam" is the manifestation of the unseen order, and "taking steam" a horrific inversion of the Eucharist. In traditional Christian theology, the willingness of the sacrificial victim is the operative principle: Christ voluntarily takes on the sins of the world and goes to the cross as an act of vicarious atonement. Christians believe that through his suffering and death, they find eternal life—a myth ritualized and reenacted in hundreds of thousands of churches in almost every country on Earth. For True Knot members, prolonging their own lives is the supreme good, and the sacrifice of unwilling victims the unfortunate cost of harmonious adjustment with their vision of the unseen order. It may not look like it to many people, but for the True Knot "taking steam" is its sacrament, and the group's leader, Rose the Hat, its de facto priest. Seen through the lens of a story such as this, far more often than not, it is the sudden fracture of our illusions about religion that reveal most clearly the cracks in the world.

Seeing the Cracks in the World

"If you think that the shining begins and ends with paltry shit like telepathy," Danny Torrance tells his close friend, pediatrician John Dalton, in *Doctor Sleep*, "you're way short. There are other worlds than these."[24] This is the point King repeatedly strives to make. From *The Shining* and *Doctor Sleep* to *The Dead Zone*, *Desperation*, and *Revival*, his novels explore a myriad of ways different orders of reality rub up against each other. His short fiction exposes the various cracks in the world through which elements of the unseen order peer and pass. Specifically, we catch glimpses of its *quintessence*, while we encounter it as a problem of *perception*, as a function of *difference*, and as a locus of *communication*. None of these are discrete elements in King's storytelling, but are instead mutually informing and reinforcing aspects of how he questions our evolving relationship with these different orders of reality.

Ackerman's Field: Quintessence

In his introduction to *Fear Itself*, one of the first volumes of criticism on King's work, fellow horror author Peter Straub describes the delightful *frisson* he felt reading *'Salem's Lot* for the first time. We're more than 150 pages in, Straub tells us, more than a quarter of the novel, when we realize that one of the main characters, Kurt Barlow, is a vampire. "Great, another *vampire* story," we might have said wearily. For Straub, though, with whom King would later collaborate on *The Talisman* and *Black House*, at that moment "everything clicked together like a good lock."[25] Despite the fact that the vampire tale was by then a hoary and much discredited generic convention, because of his "wonderfully assured technique, King had *disarmed my capacity for doubt*."[26] A telling phrase, in terms of storyworld creation this is much more powerful than Coleridge's oft-quoted but anemic "willing suspension of disbelief." Whether in horror fiction such as *'Salem's Lot* or in religious mythology such as the birth of the Buddha or the resurrection of the Christ, the ability to disarm doubt demonstrates the power of narrative. Rather than momentarily "suspending our disbelief" in a story that could not possibly be true, we come to believe that it is true, even as we sit there knowing it's not.

When the two authors, by then mutual, ardent fans, arranged to meet for the first time while King was spending a year in London, Straub recalls the initial difficulty in getting together. "It was raining," he writes (it is *London*, after all), and King "couldn't find a cab. When he did find one, the driver didn't want to come all the way north to Crouch End." Straub adds, "I'd had that problem myself."[27]

More than a decade later, King himself uses this incident to underwrite the supernatural dread of his Lovecraftian homage, "Crouch End."[28] Two police constables, a rookie and a seasoned veteran, are mulling over recent events in the normally quiet North London suburb. In this neighborhood, where things are usually buttoned up well before midnight, strange things have been happening. "What about Lovecraft?" asks PC Vetter. "Ever read anything by him?"

> Well, this fellow Lovecraft was always writing about Dimensions. . . . Dimensions close to ours. Full of immortal monsters that would drive man mad at one look. Frightful rubbish, of course. Except when one of these people straggles in, I wonder if all of it *was* rubbish. . . . Places where the barriers are thinner. Do you get me? . . . And I think Crouch End's one of those places.[29]

In the same way "Crouch End" self-consciously reiterates the "weird fiction" of H. P. Lovecraft,[30] "N.," writes King, "was strongly influenced by Arthur Machen's 'The Great God Pan,' a story that (like Bram Stoker's *Dracula*) surmounted its rather clumsy prose and works its way unrelentingly into the reader's terror-zone."[31] In his introductions and afterwords, as well as in his storyworlds themselves, King regularly acknowledges his debt to the horror writers who have come before him, the ones who told the same stories in their own ways, who peered into the same shadows and poked about in the same dark places. Arguably, though, along with H. P. Lovecraft, few affected him more than the Welsh writer Arthur Machen.

In veiled Victorian language (but in no uncertain terms), Machen reminds us that the Church of England's tame deity, the "gentle Jesus meek and mild," is not the only god who has commanded the attention of humankind. There are older gods, more terrifying in aspect, more demanding of devotion, and far less forgiving of weakness and failure. "I think 'Pan' is as close as the horror genre comes to a white whale," King continues, "and that sooner or later every writer who takes the form seriously must try to tackle its theme: that reality is *thin*, and the *true* beyond is a limitless abyss filled with monsters."[32]

At the heart of both stories, Machen's "The Great God Pan" and King's "N.," are the literary conceits of the "dread tale passed on" and the "found manuscript." While the former are often framed as things of which we ought not speak, and then only in frightened whispers, the latter comes with an explicit warning: we would be better off if the tale were never told, and the manuscript destroyed. "I listened to her as she spoke in her beautiful voice," the derelict Charles Herbert tells his former schoolmate Villiers in Machen's story, "spoke of things which even now I would not dare whisper in blackest night."[33] Now a respected man-about-town, Villiers wonders what could possibly have brought his erstwhile friend to such low estate. "I tell you you can have no conception of what I know," Herbert continues, "not in your most fantastic, hideous dreams can you have imaged forth the faintest shadow of what I have heard— and seen."[34]

Cautionary passages such as this are standard fare in this kind of weird fiction: the certainty of knowledge that we were not meant to have, but that we relentlessly seek out and will inevitably destroy us. Once we have seen, we cannot *unsee*. Once we know something, we can never *not know* it. Taking refuge in simple ignorance is no longer an option. In a vain effort to forget, we may sink into alcoholism, addiction, or madness, but the damage is done. "I could tell you certain things that would convince you," Herbert says, "but you would never know a happy day again. You would pass the rest of your life, as I pass mine, a haunted man."[35]

The fear of supernatural contagion is also a staple of weird fiction. Whether it's something we "pick up" and transmit to others, the viral result of some grim external agency, or something entirely unknown by which we are simply and inexplicably infected, it is a function of the classic horror trope Things We Are Not Meant to Know.

Consider the central theme of three such stories: Machen's "The Great God Pan," published in 1890; Lovecraft's "From Beyond," written three decades later, but not published until 1934; and King's "N.," published in 2008 in his *Just after Sunset* collection.[36] These are not, however, simply reiterations or repetitions. That is, while they are *tellings* that draw on a common mythic narrative, they are not *variants* of the same fabulous story.[37] Each posits an unseen order populated by unfathomable monstrosity. Each proposes a breach in the barrier, a crack in the world our relentless curiosity has wedged open and through which aspects of that order slip to infect our universe. Each frames the menace in terms of a supernatural contagion restrained or curtailed by some element of the relationship between the seen and the unseen. Finally, in its own way, each assures us that we are far better off not knowing what the story will reveal—all but ensuring that we will continue to wonder.

In "The Great God Pan," years before Herbert and Villiers meet by chance, the barrier between the worlds is first broken by the obsessed Dr. Raymond. Raymond reveals to his friend Clarke that the secret of the unseen order is neither supernatural nor magical, but essentially biological. It is "a slight lesion in the grey matter, that is all; a trifling rearrangement of certain cells, a microscopical alteration that would escape the attention of ninety-nine brain specialists out of a hundred."[38] For Machen, the veil separating our world from the other is the mere thickness of a few cell walls, the scant protection offered by our primitive brains. More than that, Raymond insists, what lies beyond is the *real* world, not what we experience here. Everything we think we see, everything we think we know, everything of which we are so . . . *certain*, "all these are but dreams and shadows: the shadows that hide the real world from our eyes," he tells his terrified friend. "There *is* a real world, but it is beyond this glamour and this vision, beyond these 'chases in Arras, dreams in a career,' beyond them all as beyond a veil."[39]

H. P. Lovecraft's "From Beyond," on the other hand, takes us to the "attic laboratory" of the similarly obsessed Crawford Tillinghast, where an "accursed electrical machine" waits to "generate waves acting on un-recognized sense-organs that exist in us as atrophied or rudimentary vestiges. These waves will open up to us many vistas unknown to man, and several unknown to anything we consider organic life."[40] As with Machen's mad scientist, nothing can dissuade Tillinghast as he delights in what his experiments disclose: the stripping of illusion from our collective vision. "We shall leap time, space, and dimensions," he says, "and without bodily motion, peer to the bottom of creation."[41] Tillinghast's guest that fateful night, the story's narrator, wishes fervently that he did not know, that he had not seen, that he had not been disillusioned. "It would help my shaky nerves," he tells us, "if I could dismiss what I now have to think of the air and the sky about and above me."[42] At the beginning of the story, Tillinghast not only presents the quintessential statement of the problem, but highlights the astonishing hubris to think we can even understand the terms of the cosmic equation, let alone solve it for x.

"What do we know," he had said, "of the world and the universe about us? Our means of receiving impressions are absurdly few, and our notions of surrounding objects infinitely narrow. We see things only as we are constructed to see them, and can gain no idea of their absolute nature. With five feeble senses we pretend to comprehend the boundlessly complex cosmos. . . . I have always believed that such strange, inaccessible worlds exist at our very elbows, *and now I believe I have found a way to break down the barriers.*"[43]

Reading King's "N.," we're struck by a number of similarities and differences. A found-manuscript story, "N." consists of seven documents: a psychiatrist's case notes for a patient known only as N.; the patient's own story, written in a diary as part of his therapeutic process; Dr. Bonsaint's fragmentary manuscript on the case, perhaps the beginnings of an article or a book; two letters from Bonsaint's sister, Sheila—one introducing the documents, the other advising Charles Keen (the putative narrator) to burn the material and never return to the town of Motton, Maine; a newspaper report describing the suicides of the Bonsaint siblings—a week apart, in the same place and the same manner;[44] and, finally, an email from Keen to his receptionist, asking her to cancel his appointments for the week so he can return to Motton, despite Sheila's explicit warning. Both the title and story's fragmentary format give "N." a Kafkaesque feel, while the sense of an unnamable horror, a tenuous barrier, and a supernatural contagion locate it in the same "telling stream" with "The Great God Pan" and "From Beyond."

At their first session, N. asks Dr. Bonsaint if he's ever read Arthur Machen's story. "'It's the most terrifying story ever written,' he says. 'In it, one of the characters says "lust always prevails." But lust isn't what he means. What he means is compulsion.'"[45] An image of N. "being pecked to pieces by invisible birds" appears in Bonsaint's mind. "I see them roosting all over N., pecking away at his flesh in bloody nibbles."[46] Though neither patient nor therapist may yet realize it, this feeling of disquiet is often the experience of prodding the veil between the seen and the unseen. Little of the seen makes sense anymore, and nothing can ever look the same again. After all, whether written by Machen, Lovecraft, or King, each of their stories implies that the unseen order remains hidden for a reason. In N.'s case, the circle of stones standing in the middle of Ackerman's Field marks the grim reality that something vast and terrifying waits just on the other side of reality—and it is up to N. to keep it there.

When Bonsaint asks whether N. is ready to say why he's really there, the distraught man replies, "But, Doc . . . are you sure?"[47] That is, does he *really* want to know, "even if it puts you at risk of winding up like I am now? Because it could happen. I'm lost, but I think—I hope—that I haven't got to the drowning-man state, so panicky I'd be willing to pull down anyone who was trying to save me."[48]

In each of these stories, even a glimpse of the unseen order, a momentary contact with what lurks on the other side, can lead to madness. In Machen's tale, for example, Mary, Dr. Raymond's original experimental subject, ends her brief, unhappy life "a hopeless idiot."[49] Years later, those who encounter Helen, the demigod offspring of Mary's sexual union with "the great god Pan," are also changed in vast and terrible ways. Charles Herbert, we learn, was at one time Helen's husband, but the experience has reduced him to terrified vagrancy. Others who cross Helen's path, even in the most tangential ways, are often left mute and mindless with horror.

N., on the other hand, has both seen what lurks beyond the thin spots and is concerned with keeping it contained. His fear is exposed in the leering faces in the standing stones and the unmistakable feeling that now something knows he's there. In Ackerman's Field, what leaks through the thin spot between the worlds is equated with madness, a spiritual infection that N. believes only his obsessive-compulsive disorder keeps from becoming a pandemic. "If it's not mental—," he tells Bonsaint, "if what I saw and sensed in Ackerman's Field is real—then I'm carrying a kind of infection, which I could pass on to you."[50] Located in what the psychiatrist calls "that broken-down part of Maine," Ackerman's Field simply reeks of Lovecraft and confronts us with the same sense of *thinness* PC Vetter experiences in "Crouch End."[51] In a passage worth quoting at length, N. points to the thin spot's *quintessence*.

> Reality is a mystery, Dr. Bonsaint, and the everyday texture of things is the cloth we draw over it to mask its brightness and darkness. I think we cover the faces of corpses for the same reason. We see the faces of the dead as a kind of gate. It's shut against us . . . but we know it won't *always* be shut. Someday it will swing open for each of us, and each of us will go through.
>
> But there are places where the cloth gets ragged and reality is thin. The face beneath peeps through . . . but not the face of a corpse. It would almost be better if it was. Ackerman's Field is one of those places, and no damn wonder whoever owns it put up a KEEP OUT sign.[52]

What N. takes first to be "a trick of the evening light" suddenly morphs into faces carved into the stone pillars, "not human faces either; the faces of beasts and monsters."[53] Shifting his position, though, which is to say, shifting his perspective—as we will see, a principal goal of the ritual process—N. "saw new faces. Some of those looked human but they were just as horrible. *More* horrible really, because human is always more horrible, don't you think?"[54] Although his rational mind easily explains the formation as natural geology, part of him just as easily imagines the circle as "*planned*, like stones in a Druid circle."[55] More troubling for N. is that when he looks at the stones with his naked eye, there are only seven. Looking through his camera's viewfinder, though, he sees that there are eight, and "that sense of *thinness* swept over me again, as if the world was fragile at that particular place."[56]

This is the quintessence of the unseen order: that *this* is not all there *is*. How we understand the tenuous barriers between these different domains of existence depends on what we believe we see in them. And, very often, we base our reactions less on the reality of a thing than on our perceptions of it.

Summer Street School: Perception

If those of us who are old enough listen carefully, we can almost hear Rod Serling's iconic voice from the famous 1960s television series *The Twilight Zone*: "Meet Emily Sidley, to all outward appearances a perfectly ordinary third-grade teacher. A bit severe, perhaps, as she approaches the end of a long career, but not the sort to take twelve children into the mimeograph room and shoot each of them in the head with a pistol her older brother had taken 'from the body of a dead German.'"[57] "Suffer the Little Children," which was originally published in the men's magazine *Cavalier*, is one of the most disturbing entries in the canon of King's short fiction. This is the story we write in our heads whenever we hear of children murdered at the hands of those they trust—often, but not always a parent. This is the kind of story we write when we read about the death of a young nun in a remote Romanian monastery—starved and beaten to death when her recently diagnosed schizophrenia is interpreted by devout if misguided co-religionists as demonic possession.[58] This is the story we write when we're told any number of tales of unimaginable brutality visited upon the most defenseless among us.

"What happened?" we wonder, as the initial shock of the situation wears off and its much deeper horror sinks in. "What could possibly make them *do* that?" For grade-school teacher Emily Sidley, this is the far end of a continuum that begins the moment we think, "They're nothing but little monsters"—passing notes in class, concealing bean shooters in their pockets, *not* doing their homework—and ends in the copy room with a dead German's Luger in her hand and the reek of cordite in the air. These are stories *about* the crack in the world, but also about *whether* that crack actually exists. They're about our reaction to perception, behavior based on what we *think* is real or *believe* is real. "We see the world not as it is," writes Lisa Cron in *Wired for Story*, "but as we believe it to be."[59] Notwithstanding the gospel allusion in King's title, it is those moments when we perceive the unseen order intruding into our world that make "Suffer the Little Children" a profoundly religious story. Because religion, at its heart, is behavior based on belief, a perception of the world that, in the end, cannot be confirmed or denied.

What did Emily see that day when the world cracked open and the unseen order peaked through? Even as she took the pistol from its box and loaded it "carefully, just as Jim had shown her,"[60] how many times did she think, *This is insane, Emily, it's all in your mind. They're little boys and girls, not monsters*? What was she so convinced she saw that the end result was "a little dead boy with a round black hole above his right eye"?[61] Whatever it was, the difference between private mania and public mayhem, between one former grade-school teacher who was later "sent quietly to Juniper Hill" and angry villagers with pitchforks and torches, is often little more than the ability to get others to see as we do.[62]

In the West, possession narratives are often about who sees the possessed and whether what they see is real. From Miles Bennell in *Invasion of the Body Snatchers* to Regan MacNeil in *The Exorcist*, however, from Ira Levin's *The Stepford Wives* to Emily Sidley's grade three class at Summer Street School, getting others to believe is crucial. Does it become more real, though, simply because others see it our way? Clearly not, and this is one of the principal problems of belief, one of the reasons our various faiths require constant, ongoing reinforcement. But what, exactly, does she see?

While she waited impatiently for an inattentive student to spell his assigned word, *something* happened in the classroom. Suddenly, "Robert changed. She caught just a flicker of it, just a frightening glimpse of Robert's face changing into something . . . different."[63] *Of course*, she thinks, *I imagined it*. How absurd to think otherwise. Tired, stressed, more than a bit frustrated with the class, she was "acting like a skittish girl just out of teachers college."[64] What Emily Sidley catches out of the corner of her eye, though, are the masks of reality beginning to slip, the cracks opening between the worlds. What she saw was "something bulbous. Something that shimmered. Something that stared at me, yes, stared, and grinned and wasn't a child at all. It was old and it was evil and—."[65] And what? Demonic?

In many ways, we have tamed religion, turned it into a piece of cultural furniture, what a generation ago Canadian writer Pierre Berton dubbed "the comfortable pew."[66] It has become a weekly entertainment, rather than the life-or-death affair it was for our ancestors. Indeed, in our haste to distance ourselves from the more atrocious aspects of religious history—and the atrocities still committed each day in the name of religion—we forget that our visions of the unseen order have always had much darker sides. In other words, it's not always our guardian angels who look in on us. When Chris MacNeil asks *The Exorcist*'s Father Damien how she can get an exorcism for her daughter, he responds, incredulously, "Well, the first thing, I'd have to get them into a time machine and get them back to the sixteenth century." In *Hellraiser III*, when journalist Joey Summerskill seeks refuge in a local church, claiming that demons are after her, the smiling priest urges her back to a seat in the comfortable pew. "Demons?" he says gently. "Demons are not real. They're parables, metaphors." A moment later, though, when *Hellraiser*'s iconic Pinhead appears in the narthex, Joey replies with terrified sarcasm, "Then what the fuck is *that*?"

Early Christian history is littered with stories of demons tempting the desert fathers and mothers, men and women who abandoned everything and fled to the wastelands in search of God. While many streams of Christianity have abandoned belief in the literal embodiment of supernatural evil, others maintain that demonic threats lurk behind pop cultural phenomena ranging from rock music and scary movies to comic books and *Dungeons & Dragons*.[67] In Thailand, monastic hell gardens such as Wang Saen Suk graphically portray a Buddhist version of Dante's *Inferno*, while Tibetan Buddhists transitioning through the *bardo* state are encouraged to recognize demonic figures as products of their own mind, rather than real entities. In the latter case, what they choose for their next life depends on their perception of what happens in the space between lives.

In a third-grade classroom at Summer Street School, the dark side of the unseen order peeks in on poor Emily Sidley.

> "There's quite a few of us," Robert said suddenly, as if he were commenting on the weather.
> It was Miss Sidley's turn to be silent.

Quite evil, she thought, amazed. *Very, incredibly evil.*

"Little boys who tell stories go to hell," she said clearly. "I know many parents no longer make their . . . their *spawn* . . . aware of that fact, but I assure you it is a *true* fact, Robert. Little boys who tell stories go to hell. Little girls too, for that matter."[68]

Even then, she can't quite believe it, because it couldn't possibly be true. Could it?

Robert changed.

His face suddenly ran together like melting wax, the eyes flattening and spreading like knife-struck egg yolks, nose widening and yawning mouth disappearing. The head elongated, and the hair was suddenly not hair, but straggling, twitching growths.

Robert began to chuckle.[69]

"She ran," King tells his Constant Reader, and "fled screaming down the corridor."[70] In his author's note for this story, King writes, "Put another way, 'Suffer the Little Children' is a ghastly sick-joke with no redeeming social merit whatever." While we may disagree with King on this, he concludes, "I like that in a story."[71] Indeed, the story's value is that it discloses so precisely how powerful perception is as a motivator of behavior.

Monsters, aliens, angels and demons—these are objects of belief, in many cases far more powerful than anything so prosaic as mere reality. Far more dangerous, more horrific than, say, "lions and tigers and bears! Oh my!" What happens, though, when we take the notion of children as "little monsters" seriously? How does that affect our perception of the thin spots when we take them literally? Once again, we're back to the question of the unknown and the unseen. We've returned to the reality of our perennial, unspoken fear: What if they're right?

Traveling from a grade-school classroom to a highway rest stop in King's short story "Mile 81," we find that the setting could still not be more prosaic.[72] Even though its buildings have been boarded up for lack of government funding, the weedy patch of cracked asphalt still offers momentary respite for weary travelers. Sitting at this particular rest stop, though, off to one side, is a mud-covered station wagon of indeterminate vintage. The kind of thing one sees on countless blue highways throughout the country, this abandoned vehicle is actually camouflage for something lurking behind or beyond what we think is real. As various motorists approach this car-that-is-not-a-car, concerned that there might be someone inside, perhaps in need of help, one by one they are caught by it, sucked in, and consumed. Fundamentalist Christian Doug Clayton, female mud-wrestler Julie Vernon, the Lussier family in their 2011 Ford Expedition, even little Pete Simmons, who watches horrified from the abandoned washrooms—they are like so many flies trapped in amber by a force they cannot begin to understand.

In reality, the station wagon is a kind of grimy, mechanical pitcher plant that has learned to prey on the neighborly good will of one person for another. It is an alien presence that proves to Doug Clayton, for example, a man "who liked to call his Bible, 'the ultimate insurance manual,'" that the world is nothing like the Good Book says.[73] It is both more wondrous and more terrible than anything his friends at the Church of the Holy Redeemer could imagine.

Like "Children of the Corn" and "Suffer the Little Children," stories such as "Mile 81" call into question our perceptions of the seen and the unseen orders. Often, through characters like Doug, they directly challenge the religiously oriented hubris that claims to know what's what. In "Mile 81," another unnatural narrative warning us that things are not necessarily as they appear to be, the question of who or what will emerge from the old station wagon at the deserted rest stop is only the beginning of the horror. As the survivors battle the car-that-is-not-a-car, "it pulled in tighter and still tighter, becoming a fiery ball. Then, as Pete and the Lussier kids and Trooper Andrews watched, it shot up into the blue spring sky. For a moment longer it was there, glowing like a cinder, and then it was gone. Pete found himself thinking of the cold darkness above the envelope of the earth's atmosphere—where anything might live and lurk."[74] And that's the point. In the end, at "Mile 81" the unseen order is extraterrestrial rather than supernatural, alien not paranormal. Something else, something Other, something Different has planted itself in our reality, looking for its next meal.

Haven, Maine: Difference

An enduring myth of American UFO folklore is that many of the tech-nological advances since the end of World War II—everything from microwaves to microchips, and from supersonic flight to stealth technol-ogy—is the result of the reverse engineering of recovered extraterrestrial spacecraft. Sometimes in these enterprises we enjoy the encouragement and cooperation of the original occupants; other times, not. As a result, the story goes, humankind has leapfrogged the time scale of technologi-cal evolution, going from the Wright brothers' first flight at Kill Devil Hill to the moon landing at Tranquility Base—and beyond—in less than one human lifetime. Attempting to explain this astonishing techno-logical advance, "ancient astronaut" theorists often ask, "How could we possibly have done all that *without* help?"

Though King is careful to avoid this kind of subcultural conspiracy lore, this very myth animates *The Tommyknockers*, one of King's few novels explicitly based on extraterrestrial contact.[75] The discovery of a crashed UFO, buried for tens of thousands of years in the rocky ground of coastal Maine, leads to a series of technological advances inexplicable by any means other than alien intervention. Pulp novelist Bobbi Ander-son believes that the craft was buried deep in the glacier that covered most of what is now the Eastern Seaboard, and remained undisturbed until she tripped over a tiny portion protruding above ground on her rural property. Exposed to the craft's influence, Bobbi, who admits to limited household repair skills, suddenly "invents" an energy source that allows her to disconnect entirely from the Coastal Maine Power grid. Upgrading her "old black Underwood" allows her to "write" a four-hundred-page novel in less than three days.[76] Not only does the aug-mented manual typewriter type by itself, it does so automatically, reading Bobbi's thoughts while she digs in her garden or continues excavating the alien craft. Even as she sleeps, it accesses the deep well of her mind, the place where all her stories, including novels such as *The Buffalo Soldiers*, already exist *in toto*. The machine brings them to the surface and writes them down. In the morning, after she makes her coffee, Bobbi simply separates the pages spooled out onto the floor and stacks the manuscript.

"It's like a direct tap into the subconscious," she tells her best friend, poet Jim Gardner, "more like dreaming than writing . . . but what comes out is unlike dreams, which are often surreal and disconnected. This really isn't a typewriter at all anymore. It's a dream machine. One that dreams rationally."[77] She realizes, though, that these are not "her" inventions, that she is little more than a conduit, a programmable third-hand tool for the aliens she has come to call "the Tommyknockers." "That's what I am," she tells him, as they weigh the consequences and implications of her find. "An idiot savant. That's *all* I am, and they'd know it. Those things—customizing the typewriter, fixing the water heater—I only remember them in bits and pieces. When I'm *doing* them, everything seems as clear as a bell. But later—."[78]

When Bobbi first shows Gardner the craft, hardly his sharpest turn on life's roller coaster in the last few hours, "a line from Genesis suddenly occurred to him, making him shiver as if a cold wind had blown past: *There were giants in the earth in those days.*"[79] As he struggles to understand, almost feverish from the implications, he asks Bobbi, "People are going to change their fucking *religions* over this, do you know it?"[80]

Stephen King wrote *The Tommyknockers* between August 1982 and May 1987. He typed the final sentence—"Ninety-three million miles from the sun, and a hundred parsecs from the axis-pole of the galaxy, Hilly and David Brown slept in each others' arms"—a decade, almost to the day, after the premiere of *Star Wars*, nearly ten years after *Close Encounters of the Third Kind* and five years after *E.T.: The Extraterrestrial.*[81] When it was published, however, *The X-Files*, one of the most popular television series of the 1990s, was still years away from its network debut, while the plethora of "real UFO" pseudo-documentaries were decades over the horizon. It's easy enough to read *The Tommyknockers* now and to forget the historical context in which it was imagined and written. Forgetting to look at the publication date can easily mislead us into reading the novel through the lens of pop culture products, tropes, and concepts that did not yet exist or were not as fully formed as they are now. To understand *The Tommyknockers* in context, we must ask what products, tropes, and concepts *did* exist. What was going on in popular culture that King's novel tapped in to? "When the horror movies wear their various sociopolitical hats," he writes in *Danse Macabre*, though we could extend his description to include horror culture writ large, "—the B-picture as tabloid editorial—they often serve as an extraordinarily accurate barometer of those things which trouble the night-thoughts of a whole society."[82] So, what were those troubled night-thoughts?

"*Don't you know what you're talking about?*" Jim Gardner raves drunkenly at a party, pouring out "the inarticulate cry of the heart." "*Don't you know what the stakes are? Don't any of you remember what happened in Russia two years ago?*"[83] A little more than a year before King's novel was published, one of the worst nuclear disasters in history occurred at the Chernobyl power plant in northern Ukraine, near the border with Belarus. "They *haven't. They* can't," Gardner realizes. "*They'll be burying the cancer victims far into the next century.*"[84]

Bobbi Anderson has no idea what she's dealing with when she unearths the gigantic alien craft, nor any conception of the consequences when she begins to build her strange devices. King's terrestrial allegory is clear: Just as there are some things we're not meant to see, there is some power we are not meant to have. There is also, however, the extraterrestrial connection, an unseen order that emerges not from another dimension, but from the velvet black of night.

Although they lurk in the background like the majority of the alien ship buried on Bobbi's property, Gardner's seemingly offhand references—the *nephilim*, the "giants" of Genesis 6 and Numbers 13, and the potential shift in religious consciousness once evidence of extraterrestrial life is undeniable—speak to these other issues: questions of paleo-contact and extraterrestrial intervention in human evolution. While the former we might call the "we are not alone" problem, the latter exemplifies the "gods from outer space" dilemma, and the effect that confirmation of contact with extraterrestrial intelligence (ETI) could have on religious belief and practice.

Considered thus, *The Tommyknockers* becomes more than simply an alien invasion story or an allegory for the dangers of technology exceeding common sense. It is a colonization and planetary conversion narrative that resonates with conquests, both political and religious, going back as far as we have records. Two of the most prominent proponents of the "ancient astronaut" theory, into which *The Tommyknockers* fits precisely, are Erich von Däniken, a Swiss hotelier turned author and whose *Chariots of the Gods?* is arguably the most famous example of the genre, and Zecharia Sitchin, less well-known than von Däniken, but whose ideas hold tremendous sway among believers in paleo-contact.[85]

Sitchin's analysis begins with a not unreasonable question: "How was it, for example, that the civilization of Sumer seemed to flower so suddenly nearly 6,000 years ago without a precursor?"[86] Proposing a theory of modified catastrophism, Sitchin believed that our solar system contains a planet called Nibiru, which follows such an eccentric orbit that it enters the inner solar system (i.e., within the orbital plane of Pluto) only once every few thousand years. Previous incursions include one during which Nibiru collided with Tiamat, one of its own moons, an impact that created both Earth and the asteroid belt between Jupiter and Neptune.[87] According to Sitchin, Nibiru is inhabited by a technologically advanced race known as the Anunnaki, who first visited Earth nearly half a million years ago. Through genetic engineering, the Anunnaki created *Homo sapiens* as a slave race, eventually providing them with a framework for culture and society.

The core of the ancient astronaut theory is that these events formed the basis for human religious mythology. That is, where did "civilization" come from, and why does it seem to appear as if out of nowhere? The creation of the solar system is understood as a great battle between primordial forces, the creation of humankind the product of gods and goddesses descending from the heavens—in this case, all recorded in the ancient Babylonian epic, the *Enûma Elish*. Seen through the lens of the ancient astronaut theory, this is the unseen order as *difference*. It is the technological and spatio-political understood as all but supernatural, and it invokes Arthur C. Clarke's venerable "Third Law": "Any sufficiently advanced technology is indistinguishable from magic."[88]

Whether Sitchin's catastrophism or von Däniken's theory of paleo-contact have any validity beyond their internal consistency—which, in many ways, makes these argument their own kind of theology—matters less than the fact that such books, and dozens upon dozens of others, were enormously popular when they first appeared, and remain so today. They continue to pose those "properly human questions" of origin and meaning. In the same way extraterrestrials guided paleo-Britons to construct Stonehenge, Old Kingdom Egyptians the Great Pyramids, and primitive peoples around the world monumental structures ranging from the stone heads (and bodies) on Easter Island to the Nazca Lines etched into the high desert of Peru, the Tommyknockers led Bobbi Anderson to create a telepathic typewriter.

"The unanswered question," writes Sitchin, "is: *Why*—why did civilization come about at all?"

> For, as most scholars now admit in frustration, by all data Man should be without civilization. There is no obvious reason that we should be more civilized than the primitive tribes of the Amazon jungles or the inaccessible parts of New Guinea. . . . The obvious question, then, is this: Did we and our Mediterranean ancestors really acquire this advanced civilization on our own?[89]

For Stephen King, though, in this novel at least, the answer is obvious:

> Late last night and the night before
> Tommyknockers, Tommyknockers, knocking at the door.[90]

Once again, we return to the fifth business of weird fiction: the one thing that changes in the ordinary round of daily life, the one thing that we notice—or that notices us—and that brings us into contact with orders of reality we scarcely imagine exist. Once contact is made, however, how we communicate with whatever populates the unseen order will not only shape our perception of it, but determine our ability to navigate our relationship with whatever awaits on the other side.

Castle Rock: Communication

Communication with the various denizens and ghostly inhabitants of the unseen order has played a prominent role in the human religious imagination for millennia. Shamans travel to the spirit realm, seeking healing for the tribe or knowledge in a time of crisis. Spiritualism and spiritualist churches have been part of the Western religious landscape since the middle of the nineteenth century. Spiritualist practice is predicated specifically on the *thinness* of the veil between the seen and the unseen orders, between the living and the dead.[91] In brief, spiritualists believe that some part of each person, whether as a soul or a spirit, survives bodily death and can communicate with the living. Many spiritualist churches practice mediumship—active communication with the dead—as a part of weekly worship services. Celebrity mediums such as James van Praagh, John Edward, Sylvia Browne, and Allison DuBois are regular pop culture fare. Although skeptics just as regularly debunk spiritualist claims, their criticisms do little to diminish popular enthusiasm for ongoing contact with those we love and fear we have lost. Or, in the case of Stephen King's novel *The Dark Half*, those we have come to hate—and fear we cannot lose.

In the interconnected panoply of King's storyworlds, Thad Beaumont is yet another alcoholic writer from Somewhere, Maine. Using an old Remington 32 typewriter, he writes serious literature, Very Important Novels. Using nothing but Berol Black Beauty pencils, on the other hand, and writing under the pseudonym George Stark, he produces wildly popular genre crime fiction.[92] While the one established his reputation, the other paid for his lakeside summer house. Rather than a professionally useful figment of Beaumont's imagination, however, Stark has taken on a life of his own, a particularly horrific, vengeful life that he's unwilling to give up. Who is he? *What* is he? The reality is that Stark has been with Beaumont from the beginning—a twin brother who never developed in the womb, but never really disappeared. Through Beaumont's pseudonymous authorship, the revenant spirit of his unborn brother has taken material form in Stark, the hardened-criminal-turned-crime-novelist. To communicate with his "dark half," Beaumont practices a particular form of mediumship, a method for piercing the veil between the worlds, for communicating across the thin spots.

> The idea embodied a form of psychic contact he had read about but had never seen demonstrated: automatic writing. The person attempting to contact a dead soul (or a living one) by this method held a pen or pencil loosely in his hand with the tip on a blank sheet of paper and simply waited for the spirit—pun most definitely intended—to move him. . . . This could be extremely dangerous—that it could, in fact, lay the practitioner wide open to some form of possession.[93]

Both popular and religious culture are filled with examples of such channeled communication: from *The Urantia Book*, a religious text more than two thousand pages long that claims to be entirely the product of automatic writing, to *Sedona* magazine, which for more than two decades has published predictions, spiritual advice, encouragement, and social commentary—all derived allegedly from channeled sources. Although this form of spirit communication is now often relegated to the so-called New Age movement, its roots sink millennia deep into human religious consciousness. As Thad Beaumont recalls the classic *Rocky and Bullwinkle* line "Eenie-meany-chili-beany. The spirits are about to speak!" the veil between the worlds becomes even thinner.[94]

In stories such as these, religion, superstition, and folklore often mix and mingle, occasionally becoming indistinct one from the other. Throughout *The Dark Half*, for example, the image of sparrows and the phrase "The sparrows are flying again" mark both the boundary between the worlds and the presence of those with the power to cross back and forth. According to Greek mythology, explains one of Thad's colleagues, sparrows are a species of *psychopomp*, "meaning those who conduct." We often forget that what we now blithely dismiss as "myth" or "legend" was for thousands of years the essence of religious belief and practice.

> In this case, those who conduct human souls back and forth between the land of the living and the land of the dead. . . . Loons and whippoorwills are outriders of the living. . . . Their job is to guide newly dead souls to their proper place in the afterlife. . . . Sparrows are said to be outriders of the deceased. . . . Their job is to guide lost souls back into the land of the living. They are, in other words, the harbingers of the living dead.[95]

Although King gives *The Dark Half* his signature spin, the idea of a character escaping the pages of a book is not uncommon in fantasy literature. In Timothy Findley's *Headhunter*, for example, former librarian and "sometime spiritualist" Lilah Kemp is able to call characters out of books she reads at the Metropolitan Toronto Reference Library. "A spiritualist of intense but undisciplined powers," writes Findley, "she had once brought Teresa of Avila back into being and lost her on Yonge Street."[96] Unfortunately, as *Headhunter*'s opening line tells us, "On a winter's day, while a blizzard raged through the streets of Toronto, Lilah Kemp inadvertently set Kurtz free from page 92 of *Heart of Darkness*."[97] And that isn't the worst of it. Once, "Jack the Ripper slipped from Lilah's grasp and killed two girls in Allan Gardens."[98] Similarly, in Cornelia Funke's *Inkheart* trilogy, Mortimer Folchart and his daughter, Maggie, are "Silvertongues," people who possess the power to read characters out of books, to take literally the popular storytelling art of "bringing them to life."[99]

In the introduction to *Nightmares and Dreamscapes*, four years after *The Dark Half*, but calling back to the Cowardly Lion, King writes, "Most of all, I *do* believe in spooks. I *do* believe in spooks. I *do* believe in spooks."[100] The line also appears in *The Dark Half*, placed there in the mind of Castle Rock's sheriff, Alan Pangborn, as he struggles to explain, or at least come to terms with, the *fact* of George Stark, who by all that's rational *should not exist*. Through Pangborn, King highlights the importance and compulsion of fiction, especially stories that probe our perception of the unseen order and its quintessence, storyworlds that mark the difference between what we know and what we imagine, and characters that talk across the worlds. "*But writers invite ghosts*," Pangborn thinks, and "*maybe, along with actors and artists, they are the only totally accepted mediums of our society. They make worlds that never were, populate them with people who never existed, and then invite us to join them in their fantasies. And we do it, don't we? Yes, we PAY to do it.*"[101]

Just as *'Salem's Lot* is King's stake in the vampire story, and *Revival* his telling of *Frankenstein*, *The Dark Half* visits another classic horror trope: the thin spots marking the boundaries between the seen and the unseen. In its own way, each of these stories confronts our universal awareness of death, and our millennia-old wonderings: What happens next? What are we looking for? What are we hoping to find? Like the religious professionals who guide our varied faith lives through sermons and exhortations, "the only totally accepted mediums of our society" are expected to ask these central questions on our behalf, questions to which we now turn.

3

Deadfall

Ghost Stories as God-Talk

Death is the great and certain mystery, the *ur*-fear stalking us all. While it may take us by surprise, so far as we know only humans recognize its inevitability. Only humans have developed the ability to imagine a world in which we are *not*. At some point in history, our hominin ancestors noticed that one of their small group no longer moved about the camp and there identified the ineluctable *difference* of death. However long it took, this is the moment from which so much of our religious imagining evolved. What has happened to them? Where have they gone? Are they still, in some way, a part of us? Will they come back? Will the same thing happen to us? What should we do? These questions and more are the dark loam in which seeds of religious belief, ritual, and devotion were originally sown. Whether we are believers or not, however, the fact that "religion" is now so deeply embedded in our culture often blinds us to two important considerations: priority and story. Religious belief and practice do not precede death as a human inevitability. This may seem absurdly obvious, but because our death rituals are grounded in much larger systems of religious understanding, systems that are presented to us with an *a priori* certitude, we forget the long period of time when our ancestors simply wandered away from the body. Countless thousands of years passed *before* "religion," as it were, before as a species we wondered what happens after, and before we began to tell each other stories about it.

Stories we told before the rise of the gods. Stories we still tell.

That's the second point. How many of us have explained the loss of a beloved pet with "she's gone to live on a farm in the country"? Presumably, children anguished that they may never again play with "Hannah the best dog that ever lived" take some comfort in knowing that she's not, in fact, gone.[1] Not *really*. We loved her deeply in life and are comforted knowing that she's happy and well now that she's no longer with us. And how different is this from the stories we draw from the wells of religious experience? When a Christian dies, for example, we're told that "she's in a better place now," that "he's gone to be with the Lord" and at that very moment is sitting down to "dinner with Jesus Christ," as *Under the Dome*'s Big Jim Rennie is fond of saying, with "roast beef, fresh peas, mashed with gravy! How's that for an awesome thought? You hang onto that."[2] That is, hang on to the stories we tell each other both to blunt the sting of death and to explain its mystery.

Death, writes Stephen King in his brief introduction to "Riding the Bullet," "is probably the single greatest subject of horror fiction: our need to cope with a mystery that can be understood only with the aid of a hopeful imagination."[3] The mystery of death is the driving force behind both horror culture and religious belief, both of which in their own way respond to questions that are never fully, finally answered. We manage our mortality, the inevitability of a world in which we are *not*, through the stories we tell. "Supernatural stories," writes Brian Boyd, whether we regard them as true (religion) or fiction ("Riding the Bullet"), "attempt to offer an additional level of explanation," specifically in terms of the "unseen forces that supposedly impact our lives."[4] We may not understand what happens at death any better or more clearly, but our stories—even, and perhaps especially our ghost stories—ease the thought of passing from this life to whatever awaits beyond. If nothing else, they assure us that there *is* something "beyond."

Our ghost stories invoke our god-talk.

Forerunners and Ferrymen

Unlike so much of Stephen King's short fiction, "Mister Yummy" is not really a horror story. Nothing very scary happens. No monsters leer from fallow fields, no teachers shoot small boys in the head. There are no fifth-business surprises. Indeed, it reads more like a fictional meditation on an experience too common to be ignored, yet too easily dismissed because we cannot explain it. "Mister Yummy" has a comforting feel to it, a sense that everything is going to turn out all right at the end.

The end, of course, is death.

The setting is the Lakeview Assisted Living Center. Lately, Ollie has been seeing visions of a beautiful young man he saw only once before, decades ago at a New York "dance club called Highpockets" during the dread years of the AIDS epidemic.[5] Each time he appears, the young man he took to calling "Mister Yummy" draws closer and closer. He was "at the foot of the main drive," he tells his friend Dave, then he was "lounging on the porch steps below the main entrance," and finally "sitting on a bench outside the admission office."[6] Most recently, Mister Yummy was in the center's common room. He waved to Ollie, even "tipped me a wink."[7] "Pretty soon I'll have a room visit," the old man continues, "and that will be that. I don't mind."[8] That evening, they find Ollie on his bed, seeming to have "died as he lived, peacefully and with no fuss."[9]

A few months later, Dave sees "a young woman standing by the fountain. She wore the kind of shin-length, frilly-collared dress you only saw nowadays in old black-and-white movies."[10] "*Hello, Miss Yummy,*" Dave thinks as "the pretty redhead tipped him a wink," knowing that "next time she would be closer."[11]

Now, it may be that in the moments surrounding death our brains create a comfort zone, an illusion to cushion the terror that overwhelms us. As Dave tells Ollie at first, "it was just a trick your brain played on you."[12] That is, the forerunners, the apparitions, the ghostly conductors, the mothers and fathers, friends, family, and, in my case, I hope, the dogs, may all be hallucinations, nothing more than synaptic misfires at a time of extreme crisis. If so, though, their misfiring is remarkably consistent, and has inspired countless stories, from the reassuring to the terrifying.

In Ireland, banshees keen impending death, while on the west coast of Canada, owls are said to call the name of one about to die. For the Greeks it was Charon, the mythical ferryman who took them across the river Styx, while ancient Egyptians built elaborate funerary boats to convey the souls of the dead to the afterlife. Around the world and in myriad forms, the Grim Reaper comes to collect us when our time is done. While these are only a few of the countless ways we have imagined our passage from the seen to the unseen, what they all have in common is that they do imagine such a journey. "I'm not scared of hell," ninety-one-year-old Charlie Hayes says to Danny Torrance in *Doctor Sleep*. "I'm scared there's *nothing*. There was nothing *before*, we all know that, so doesn't it stand to reason there's nothing after?"[13] From that moment in the cave so many millennia ago to the most extravagant burial rituals today, none of our death rites imagine there is simply nothing.

If you doubt this claim, consider "Riding the Bullet." Unlike "Mister Yummy," "Riding the Bullet" is pure horror, King's "telling of a tale you can hear in almost any small town."[14]

Somewhere deep in the Maine night, the heavy rumble of an old Mach 1 Mustang winds down as the driver stops to pick up a hitchhiker. Alan Parker climbs in, desperately grateful for the ride. Many miles away, his mother has had a stroke, and long hours on lonely roads have convinced him she's already gone. "Nice to meet you," says the young man behind the wheel. "I'm George Staub." He extends a hand that "seemed to float out like a hand in a dream."[15] A chill runs down Alan's spine, suddenly, inexplicably certain he will never see his mother again. His mind's eye flashes back to a moment just minutes before the Mustang's lights came around the bend: the inscription on a tombstone.

GEORGE STAUB
JANUARY 19, 1977–OCTOBER 12, 1998
Well begun, too soon done.[16]

As the small rural graveyard dwindled rapidly in the vintage muscle car's rearview mirror, it was the smell that really gave the game away—that, and "the heavy black line that encircled his neck."[17] What might pass at first for a tattoo clearly wasn't. "Dozens of black marks crossed it vertically. They were the stitches," Alan realizes in horror, "put in by whoever had put his head back on his body."[18]

"I was riding with a dead man."[19]

Unlike Ollie or Dave, though, who recognize and even welcome the ones who have come for them, Alan knew instinctively that he "must not let the driver of the Mustang know that I sensed something was wrong. It was my only chance."[20] Instead of embracing the harbinger, he seeks refuge in denial, in the desperate hope that the driver might not be here for him, that he might yet live to see the Mustang's taillights disappear. But as they tear through the night, George Staub turns to him. "Do you know who I am, Alan?"

"You're a ghost."[21]

"Come on, man," Staub says, giving "an impatient little snort," "you can do better than that. Fuckin *Casper*'s a ghost. Do I float in the air?"[22] When he holds his hand up, Alan "could hear the dry, unlubricated sound of his tendons creaking."[23] If not a ghost, not a revenant spirit, then what?

"I'm a kind of messenger," Staub said "Fuckin FedEx from beyond the grave, you like that? Guys like me actually come out pretty often—whenever the circumstances are just right. You know what I think? I think that whoever runs things—God or whatever—must like to be entertained."[24]

Casting George Staub as a psychopomp, a four-barrel ferryman for the dead, "Riding the Bullet" inverts a couple of classic spooky tales: the vanishing hitchhiker and the ghostly conductor. An enduring motif found around the world, the vanishing hitchhiker's basic structure is simple: a person, usually a young woman, is offered a ride, either spontaneously or in response to a request for help. Invariably vague about details, she occasionally does not speak at all. When they reach their destination, however, the driver and other passengers turn to find her seat empty.[25] More than this, though, more than simply ghosts, King points to the ongoing uncertainty we harbor about the nature of the unseen order. From whom is George Staub a messenger? From "God or whatever"? And what is the message?

It is not the case that we craft scary stories on the basis of religion, as though the one grows from the other like some phantom limb we can ignore at will. Nor can we turn away from ghost stories because "they're not our thing," and then with no hint of irony sit in church and nod faithfully over the minister's thrilling exposition of 1 Samuel 28:3–25—King Saul demanding that the witch of Endor summon the spirit of the prophet Samuel. It's not that we can mock the current pop culture fascination with zombies, which seems to have taken over from vampires (which had previously sucked the celebrity out of witches), but then listen with rapt attention to the story of Lazarus—or, for that matter, Jesus. Ghost stories are not epiphenomenal to religious myth and legend; they emerge and take shape from the same place in the human imagination. Indeed, in a relatively rare moment of autobiography, King tells us that "Riding the Bullet" was his "attempt to talk about how my own mother's approaching death made me feel."[26] Both are ongoing attempts to answer the same simple question: What happens when we die?

Believing in Ghosts

In 2005 paranormal entertainment in America enjoyed a banner year. Major television networks premiered six new series, divided neatly along two lines. Three explored the idea of extraterrestrials (*Surface*; *Threshold*; *Invasion*), while three others, aspects of the supernatural (*Medium*; *The Ghost-Whisperer*; and the eponymous *Supernatural*). All ran with large budgets and the enthusiastic backing of their parent studios; most featured well-known actors in lead roles. Yet their success split precisely along their subject lines. None of the alien-themed shows survived its first season, and two were cancelled after airing only a few episodes. *Medium* and *The Ghost-Whisperer*, on the other hand, each ran for seven seasons, and *Supernatural* for more than a dozen. All this, even though surveys regularly indicate that belief in UFO and ETI phenomena lags not far behind belief in haunting spirits. What explains the durability of one domain of storytelling over the other? Why do we return more often and more readily to ghost stories than to alien invasions?

We are pattern-seeking creatures, and one of the cognitive processes that gradually emerged in our developing brains, and that helped to select us for survival, is known as the *availability heuristic*. Basically, the more readily we can recall an example of something, the more likely we are to regard that thing as true. The more easily we can distinguish predator from prey, the more likely we are to eat than be eaten. Reinforced by such other social and psychological mechanisms as the *validity effect* (the more often we hear something, the more likely we will think it reliable), *source dissociation* (our tendency to forget where we learned something, especially if we agree with it), and the *in-print fallacy* (they wouldn't be allowed to print it if it wasn't true, right?), this helps to explain why supernatural stories prove more resilient and popular than their extraterrestrial competitors. Rummaging through the footlocker of life experience, we far more easily find examples of spirit manifestation than alien visitation—Erich von Däniken and Zecharia Sitchin notwithstanding. No matter how many people *say* they believe in the possibility of extraterrestrials, the cultural depth of belief in haunting spirits is far greater than in ET.

Many cities and towns, perhaps even most, have their local legends about haunted places—houses, train stations, abandoned churches, schools, or derelict hospitals. The old Walker place out on Marsden Road. Epperson House, for example, now home to the School of Architecture at the University of Missouri–Kansas City, is reputed to be haunted by the ghost of Harriet Barse, a local music student who died there in 1922. Nearly a century later, both students and staff claim to have seen her shade walking the halls. While thousands of places have similar legends, far fewer have local myths about "that place where the flying saucer landed." Put differently, there may be tens of thousands of "Epperson Houses," but only one Roswell, New Mexico, only one Rachel, Nevada, only one Rendlesham Forest.

In late 2005, perhaps in response to the popularity of these new TV shows, Gallup surveyed Canadians, Americans, and Britons about the supernatural and the paranormal. Among other things, respondents were asked about belief in haunted houses, extraterrestrial visitation, and the possibility of communication with the dead, each of which implies its own species of god-talk, its own understanding of "how the world works." It turns out that roughly 40 percent of Americans and Britons say they believe in haunted houses.[27] About one-third of Americans believe in ghosts, and "that spirits of dead people can come back in certain places/situations."[28] Roughly the same number think that "haunted houses and otherworldly inhabitants go hand in hand, so it makes sense that a similar proportion of Americans believe in ghosts as believe in the houses they haunt."[29] This is the stuff of horror fiction going back nearly three hundred years. And, while these numbers are interesting, they don't really tell us much on their own.

Gallup also polled Americans on their beliefs in eternal destinations. Seventy percent indicated that they believe in Hell, that number rising to over 80 percent when we add those who "weren't sure." On the other hand, just over 90 percent say they believe in Heaven.[30] Although it may not be immediately apparent, this suggests that tens of millions of Americans have their concept of postmortem existence only partially shaped by their religious beliefs. For many, notions of the afterlife are also clearly inflected by folk belief in ghosts, and by the stories people tell about haunting spirits. Of course, polls such as these only ask *whether* people believe in this or that phenomenon, not *why*. Despite the fact that Christian theology makes no explicit room for ghosts and haunting spirits—some denominations forbid attempts at spirit communication, while others insist that haunting spirits are inevitably demonic—ghosts as god-talk have a lengthy history.

"In medieval England," writes historian Keith Thomas, "it was fully accepted that dead men might sometimes return to haunt the living. The Catholic Church rationalized the ancient belief in ghosts by teaching that such apparitions were the souls of those trapped in Purgatory, unable to rest until they had expiated their sins."[31] On the other hand, one unnamed fifteenth-century author suggests that "ghosts of the dead might well be sent back by God, 'sometimes for to have help; sometimes to show that the souls live after the body to confirm them that be feeble in the faith.'"[32] Thomas's use of the word "rationalized" is key here: the Catholic Church in the Middle Ages did not let dogma exclude entirely the folk beliefs of the faithful, but instead found a way to integrate them, to *rationalize* them within the context of the faith. "Father Patrick might say there be no such thing as ghosts," we can almost hear them say over a pint of ale, "but I *know* that ol' Headless Bob walks of a night o'er the moors."

"Most surviving medieval ghost stories," Thomas continues, "are to be found in anecdotal compilations made by the clergy for didactic purposes. But their details are usually sufficiently precise to suggest that the tales were not invented, but related to the experiences of real people."[33] Despite official church pronouncements, the durability of folk belief in haunting spirits was woven into the popular god-talk, the people's theology, and continues through the work of writers ranging from M. R. James and V. C. Andrews to H. P. Lovecraft and Shirley Jackson. Stephen King's spooky stories ask the same questions, though in two different ways: how do we react *to* ghosts, and how do we react *as* ghosts?

Coming to Grips with Ghosts

Our reaction to ghosts and haunting spirits is inevitably about the slippage between skepticism and belief. Mike Enslin, for example, the main character in King's short story "1408," epitomizes the hard-bitten journalist.[34] A debunker writing regularly for magazines like *Skeptic* and *Skeptical Inquirer*, he claims to want to find evidence of the paranormal—he just never does. That is, until he checks into room 1408 at the Dolphin Hotel. There, the manager tells him, his skepticism could be his undoing. "In an abandoned house or an old castle keep," Mr. Olin says, "your unbelief may serve you as protection. In room 1408, it will only render you more vulnerable."[35] On the other hand, many people give neither spooks nor spirits a second thought—until they are confronted with the inexplicable and feel their axis of belief tilt beneath them.

New York City: "The Things They Left Behind"

Psychologists call them "flashbulb memories," incidents or events of such singular importance that they engrave themselves onto our consciousness in ways that the vast majority of experiences simply don't. Most often, they take the form of *Do you remember where you were when . . . ?* questions. Those middle-aged and older often ask, Do you remember where you were when you heard that President Kennedy had been shot? (In my case, coming up the stairs to find my mother on the floor, weeping in front of the television set.) Others wonder where you were when the space shuttle *Challenger* exploded on January 28, 1986, just seventy-three seconds into its flight. (Watching the launch during my second semester at seminary, and marveling at how little the tragedy meant to my classmates.) Or 9/11? (Teaching an early-morning class at the University of Missouri–Kansas City, and watching the World Trade Center's North Tower come down at 10:28 a.m.)

In King's short story "The Things They Left Behind," Scott Staley wasn't at his World Trade Center office that sunny September morning. And he lived. His friends, though, his coworkers and acquaintances, those he passed in the lobby every morning as he got his coffee, men and women with whom he rode the elevator to the 110th floor—they didn't. But on that morning, a voice in his head (sounding strangely like James Brown) told him to call in sick. He did. And he lived.

Eleven months later, items belonging to people who died on September 11 begin to appear in his apartment. A pair of novelty sunglasses. A baseball bat. A conch shell. A small Lucite cube containing a rare steel penny. None of them should be there, obviously, but they are. And they won't go away. No matter how he tries to get rid of them, they always reappear. In the end, they won't leave his home until Scott Staley returns them to *their* homes.

Slightly more unnerving than "Mister Yummy" but not as horrifying as "Riding the Bullet," "The Things They Left Behind" is, as King puts it, "an act of willed understanding"[36] that seeks a voice, that tells of real-life horror and becomes, as science fiction author Orson Scott Card would say, a "speaker for the dead." When it comes to the important things, things that *matter*, as King notes in his introduction to *The Bazaar of Bad Dreams*, which was published more than a decade after 9/11, "only fiction can approach answers to those questions. Only *through* fiction can we think about the unthinkable, and perhaps obtain some sort of closure."[37]

"The Things They Left Behind" is a many-faceted tale. Part ghost story, though one that deals with the material culture of ghosts; part poltergeist account that questions the nature of the barrier between this world and the next; part survivor-guilt narrative, though Scott denies that the manifestations are part of the emotional baggage he carries because he lived when so many others did not. Part revenant story—Scott and his erstwhile friend Paula Robeson can achieve some measure of closure only when the 9/11 objects are returned to the families left behind by their original owners. This need for closure, for peace, for rest, even for understanding are traditional elements in ghost stories. In such "caught dead" tales, before they can move on in death, vengeful revenants seek to redress wrongs done them in life. It is also part relic story—for the real survivors, those friends and family left behind, these ordinary, everyday objects become sacred touchstones, reliquaries of blessed memory.

"It occurred to me," Scott thinks at the end of the story, "that other items might show up in time. And I'd be lying if I told you I found that possibility entirely unpleasant. When it comes to returning things which people believe have been lost forever, things that have *weight*, there are compensations."[38] Not everyone is equipped to handle the fact that the world is no longer as simple as it seems, that everything we think is true can be turned on its head by some cheap sunglasses or a souvenir seashell.

"How important to you is it," asks Paula, when Scott first tries to explain his dilemma, "that I believe your story about those things coming back?"

"I thought this was an excellent question," he mused, "even though the Lucite cube was right there next to the sugar bowl."[39] Whatever Paula and Scott thought they believed about the spirit world, whatever childhood stories they thought they had outgrown, and whatever each was willing to admit in the face of the small Lucite cube, nothing could ever look the same as it did before discovering "the things they left behind."

Derry, Maine: It

Unlike either "Mister Yummy" or "The Things They Left Behind," *It* is the quintessential monster story, and one about the most monstrous of crimes: the murder of children. During the late 1950s, six friends battle the entity known as It—and survive. Three decades later, believing that the horror has returned, five of them travel back to Derry, Maine, King's literary stand-in for Bangor and the dark heart of his storyworld complex.[40] Much of *It* passes with only an occasional reference to religion, either explicit or implicit. On Neiboldt Street, for example, stands a "Church School which was run by people Ben's mother called 'the Christers.'"[41] Or, imprisoned for the bludgeoning death of his four-year-old son, a man begins "taking instruction in the Catholic faith shortly after beginning his prison term" and experiences something of a jailhouse conversion.[42] Several years later, only a few months after his release, the man commits suicide, a clear contravention of Roman Catholic teaching. This is a measure of how deep he felt his need for repentance, or how unforgivable he believed his sin. The note he left read simply, "I saw Eddie last night. He was dead."[43] As Michael Cox and Robert Gilbert point out in their introduction to *The Oxford Book of Ghost Stories*, "Whatever we do with the dead they will not go away."[44]

When ten-year-old Bill Denbrough claims to have seen the ghost of his younger brother, George, who was among It's first victims, his friend Richie believes him without question.

The idea of ghosts gave his child's mind no trouble at all. He was sure there was such things. His parents were Methodists, and Richie went to church every Sunday and to Thursday-night Methodist Youth Fellowship meetings as well. He knew a great deal about the Bible already, and he knew the Bible believed in all sorts of weird stuff. According to the Bible, God Himself was at least one-third Ghost, and that was just the beginning.[45]

A child's grasp of Trinitarian theology notwithstanding, he's not wrong. "The Bible believed in demons. . . . The Bible believed in witches."[46] Indeed, for Richie Tozier, "some of the stuff in the Bible was even better than the stuff in the horror comics"[47]—the very comics that in the late 1950s were the target of virulent moral crusades, both at home and abroad.[48] Richie knew that the Bible often attributed accidental death to divine intervention. He knew that there were "mass baby-murders that had accompanied the births of both Moses and Jesus Christ; guys who came out of their graves or flew into the air; soldiers who witched down walls; prophets who saw the future and fought monsters."[49] What parent wouldn't want their child protected from such horrors, taken by themselves and stripped of their religious provenance? But these aren't comic books. They aren't horror pulps or B movies at the Aladdin. "All of that was in the Bible and every word of it was true—so said Reverend Craig and so said Richie's folks and so said Richie."[50]

While Christian doctrine acknowledges the existence of ghosts and haunting spirits, it does so almost grudgingly. Unlike Buddhism, Hinduism, Shinto, or varieties of modern Paganism, Christian theology makes no official room for these discarnate entities, especially not the kind that leak and bleed from the school portraits of murdered six-year-olds. In other religions, though, according to other dialects of god-talk, these entities can remain as tortured spirits, hungry ghosts so traumatized by the terror of their passing that they are unable to move from this plane of existence to whatever awaits beyond it.[51] Still other visions of the unseen order insist that the dead never really leave, that we remain connected to them in inexplicable, often terrifying ways.

Ludlow, Maine: Pet Sematary

"It's probably wrong to believe that there can be any limit to the horror which the human mind can experience," King writes in *Pet Sematary*, a novel he originally intended not to publish, thinking that this time he might have gone too far.[52] In this case, it's the death of a small child, two-year-old Gage Creed. Here, though, unlike *It*'s George Denbrough, Gage is brought back to a horrific semblance of life by a father seeking nothing more than relief for his own heartache. Although King maintains that he does relatively little plotting, here he tells his Constant Readers exactly what's going to happen, then dares us to follow him into the woods. In the hands of many other writers, any passage that says in whatever way, "In the next several pages a small boy will die," would utterly defeat the purpose of the story. Not *Pet Sematary*. Like death itself, in King's hands knowing what's coming only increases the tension.

The story doesn't begin with the small boy, though, but with a cat named Church—short for Winston Churchill, lest we be tempted to read too much into the name—who is run over in the road. Could there be a more sadly common occurrence? Louis Creed and his neighbor, octogenarian Jud Crandall, take the unfortunate cat's body into the woods to bury him in the "Pet Sematary." The child's misspelling notwithstanding, it's exactly what you would imagine. Off to the side about a mile up the trail is the animal graveyard, bounded by a massive deadfall, a tangled mass of branches and fallen tree trunks. Instead of stopping there, though, and simply burying Church, Jud leads Louis up and over the treacherous heap of downed trees, and deeper into the woods. Eventually, they arrive at an ancient Micmac burial site. The difference between the two graveyards is that whatever is buried on the Pet Sematary side of the deadfall stays dead.

Or at least it stays buried.

Later that night, when Church strolls back home, seemingly alive, though somehow not, Louis's rational mind searches for an explanation. They buried a cat that looked like Church. His daughter's pet was still alive, probably hunting mice in the fields. They buried Church, but the cat was only stunned and not dead. Somehow, he revived. Somehow, he managed to claw his way out and escape a grave "about two feet wide and three feet long," "perhaps thirty inches deep," one dug right down to bedrock, then covered with "a low conical pile of stones."[53] These are less explanations, though, than rationalizations. In the end, they are little more than comforting fictions. As part of the mystery falls away and the horrific truth dawns on Louis Creed, it is as if he "had known in some deeper, more primitive part of his mind what their night hike up to the Micmac burying ground had meant all along."[54] It is this "deeper, more primitive part of his mind"—which is to say, *our* mind, since Louis is *Pet Sematary*'s everyman—that the story speaks to in us, the part that "gets you to believe the unbelievable," as one media blurb put it.

As Louis listens to the story of Stanny B., Jud's dog who survived death more than once courtesy of the Micmac burying ground, his mind pivots between the modern/rational and the deeper/primitive, between the way things are supposed to be and the way his growing terror tells him they are. Church's ghastly resurrection, he slowly realizes, is only a shadow of a much darker reality.

Pet Sematary includes what amounts to a mini-seminar in comparative religion, a crash course on the different ways people deal with death, performed for King's Constant Reader by a five-year-old girl and a father whose whole world has been turned upside down. "Catholics believe in heaven and hell," Louis tells Ellie, "but they also believe there's a place called Limbo and one called Purgatory."[55] "Hindus and Buddhists believe in Nirvana."[56] Rebirth, what Ellie calls "carnation," is on the syllabus as well. "Like what happened to Audrey Rose in that movie on TV," she tells her father sagely, though whether a five-year-old should be watching Robert Wise's classic horror film is left unaddressed.[57] "What it comes down to, Ellie," Louis tells her in words more than a few religious believers would do well to heed, "is this: no one knows," though he allows, "I believe that we go on. . . . It may be that it's different for different people."[58]

> What we *know* is this. When we die, one of two things happens. Either our souls and thoughts somehow survive the experience of dying or they don't. If they do, that opens up every possibility you could think of. If we don't, it's just blotto. The end.[59]

Among the many things *Pet Sematary* challenges is the notion of "safe" religion, of religion as a means of compartmentalizing all the scary things about life, death, and the razor-thin abyss that stands between them. Many people simply craft the kind of god that suits them, not out of whole cloth, but by choosing the bits they like from their religion, and discarding whatever make them uncomfortable. Participating in what is called "cafeteria" or "salad bar" religion—"Sheilaism," to sociologists[60]—believers often steadfastly refuse to face not only the dark side of religion, but the even darker potential of the unseen order. For Louis, the Micmac burial ground has come to embody "a place that was always considered to be a holy place . . . but not in a good way."[61] Holiness, he warns, should never be automatically taken for goodness. None of that matters, though, when it's the crumpled and lifeless body of your child you carry in your arms.

"Let there be God," Louis pleads later in the book, as he carries Gage's body past the deadfall and through Little God Swamp, pivoting between the desperate love he has for his son and the insanity of bringing him back through the power of the Micmac burial ground. "Let there be God, let there be Sunday morning, let there be smiling Episcopalian ministers in shining white surplices"—that is, let everything be as it was, before he became privy to what *is*. Above all, "let there not be those dark and dragging horrors on the night-side of the universe."[62]

More than anything else, Louis Creed wants to take some small measure of comfort in the stories we have crafted to manage our fear of what lies beyond the deadfall. He wants to believe the cruel platitudes so many clergy offer in the face of unfathomable grief. "He's in a better place now." "At least she's with the angels in heaven." "We just have to know that this is all part of God's plan." What Louis knows, however, is that what lives on "the night-side of the universe" has little to do with anything we might call "God."

Dark Score Lake: Bag of Bones

Stephen King routinely breaks what fantasy legend Fritz Leiber calls the cardinal rule of writing: casting writers as characters. Indeed, from within his own storyworlds King often digs slyly at his reputation as a horror-*meister*. As *The Tommyknockers*' Ev Hillman, for example, struggles to understand what's happening to his family and his community, he thinks about Bobbi Anderson, the woman who unearthed the Tommyknocker ship. "She wrote good old western stories that you could really sink your teeth into," he tells us, "not full of make-believe monsters and dirty words, like the ones that fellow who lived up Bangor wrote."[63] Indeed, Ev's preference for "oat operas" notwithstanding, throughout his work King takes seriously Alan Pangborn's belief that "*writers invite ghosts*," and more than a few monsters, and that "*along with actors and artists, they are the only totally accepted mediums of our society*."[64]

We learn early in *Bag of Bones*, which was published nearly a decade after *The Dark Half*, that Thad Beaumont has committed suicide, though we're never told why. Perhaps the shade of George Stark was simply too deep and too dark. Instead, *Bag of Bones* introduces us to another successful author, another thin spot between the worlds, and another opportunity to wonder about ghost stories as god-talk. Following his wife's sudden death, horror novelist Mike Noonan struggles with writer's block and seeks refuge at Sara Laughs, their vacation home on Dark Score Lake, an hour or so north of Castle Rock.[65] Rather than a supernatural tale, *Bag of Bones* could be read as a straight-up psychological thriller. Written in the first-person, stories in which everything takes place as a function of one character's perception and uncorroborated experience can more easily be explained as the product of delusion, dementia, or depression. This is considerably more difficult when different characters experience the same inexplicable events. "If one person sees a thing," notes *Duma Key's* Edgar Freemantle, "it could be a hallucination. If two people see it, chances of reality improve exponentially."[66]

When Noonan returns to Sara Laughs and hears the sound of a child weeping, he explains it away as air in the pipes. Since the house had been unoccupied for several months, this seems entirely reasonable. When he first sees the woman he describes as an "old bag of bones," but who disappears "as if she'd been a ghost herself," we're less inclined to see it as a forerunner and more willing to accept it as an illusion, a trick of the light like the standing stones in Ackerman's Field.[67] Even when Noonan sees a second "ghost," this one "as thin as the one I'd seen down at Warrington's," we're still not convinced it isn't all in his mind. "This one was green," he tells us. "Green and pointing north along the path like a dryad in some old legend."[68] At this point in the story, the natural trumps the supernatural. A grief-stricken man sees things that aren't really there. "The woman was green because she was a birch growing a little to the north of where my set of railroad tie-steps ended."[69]

In just a few short sentences, though, King presents the conflict between the modern, rational mind—the mind that knows it's only air in the pipes or a tree by the road—and the pattern-seeking part of our brain that has for millennia controlled the "fight or flight" system. "It wasn't the first time I'd spooked myself like that," Noonan continues. "I see things, that's all."[70] The question is, Why does he see things? Once again, we are confronted with the overwhelming power of story to affect not only how we see the world around us, but what we see in that world. "Write enough stories," he tells us ruefully, "and every shadow on the floor looks like a footprint, every line in the dirt like a secret message."[71] We may hear the air in the pipes, see the shadow or the line, but the security those answers offer is elusive and temporary. The primitive mind, the part still cautiously peering out from the cave, looks around and wonders, What the hell is out there?

Horror writers often spin their stories in real time, as it were, refusing to tell readers what's going to happen until it does. This way, whatever jumps out of the closet comes as something of a surprise. Many of King's novels, on the other hand—indeed, his most effective at evoking the creeps, the delightful *frisson* of horror—are written retrospectively. They look backward at terrifying events we've experienced together and survived—if only just. More than a few novels have been ruined by injudicious foreshadowing, but King uses it like a cold breath whispering across the hollow of your neck, a bony finger beckoning you along the story's path.

It *was* just air in the pipes; it *was* just a birch tree by the steps . . . wasn't it? There's nothing there. Nothing to be afraid of. That's what we tell ourselves. There's nothing in the dark that isn't there in the light. That is, until the moment "when I first began to really believe that I wasn't alone in Sara Laughs. *So what?* I asked myself. *Even if it should be true, so what? Ghosts can't hurt anyone.*"[72]

"That's what I thought then," Mike concludes.

For Mike Noonan, his first experience of the crack in the world, his encounter with whatever haunts Sara Laughs, is like peering over "the rim of the universe."[73] Suddenly, like Louis Creed, he realizes that little of what he thought he knew makes sense, and he gradually recognizes that there is a battle ongoing in the unseen order that mirrors the one taking place on the shores of Dark Score Lake. A guiding spirit, perhaps his deceased wife, Johanna, points the way for him to help a young widow and her daughter, and gives Mike the strength to survive when he is attacked in the lake by the novel's principal villain. In the midst of a horror story, her help raises the not-unreasonable question, Why are we afraid of ghosts, especially the spirits of those we have loved in life and who have loved us? Or, put differently, why do we tend to imagine our fears far more easily than our hopes? To understand these questions in terms of *Bag of Bones*, we have to consider the terrible events that cracked the world open on the shores of that small Maine lake: the rape and murder of a young black woman, a blues singer named Sara Tidwell, more than a century before Mike Noonan bought the house that came to be known as Sara Laughs.

In many ways, if *Needful Things* is Stephen King's fable of life under Ronald Reagan, the natural and supernatural battles around Dark Score Lake consider the brutal legacy of Northern racism that still haunts the United States. Almost worse than slavery, which could at least be recognized and brought to an official end, the racism of the characters in *Bag of Bones* is bred in the bone. This is the racism that continues to rear its head no matter how fervently we believe we're past it. Indeed, the more often we tell ourselves we've left the ugly notion of someone "knowing her place" behind, the more our stories betray the questions that still haunt us as a society.

During the long pages of Sara's gang rape and murder, and the killing of her eight-year-old son, King inserts a number of brief moments, counterpoints that serve to deepen the horror: the local Methodist congregation at Sunday worship, Dark Score Baptists celebrating the opening of their new church building. Consider, though, that in the flow of the narrative these details are largely unnecessary. The horror of Sara's ordeal is more than enough to carry the story, but these grace notes provide a poignant, telling antiphon to the screams that find voice only in the young singer's head. They raise the pitch of our revulsion. Rather than overt racism, they say, this is the blindness of the organized church, the fact that congregation members sing hymns and offer prayers in the midst of seething prejudice. Indeed, the murders themselves proceed almost like a racist liturgy. During the approach, while Sara is as yet unaware of the men lying in wait, "faintly, from the other side of the lake, she can hear the Methodists singing. The sound is sweet and faint and beautiful; distance and echo has tuned every sour voice."[74]

Then the small knot of men, led by Jared Devore, step into The Street, the small town's main thoroughfare. "That's what Jared hated most of all, wasn't it?" Mike asks, as the unseen order intrudes and puts the visible world in proper perspective. "That they didn't turn aside, didn't turn away. She walked on The Street and no one treated her like a nigger. They treated her like a neighbor."[75] Even as Sara demands to know what's going on, as a young black woman in turn-of-the-century Maine she knows perfectly well. She looks around. "Where is everybody? Where can they all be? God damn! Across the lake, the Methodists have moved on to 'Trust and Obey,' a droner if there ever was one."[76]

Bag of Bones lacks the kind of scene-chewing abandon of *Needful Things*, where King presents sectarian conflict with all the finesse of a blunt object. Instead, this story reflects with surgical precision the blind eye and the deaf ear the Church has so often turned to the varieties of malevolence that have arisen both around it and within it. This could as easily have been written about the systematic rape of children by Roman Catholic priests, about the horror of Native residential schools, about the countless times religious belief has entered into a concordat with evil, rather than stand in solidarity with its victims.

As Sara is stalked, raped, and murdered—all while having to watch as they drown her young son—the sound of Methodists singing floats over the surface of Dark Score Lake. The congregants may not be there when it happens, but many of them are there in spirit because "almost everyone on the TR knew that Sara and her boy had been murdered, and almost everyone had a good idea of who'd done it."[77] Once more, the silence of the complicit has drowned the cries of the dying.

Before the end begins, though, when Sara tries one last time to force her way through the valley of the shadow of death, for there's no doubt that's what Jared and his cronies represent, the liturgy's next movement begins. "Faint and sweet are the Methodists, faithy music carrying across the lake's still surface. A droner of a hymn, but sweet across the miles."

> When we walk with the Lord
> in the light of His word,
> what a glory He sheds on your way . . .[78]

Finally, as the end nears for Sara as well, there is the recessional. "By the time the last one is finished, oh God, the first one is ready again. Across the river the Methodists are now singing 'Blessed Assurance, Jesus Is Mine.'"[79]

King has said many times that "the writer of horror fiction is neither more nor less than an agent of the status quo."[80] Just so for organized religion. Indeed, for decades deviation from social or cultural norms was used as a way to distinguish between "church," "sect," and "cult."[81] Put simply, "churches" reflect most clearly and hew most closely to accepted cultural values. Essentially conservative, religions are uncomfortable with change. Too much is at stake. Presumably, none of Dark Score's Methodists would approve of racial hate crimes. Yet, though few would go so far as to say that Sara "had it coming," they might nod sadly, even a bit primly, and make comforting noises to each other about "knowing one's place." Knowing *about* the racism that permeates their small community, though, knowing about it and living with it every day in the remote tracts of rural Maine, they may just find it easier to look down at their hymn books and sing the old familiar songs. Once again, in the storyworlds of Stephen King, God's people are present and accounted for. God, on the other hand, is noticeably absent. The god they worship, at least.

Ghosts imply god-talk. Postmortem survival of any kind suggests some conception of the way things work, a spiritual cosmology. While they may disagree on the fine details of the faith, both the Baptists and the Methodists of Dark Score Lake believe that Christians join their Lord in an eternal afterlife, while nonbelievers and those deemed unworthy of heaven spend eternity writhing in hell. The incredible yet all-too-common violence of Sara's death, however, the agony of watching her child murdered just seconds before she joins him, challenges the essentials of the "blessed assurance" that both groups of Christians claim. In *Bag of Bones*, one revenant spirit swears vengeance, while another, caught up in the story almost as an innocent bystander, battles to protect the one she loved in life.

With Stephen King, though, even this alignment of supernatural forces is rarely that simple. God may not be there on the shore of Dark Score Lake, but in her century-long rage "the Sara-thing" is. As Johanna's spirit tells Mike, "It's not really her anymore. She's let one of the Outsiders in, and they're very dangerous."[82] We never learn what the Outsiders are, or where the "Outside" is, but we are suddenly faced with an entirely different, almost Lovecraftian understanding of the unseen order. Like Louis Creed wishing for nothing more than the mundanity of "smiling Episcopalian ministers in shiny white surplices,"[83] Mike Noonan suddenly wonders whether anything he thought he knew is real.

While the Baptists laid the foundations for their church, raised its walls, and set its polished new pews in place, the Outsiders watched. While the Methodists sang hymns and prayed to their God as Sara Tidwell was raped and murdered, the Outsiders stood by, their patience challenging the very notion of eternity. They waited for someone to invite them in, someone whose rage and fury were sufficient to force a crack between the worlds. All theology is built on a scaffold of speculation, which is then given shape and consistency through common vocabulary and shared meaning. If they suspected their existence at all, Baptists and Methodists alike might call the Outsiders "demons," but what does that even mean beyond the limited conceptual framework of Protestant god-talk? Apart from the centuries of supposition, guesswork, and simple fiction that comprises Christian demonology, how much more do we know?

Once again, King highlights the uncomfortable truth that whatever answers we think we have are contingent at best, and that however we frame the answers, our questions remain, lurking just outside. Are they "demons," supernatural beings limited by Iron Age cosmology on a speck of cosmic dust tucked away in a backwater arm of the galaxy? On the other hand, perhaps they are something more primeval than demons, something unknown to us or remembered only in the stories we tell to frighten children, something that has been here so much longer than we that all of our gods pale to insignificance beside them? In terms of answers, the Baptists will have to be happy with their shiny new pews, the Methodists with their hoary old hymns. *Bag of Bones* suggests that they have little more to offer than that.

For millennia, such specters as these have shaped and influenced how we process the mystery of death, the fundamental enigma of which grounds so much of our religious thinking. Although it works itself out differently across time and around the world, one of our most common fears is not so much of death itself, but of dying, of dying badly, and either not remaining dead or not transitioning naturally to whatever awaits on the other side.

Being Dead

What is it like being dead? A more difficult question even to ask than what it means to encounter a ghost, what does it mean to *be* one? Will it be what we expect? Will it be what we want? Will we even know? Many of King's short stories invite his Constant Reader to consider the different ways of being dead, and the different, often terrifying visions of the unseen order each of these implies. One of humankind's oldest fears, for example, is *tapophobia*, the fear of being buried alive, that those who love us won't realize we're not gone as they close up the coffin.[84]

What happens, though, if we open our eyes and realize, "Dear God, I'm in a body bag"?[85]

As he's being wheeled down to "Autopsy Room Four," the only thing more terrifying for stockbroker Howard Cottrell is the possibility that he really *is* dead, and that he will posthumously experience his own postmortem examination. "What if I'm dead?" he wonders, listening to the doctor sign the forms consigning his body to the morgue. "What if this is what death is like? It fits. It fits everything with a horrid prophylactic snugness."[86]

Put differently, what if everything anyone has ever told us about death is wrong? "If I'm dead," Howard continues, trying desperately to work out whether he is or not, "why aren't I either gone or in the white light they're always talking about on *Oprah*?"[87] In this story, no comforting presence waits on the other side. No loving family or friends greet us as we "cross over." Indeed, King suggests, what if it's so much worse than that? What if our consciousness does survive, and we still actually feel everything that happens to us after death? We just can't *do* anything about it. Eaten by a shark? After the terrifying pain of ingestion, you'll experience the slow process of digestion and absorption. Washed, dressed, and buried after an unremarkable death? You lie in your coffin, sightlessly staring at the cheap satin lining you know is there but can't see because of the Stygian black. Depending on how well you've been embalmed and where you're buried, the slow process of decomposition could take years, even decades. And you'll experience it all. What about cremation? Does your consciousness eventually let go? Do *you* let go once you've endured the unimaginable agony of fire reducing your body to ash? And then what? We are unsure until the last pages of the story whether Howard is alive or dead. Think on this, King implies, then tell me: Are there really worse things than death?

Few cultures in the world lack ghost stories. Whether we find them embedded in myths, legends, or sacred texts, whether they come to us through epic poetry, campfire tales, or genre fiction, ghost stories help us think through the possibilities of life after death. "Though we know at any moment that we must die," wrote the German philosopher Kurt Reizler during the bleakest days of the Second World War, "we do not fear death all the time, except in some remote or dark corner of our mind."[88] It is these "remote or dark corners" that our ghost stories explore in detail. Perhaps understanding that we have died takes a much longer time, and we require much more in the way of evidence before we finally accept the reality of our death.

"Willa," David Sanderson asked his fiancée as they walked along the moonlit road leading back to the railway station, "what year is it?"[89]

> She thought it over. The wind rippled her dress as it would the dress of any live woman. "I don't exactly remember," she said at last. "Isn't that odd?"[90]

Though it's taken nearly two decades, David and Willa gradually realize that they're dead. The Amtrak train they were on had derailed between Chicago and San Francisco, plunging into a gorge somewhere in Wyoming's Wind River Range. Unlike the many stories of forerunners and ferrymen, of midnight Mustangs and Mister Yummy, King's short story "Willa" considers the possibility that in some cases the transition from life to death may be so sudden, so unexpected that we miss it altogether. We are "caught dead," as it were, unaware even that we have died. Such a claim is not so far-fetched as it may at first appear.

In Tibetan Buddhism, part of the *phowa* ceremony is intended to convince the one who has died and to calm her fears once the realization takes hold. For a period of forty-nine days, instructions from *Bardo Thodol*, known in the West as *The Tibetan Book of the Dead*, are read each day. Since the dead person's spirit is believed to linger for a time, a *lāma* reads the text aloud in the presence of the body, to comfort and to guide. "O nobly-born," the ancient ritual begins, "that which is called death being come to thee now, resolve thus: 'O this now is the hour of death. By taking advantage of this death, I will act for the good of all sentient beings, peopling the illimitable expanse of the heavens, as to obtain the Perfect Buddhahood, by resolving on love and compassion."[91] Even for those who spend a lifetime preparing, it seems, the realization of death can overwhelm.

"That Feeling, You Can Only Say What It Is in French," on the other hand, begins with a midair collision between a Lear 35 and a Delta airliner. Here, in the psychic wasteland between precognition and déjà vu, the extraordinary accounts that cluster around imminent death, King raises explicitly the question of what happens next:

> She remembered asking him what he believed you got, you know, *after*, and he had said you probably got what you'd always thought you *would* get. . . . Heaven, Hell, Grand Rapids, it was your choice—or the choice of those who had taught you what to believe. It was the human mind's final great parlor-trick: the perception of eternity in the place where you'd always expected to spend it.[92]

How many of his Constant Readers latch on to this as a postmortem explanation? How many think to themselves, *This makes sense*, if only because it's more palatable than any of the alternatives? After all, how many would *choose* the afterlife of the spirits haunting Dark Score Lake or the Overlook Hotel? How many would choose the horrific implications of "Autopsy Room Four"?

Carol Shelton, the woman having the precognitive dream, was raised in a particularly strict version of Roman Catholicism. Although she describes her husband, Bill, as "the secretary-fucking man she had married," in these last moments she chooses to remember him as the man who "rescued her from people who thought that you could live forever in paradise if you only lit enough candles and wore the blue blazer and stuck to the approved skipping rhymes."[93] Rather than Catholic dogma, in the story's linchpin passage, he tells her "you probably got what you'd always thought you *would* get. . . . Heaven, Hell, Grand Rapids, it was your choice—or the choice of those who had taught you what to believe."

Here, King reflects an important stream of Tibetan Buddhism called Yogacara. Also known as the *citta-matra* (mind-only) tradition, Yogacara posits that because everything we experience after death, everything that happens to us in the *bardo* state, is a product of our own consciousness, whatever we believe will happen determines what does happen.

King, though, has his own thoughts on the matter. "I think this story is about Hell," he writes in a brief afterword, "a version of it where you are condemned to do the same thing over and over again."[94] If Bill Shelton is correct, though, if the Yogacarans are right, then that is a truly horrifying prospect. Together, "That Feeling . . ." and King's brief explanatory sentence compress into a few mass market pages the horror of rebirth, the terror that hundreds of millions of people feel at the prospect of reincarnation, of *samsara*. Indeed, at the heart of both Buddhism and Hinduism is the drive to escape the cycle of rebirth, to get off the wheel, to finish the cosmic game played between the seen and the unseen orders.

More particular to the *citta-matra* tradition, however, if what we have been conditioned to expect after death is what we experience, then what we are taught to expect by those who think their maps of the unseen order actually mean something is of no small consequence. We fear the "pains of hell" because those we trusted, those who taught us their church's version of the "approved skipping rhymes," told us they were real. If "you probably got what you always thought you would get," who tells us what that is, and what are the consequences of their words? This is the question to which we now turn.

4

A Jumble of Whites and Blacks

Becoming Religious

What do we see when we look at something? What's actually there? What we expect to see? What we want to see? Or do we see what we've been told to see, and what we are rewarded for seeing? Since we are pattern-seeking creatures, one of our most powerful cognitive instincts is to separate the signal from the noise, to bring order to chaos, and so find meaning in our experience. As Stephen King writes in *Danse Macabre*, we are continually "expressing our faith and belief in the norm."[1] This is one reason we force familiar concepts onto nonhuman objects. We see human faces in our pets, in household appliances, in strange geological features. We've been told there's a "man in the moon"—and there he is. Shadows patterned on the surface of Mars suggest artificial structures on the red planet—and millions of people see them. We even impose stories onto random arrangements of dots and lines.[2] We are shaped not only by the stories we are told, but also by the things we are told to expect.

Bill and Carol: Incipience and Indoctrination

We met Carol and Bill Shelton at the end of the last chapter. In the timeless instant of the midair collision that took her life, Carol remembers asking Bill "what he believed you got, you know, *after*." There, we introduced the "mind-only" concept of Yogacara Buddhism, the belief that "you probably got what you always thought you would get. . . . Heaven, Hell, Grand Rapids, it was your choice."[3] This last bit is particularly important: "it was your choice—*or the choice of those who had taught you what to believe*."[4] If our earlier discussion explored the possibility of the afterlife as "the perception of eternity in the place where you'd always expected to spend it," Bill's comment points us toward far darker and potentially horrific prospects.[5] What if we get what we expect because that's what we've been told we deserve? And if so, who gets to tell us?

Bill might have been an unfaithful husband, but recall that to Carol, who was raised in a particularly strict version of Roman Catholicism, he was also the one who "rescued her from people who thought that you could live forever in paradise if you only lit enough candles and wore the blue blazer and stuck to the approved skipping rhymes."[6] King's finger-wagging at the antiphonal nature of the Catholic liturgy is of no small existential importance here. If you had been taught from childhood that unending torment in hell awaits you if you die unshriven, getting what you expect in the afterlife takes on a whole different meaning in the context of religious socialization.

To step away from Stephen King for just for a moment, consider poor Police Inspector Neil Howie in Robin Hardy's classic 1973 film *The Wicker Man*. Investigating a supposed murder on a remote Hebridean island, Howie encounters a community of modern Pagans struggling to live as they believe their ancestors did—a project that includes, on occasion, human sacrifice. Lured to a windswept cliff on the western side of the island, Howie is imprisoned in a giant human effigy made entirely of branches and twigs. The Wicker Man. "While Howie dies hoping for the life everlasting his religion has promised him, the Summerisle pagans continue hoping that their propitiatory sacrifice will bring back a bountiful harvest. Both, though, are caught between fear and faith: with his dying breath, Howie entreats his god, 'Let me not undergo the real pains of hell because I die unshriven!'"[7] Since he dies without the opportunity to make his confession and receive absolution, everything his religion has taught him reinforces the notion that nothing but hell can await him—eternal flames instead of a momentary blaze. His is another soul caught in the web of "those who had taught you what to believe."[8]

This is the disturbing question of religious socialization. In terms of King's story, what if Yogacara Buddhists are correct, and their understanding of the relationship between the seen and the unseen order is the right one? What if the reality is that what we believe about death and the afterlife actually creates our experience of both? How would you escape what you've been taught? After all, how many people know enough, or are sufficiently independent, to tell their parents, their religious leaders, and all the other significant voices in the chorus of their lives that they're wrong? Or at least that they don't believe they're right? Such as it is, our faith commitment is more than anything an accident of birth and the product of religious socialization. To leave it behind often takes a great deal of time, and is the result of social and cultural forces having little or nothing to do with specific theological or doctrinal belief. Throughout religious history, conversion has been a relatively rare phenomenon. The vast majority of believers live and die in the tradition to which they were born. Parents and family, religious leaders, and a host of others provide them with a "map of the territory," as it were. But, as Polish philosopher Alfred Korzybski reminds us, "the map is not the territory it represents."[9] The territory often contains dense, unmarked areas, seas and mountains and deserts, all labeled in our imaginations, *Hic sunt dracones*.

Here be dragons.

The problem with religion, with any supposed understanding of the unseen order, is that all we have are maps—incomplete, often poorly drawn, and filled with vast areas marked ???. Many of those maps, though, are proclaimed as the definitive guide not only to one's own territory, but to everyone else's as well. As we have seen, the biggest blank space on the map, the one that looms largest in our imagination and that our religious storytellers rush to fill with their myths, legends, promises, conjectures, and fears, is death.

Consider that, for ancient Egyptians and for at least fifteen hundred years, *The Book of the Dead* was the ritual and mythological manual for death, the afterlife, and everything in between. It governed what hundreds of thousands of men, women, and children believed about the unseen order, yet how many know it today as anything other than a *Mummy* movie set piece? This particular religious socialization held firm for at least a millennium and a half, yet today is no more than a historical curiosity, a footnote to an undergraduate classics paper. Its power is gone.

Once more, through stories such as "Autopsy Room Four" and "That Feeling . . . ," King offers us the choice between unpleasant alternatives. Which would be worse? That the Yogacarans are wrong, and we don't get what we expect in the afterlife, or that they're right, but that our expectations are shaped and controlled by institutions that may be working with inaccurate or incomplete cartographies? Although King doesn't quite come out and say it, because his stories always pose questions rather than provide answers, underpinning them all is the brute reality: Truth Matters.

In his now classic essay on the nature of mystical experience, philosopher Steven Katz highlights the importance of religious socialization in shaping our conception of the unseen order: those who experience mystical states of consciousness rarely report seeing things they do not expect to see. Roman Catholics don't see Ganesh, they see the Virgin Mary. Sufi dancers don't experience ETI, but *jazbah*, the Divine Love. Buddhists seek the direct experience of one's true nature, not the illusion of this god or that. As Willa asks her fiancée rhetorically, "Perception isn't everything, but perception and expectation together?"[10] Katz stresses the centrality of perspective and expectation when the veil between the seen and the unseen orders is parted. Indeed, this is his "single epistemological assumption": "*There are* NO *pure (i.e., unmediated) experiences.*" Further, he argues that "the experience itself as well as the form in which it is reported is shaped by concepts which the mystic"—in this case, we can insert "the religious believer"—"brings to, and which shape, his experience."[11]

The reality of the mystical experience notwithstanding, Katz points directly to the power of religious socialization. A young woman may have left her Roman Catholic roots behind, but that doesn't mean that she won't insist on having her new baby baptized. Residual thoughts of an eternity in hell remain powerful motivators in defense of her child. A grown man may no longer consider himself even moderately religious, but, whether he knows it or not, the maps he was given as a child still influence his life choices and moral decisions. Investigating how these maps are spread out in the storyworlds of Stephen King will take us from the windswept peaks of the Colorado Rockies to Cold Mountain's death row, and from the sewers beneath Derry, Maine, to a tiny curio shop in Castle Rock.

Jack Torrance: A Jumble of Whites and Blacks

As he sinks deeper into madness and paranoia in *The Shining*, falling further under the malevolent sway of the Overlook Hotel, Jack Torrance remembers a moment from his childhood in Sunday school. That morning, Sister Beatrice showed her catechism class a picture that she claimed was "a miracle of God." This is the kind of "trick picture" with which many of us are acquainted: a familiar image is "hidden" in what seems at first nothing more than a random scattering of shapes. Staring at it directly rarely reveals the pattern, the signal buried in the noise. Only when we change our perspective—moving farther away, for example, or shifting to one side, looking at the picture with our peripheral vision—does the image appear. Only then do we see what we are meant to see.

At first, Jack recalls, "The class had looked at it blankly, seeing nothing but a jumble of whites and blacks, senseless and patternless. Then one of the children in the third row had gasped, 'It's Jesus!' and that child had gone home with a brand-new Testament and also a calendar because he had been first."[12] This is the moment when perception and expectation collude, when children are told what to see—and then rewarded for seeing it. A faithful if budding Roman Catholic, little Bobby or Sally knew the picture wouldn't contain dragons or rocket ships. Not in Sister Beatrice's class. The Blessed Virgin Mary was a good bet, so was an angel, perhaps Gabriel or Michael. In this case, the miracle picture was Jesus. "One by one the other kids had given a similar gasp, one little girl transported in near-ecstasy, crying out shrilly, 'I *see* Him! I *see* Him!' She has also been rewarded with a Testament."[13]

Whether it happens through our family, our religious or educational communities, a particular subculture, or some combination of these, *socialization* is the process of framing norms and passing on expectations. It establishes the structures of everyday life that allow us to think ahead by referring back. Socialization invites specific rewards when we are successful, and incurs specific penalties when we're not. It is most effective when these norms and expectations not only become self-reinforcing, but become so much a part of our taken-for-granted "recipe knowledge" that no other way of thinking even occurs to us.[14] We forget that we have been "taught" anything at all, and the truth, as it were, becomes self-evident. Thus, a classroom full of Roman Catholic children would no more expect to see the Buddha or Ganesh in the "miracle" picture than they would Godzilla or Frankenstein's monster. There are a number of points to consider here.

First, what Jack remembers is one of the most common exercises in the pursuit of religious socialization. We frame the expectations of the faith, in this case the assumption of miracles and the presence of the Savior, then we reward those who meet them. The children with him in Sister Beatrice's class are the churchgoers of the next generation, the ones who will support the church practically and financially, and who will at some point endeavor to teach their own children to do the same. It is axiomatic that religious groups that do not successfully indoctrinate succeeding generations quickly decline and pass into history.

Second, we know that, in some ways, this *is* a trick. Though hidden, the image of Jesus is already there in the picture. The only question is whether Sister Beatrice's class can see him. It's not as though there are a number of different signals buried in the noise and the children must identify the correct one. The obvious moral of the day's lesson is that the children should look for the face of the Savior in the jumble of their daily lives. The good Sister calling it a "miracle," however, leaves us with a couple of uncomfortable options in terms of religious socialization: either she is foolish enough to believe that seeing Christ's face in a trick picture is an actual miracle, or she is comfortable lying about the nature of miracles to the children in her care. Either possibility cheapens the supposed power of her God considerably.

Following from this, it is important to note that religious socialization has not only positive, but negative aspects—some of which may not manifest for years to come. The young boy who first identified the illusion gained not one but two rewards. Once the other children know that there's something tangible at stake, every time one or another of them squeals, "I see Him, too!" and holds out a hand for the prize, the authenticity of their perception (and, by implication, their socialization) is called into question. Did they really see the image, or did they simply lie to get the reward? More than that, cheap tricks such as this quickly establish in-groups and out-groups: those with sufficient "faith" see the "miracle" of the Savior, as opposed to those who "have eyes, but fail to see" (Mk. 8:18). No child wants to be left behind, especially when there are prizes in the offing, so the pressure to lie is enormous. Sister Beatrice's praise and the reward of a New Testament, however, also invoke a negative reinforcement in those who cannot find the image, and for whom the implication is that they lack faith, or worse. In that case, what happens to those "who have not eyes to see"?

> At last everyone had seen the face of Jesus in the jumble of whites and blacks except Jacky. He strained harder and harder, scared now, part of him cynically thinking that everyone else was simply putting on to please Sister Beatrice, part of him secretly convinced that he wasn't seeing it because God had decided he was the worst sinner in the class.[15]

Bear in mind that in this memory Jack Torrance is a small boy, probably only a little older than his own son, Danny, and that he alone of all the children couldn't make out "the face of Jesus in the jumble of whites and blacks." On the one hand, he's probably right. Little Suzy Fitzpatrick probably *did* say she saw Jesus just to get a shiny New Testament. Dumb old Mikey MacLean probably *did* put his hand up because he couldn't stand to be last at something again. It doesn't really matter. Young Jacky is right; once the answer's out there, the whole game is suspect. How many millions of people continue to believe they see God only because they've been told for decades that they should expect to, and are too afraid to admit that they don't? How many claim the experience of faith—from miracles to mystical union—because the other possibility is simply too frightening?

Indeed, consider the chilling alternative: Jacky thinks there's something wrong with *him*, that he can't see the Savior's image in the optical illusion because the Creator of the universe has decided that he isn't worthy as a human being or a child of God. Whether it's deliberately induced or simply a horrifying by-product of Roman Catholic socialization, it's precisely this kind of experience that leads anti-theists such as Richard Dawkins to declare, "I am persuaded that the phrase 'child abuse' is no exaggeration when used to describe what teachers and priests are doing to children whom they encourage to believe in something like the punishment of unshriven mortal sins in an eternal hell."[16] Because isn't that precisely where "the worst sinner in the class" would end up?

But the story doesn't end there.

It's important to remember that King's Sister Beatrice does not represent the kind of yardstick-and-hellfire nun that is the stock-in-trade of so much pop culture. In fact, Jack Torrance remembers her "sad, sweet manner," that she brought presents for the class, and that it was *just a picture.*[17] Wasn't it? In many ways, this is as offensive as it gets in terms of religious socialization. It is, in the manner of Stephen King, relentlessly *ordinary*, the stuff of thousands of church school classrooms across the country every week of the year. Yet it becomes more horrifying precisely because of its predictability. It is these mundane, routine encounters that encourage us to forget the fundamentally unnatural nature of religious myth. "'Don't you see it, Jacky?' Sister Beatrice had asked him."[18] Once again, he stares hard at the picture.

> He began to shake his head, then faked excitement and said: "Yes, I do! Now! It *is* Jesus!" And everyone in the class had laughed and applauded him, making him feel triumphant, ashamed, and scared.[19]

Later, clutching *his* shiny New Testament, looking at the picture after everyone else has left, Jacky realized that "he hated it. They had all made it up the way he had, even Sister herself. It was a big fake. 'Shitfire— hellfire—shitfire,' he had whispered under his breath."[20] As with so many hidden-image pictures, staring at it, willing yourself to see what you're supposed to see, only makes seeing anything more difficult. The images are there, waiting to be discovered, but our minds must be tricked into seeing. We need to be surprised into putting the pieces into some meaningful arrangement. We catch the picture as we move our heads, glimpse it when our attention is elsewhere. Once that happens, though, we can't *not* see it. As Jacky turns away in disgust, his peripheral vision suddenly racks the image into focus. From the same place we imagine we see ghosts and ghouls, shadows that move on their own, "he had seen the face of Jesus from the corner of his eye."[21]

> He turned back, his heart in his throat. Everything had suddenly clicked into place and he had stared at the picture with fearful wonder, unable to believe he had missed it. The eyes, the zigzag of shadow across the care-worn brow, the fine nose, the compassionate lips. Looking at Jacky Torrance. What had only been a meaningless sprawl had suddenly been transformed into a black-and-white etching of the face of Christ-Our- Lord. Fearful wonder became terror.[22]

For Jacky, though, rather than experiencing reverence and awe, two of the most common ways "the fear of the Lord" is made palatable for those in the pews on Sunday morning, "fearful wonder became terror. He had cursed in front of a picture of Jesus. He would be damned. He would be in hell with the sinners. The face of Christ had been in the picture all along."[23] Here, we see the awful power of religious socialization: although the picture had been there all along, that doesn't mean that anything else about it is true. Sister Beatrice notwithstanding, there is no miracle. Someone disguised the image and created the illusion; someone hid the signal in the noise. Then someone else claimed that this map *was* the territory. The result? A small child is reduced to terror because he saw the trick for what it was and refused to play along. Indeed, this is the grand, cosmic version of the numberless times parents and grandparents—thinking themselves amusing—grasp at a toddler's face, show them a partially hidden thumb, and then exclaim, "Ha! Got your nose!"

At that moment, King suggests, we should realize that significant parts of organized religion are little more than a disturbing species of optical illusion. This is the terror instilled in Jack as a small boy, the fear that he brought with him to the Overlook:

> He knew that it was all true. . . . The hedges really walked. There was a dead woman in 217, a woman who was perhaps only a spirit and harmless under most circumstances, but was now an active danger. Like some malevolent clockwork toy she had been wound up and set in motion by Danny's own odd mind . . . and his own.[24]

But Jack is no less suggestible than his son, so the question remains, poised on a knife edge: Is it true? *What* is true? As he struggles to make sense of the data, to find the signal in the noise, to impose meaning on "the jumble of whites and blacks" that his life has become, what *is* the reality that Jack has perceived? Because Jack is no longer afraid of leaving the Overlook; he's not even afraid of dying there, snowbound. Instead, he's horrified by the thought of dying there, but still never being able to leave. If the hotel "played its cards right they could end up flitting through the Overlook's halls like insubstantial shades in a Shirley Jackson novel."[25]

This is one of *The Shining*'s most important chapters, a skeleton key to King's particular Overlook. Once you go down the rabbit hole, though, once you step through the wardrobe or peek behind the curtain, all bets are off. The principle of the hidden-picture optical illusion is that once we make sense of the data, once we solve the puzzle and force order onto chaos, we are left with the sense and meaning we impose. It becomes all but impossible *not* to see. Suddenly, revenant spirits and menacing topiary *are* the order of the day. "Once you saw the face of a god in those jumbled blacks and whites," Jack suddenly understands, "it was everybody out of the pool—you could never unsee it." Indeed, "you were damned to always see it."[26]

This is the power of religious socialization on full display. The picture contains not simply the face of a man, but an image of the Savior, perhaps derived from illustrations common in Sunday school curricula around the world. A man young Jacky Torrance could easily forget, but this isn't just a man. The image of Jesus comes with the full weight of Roman Catholic teaching behind it: the Word made flesh, very God of very God. The "zigzag of shadow" could easily be the darkness of the cross; the cares that crease his brow are precisely the sins young Jacky thinks he has committed. Indeed, not only does Jack realize that he can never unsee the image, he knows that he is never free of God's watchful gaze.

Once we accept an explanation for something, no matter how far-fetched it may have seemed a moment ago, it becomes increasingly difficult to find alternate explanations, and easier to fit formerly disparate packets of data into the new pattern. It's a truism, a fact in the life of human beings as *Homo narrans*: Repetition breeds familiarity. The more we tell a story, even (and especially) to ourselves, the more we come to believe it and the more believable it becomes. This doesn't mean, of course, that we all tell the same story the same way.

Mike and Richie: Vocabulary and Expectation

By the time readers reach chapter 13 of *It*, called "The Apocalyptic Rock-fight," they have met It in the guise of the malevolent Pennywise the Clown a number of times. Even by this point, though, King offers no hint of what It *is*, where It comes from, or what It wants—apart from the murder and mayhem It visits upon Derry, Maine. Will we ever know? Will King let us in on the cosmic joke? Or will he follow M. R. James's advice about ghost stories: just let them be what they are, without explanation? In "Some Remarks on Ghost Stories," James, clearly another of King's principal influences, advises authors that "when the climax is reached, allow us to be just a little in the dark as to the workings of their machinery. We do not want to see the bones of their theory about the supernatural."[27] In what amounts to a young boy's version of a sweat lodge ceremony, however, after the other members of the Losers Club have been driven out of their improvised ritual space, King does let the veil slip. Inside, in the heat and smoke, Mike Hanlon and Richie Tozier share a vision in which they both witness the arrival of It.

Untold millennia ago, eons before the last ice age, It came from the sky. "It was burning so hot you couldn't really look at it," Mike tells his friends later. "And it was throwin off electricity and makin thunder. The noise. . . . It sounded like the end of the world. And when it hit, it started a forest fire. That was at the end of it."[28] While both boys agree on what they *saw*, they disagree on what it *was*.

As we have seen, our awareness and interpretation of phenomena are shaped by a variety of filters, perceptual schematics, and, in this case, *expectation bias*. Put simply, we often see (or don't) what we have been programmed to see (or ignore). During their makeshift sweat lodge, the Losers learn that this unimaginable evil has been in what is now Derry for an unimaginably long time.

> "Was it a spaceship?" Ben asked.
> "Yes," Richie said. "No," Mike said.
> They looked at each other.[29]

Whatever King imagines himself to be writing about at this point, however he as the author ultimately understands It, through the Losers Club he once again highlights the power of religious socialization. In this case, it's not so much how something is *explained* as the *vocabulary* used to explain it. Despite his Methodist upbringing, Richie Tozier, who will grow up to be a famous radio personality, has no language beyond "spaceship" to describe what they saw. Long before the advent of multiplex theaters and their plethora of cinematic choices, this is the era of

B-grade science fiction movies shown on a weekend double bill at the local movie house, the Aladdin: *It Came from Outer Space, It Conquered the World, It! Terror from Beyond Space* (which inspired Ridley Scott's iconic *Alien*), and hundreds more.[30] The imaginative staple of a young boy's entertainment, these films both shape and limit Richie's vocabulary for It's arrival. Something vast, burning, and deadly comes from the sky? What could it possibly be but a spaceship?

Mike Hanlon, on the other hand, has the same vision, but sees something very different. Both boys take in the same movies; they both watch "*Science Fiction Theater*, with Your Host Truman Bradley," who each week asked, "Who knows what strange things the universe may hold?"[31] Pulp science fiction magazines—*Amazing Stories, Super-Science Fiction, Captain Future*, and dozens more—were readily available to them at the Center Street Drug Store. The language of science fiction, of UFO panics and alien invaders, was part of their shared experience, yet this is not how Mike understands their vision of It.

> "It came out of the sky," Mike repeated, "but it wasn't a *spaceship*, exactly. It wasn't a meteor, either. It was more like . . . well . . . like the Ark of the Covenant, in the Bible, that was supposed to have the spirit of God inside of it . . . except this wasn't God. Just feeling It, watching It come, you know It meant bad, that It *was* bad."[32]

The Ark of the Covenant, known to a generation of moviegoers more through *Raiders of the Lost Ark* than through the scant biblical references to it, is reputed to be a chest designed by God. Built by Moses to exacting specifications, it was made of acacia wood and clad in gold, and it contained in some way the enormous power of the Divine. The Ark was the portable vessel for the Word of God, the Tablets of the Law Moses brought down from Mount Horeb. Before it, the walls of Jericho fell, enemy armies were laid waste, and those who dared to touch it without the Almighty's permission perished.

The Losers turn to Richie, who nods. "'It came from . . . *outside*. I got that feeling. From *outside*.' 'Outside where, Richie?' Eddie asked. 'Outside everything,' Richie said."[33] As Richie Tozier struggles to find words for his experience, Mike Hanlon puts their vision in perspective.

It's *always* been here, since the beginning of time . . . since before there were men *anywhere*, unless there were maybe just a few of them in Africa somewhere, swinging through the trees or living in caves. . . . It was here, then, sleeping maybe, waiting for the ice to melt, waiting for the people to come.[34]

Whatever It was, whatever It is, Mike locates Its arrival in scarcely veiled theological terms. "And he said unto them," Luke's gospel claims Jesus told his disciples, "I beheld Satan as lightning fall from heaven" (10:18). Although Richie and Mike are the only two who go to church regularly, other religious traditions are represented among the Losers Club. Eddie Kasprak, for example, is also a Methodist, a fairly progressive denomination by the late 1950s. Only a few years later, the church would introduce a new, much more liberal Sunday school curriculum, one that nearly split the denomination and provoked a potent conservative reactionary movement.[35] By this time, among many Methodists, Satan—understood as a literal entity—was no longer theologically fashionable. Not so with the "Christers," as fellow Loser Ben Hanscom's mother calls them, the Bible-believers of Derry's Neibolt Street Church.[36]

Unlike the Methodists, Neibolt Street Church is a conservative, separatist congregation, what today we would call nondenominational, with its own church-run grade school. As a result, Mike is both religiously and educationally socialized very differently from other members of the Losers Club. "His mother was a devout Baptist," King tells us, "and Mike was therefore sent to the Neibolt Street Church School."[37]

> In between geography, reading, and arithmetic there were Bible drills, lessons on such subjects as The Meaning of the Ten Commandments in a Godless World, and discussion groups on how to handle everyday moral problems (if you saw a buddy shoplifting, for instance, or heard a teacher taking the name of God in vain).[38]

Like *The Shining*, indeed like many of Stephen King's storyworlds, *It* is not a "religious" novel in the way critics often judge *The Stand*. Rather, his exploration of religion—in this case, religious socialization and its unintended secondary effects—underpins the plot, highlighting how different faith backgrounds affect the ways we see the world and react to what we see. That is, King never says, "This you must believe," or "This you should believe." His storyworlds may be didactic, but they are never homiletic, and, as we have seen, he proposes no "dark theology" of his own. Rather, consistent throughout his more than four decades of horror fiction, it is as if he says instead, "This is what some people believe, and these are the consequences of their belief." He investigates what people *do* claim about the world and how those claims shape their decisions, making them not religious per se, but human.

Reinforced at home, church, and school—the three principal loci of socialization—Mike Hanlon's fundamentalist Protestant upbringing filters his vision of Its arrival: not a spaceship, though Its intelligence is definitely alien, but the Morning Star, the first fallen angel. Lucifer. Peering through a child's mind, King wisely avoids trotting Satan on stage like some clown-faced *diabolus ex machina*. This is not witless exposition, but explanation through the lens of the available concepts and vocabulary. Which is to say, socialization. Mike isn't the Greek chorus informing the audience of Its true identity; he's one of the characters wandering the stage and wondering aloud what It might be. For, as we shall see later, the reality of It is far stranger than any of the Losers can imagine, and makes the notion of a child-stealing demon seem almost pedestrian by comparison.

Richie Tozier Redux

In mass market paperback, *It* is a very thick book with very small type, and somehow, for whatever reason, King loses track of Richie's back-story in the latter chapters. When we first meet him, during the Losers' impromptu sweat lodge, we're told he's a Methodist. Later, as the kids prepare for the final battle with It, Richie refers to his family as "us Catholics" when he lectures the others on the finer points of Roman dogma.[39] It could be that Richie was raised Roman Catholic, but now his parents send him to the Methodist church, or that King intended this to be one of the other Losers—Ben Hanscom, perhaps, or Beverly Marsh. We don't know, and the reason is actually less important than that it give his Constant Reader another perspective on the characters' religious socialization.

As children so often do, Stan Uris, a secular Jew, and Eddie Kasprak quiz Richie the Catholic about beliefs and practices that seem in the 1950s as much a part of another culture as a different denomination. Here, King shows us the secondary effects of religious socialization. "I figure all religions are pretty weird," Richie tells his friends.[40] Stan agrees, pointing out that his family rarely observes Jewish holy days and everyone eats "ham and bacon" at home. "I hardly know what being a Jew is," he says. Stan's comment reveals the other side of religious socialization. When it is superficial or unsuccessful, when it is not reinforced through regular religious participation, any sense of one's identity as a believer gradually collapses into the rubric, "in name only." "'That's weird,' Eddie said, and burst out laughing. 'I never heard of a religion that told you what you could *eat*.'"[41]

This brief scene confronts us not only with the failure of religious socialization on the one hand (Stan), but with its often narrow, provincial nature on the other (Eddie). In the late nineteenth century, philologist Max Müller, who first coined the term "science of religion," famously told his students, "He who knows one, knows none." Referring specifically to the intellectual and cultural poverty of knowing only one *language*, Müller's oft-quoted insight has informed the field of religious studies since its founding more than half a century ago. Any person who knows something about one religion, and one religion only, cannot claim to know anything about *religion* at all.

When Richie points out that "it *is* pretty weird" that he's not allowed to eat ham, or sausage, or even bologna, that American staple of the adolescent diet, "just because you happen to be Jewish," Stan asks him, "'You eat meat on Fridays?' 'Jeez, no!' Richie said, shocked. 'You can't eat meat on Fridays, because—' He began to grin a little. 'Oh, okay, I see what you mean.'"[42]

This brief section, less than three pages in a book that is more than a thousand long, tells us a lot about religious education and socialization. First is the simple fact of socialization, in one case without reinforcement, in another with no supporting context. Stanley Uris may know that he's Jewish because his parents have told him so, and because "sometimes we go up to synagogue in Bangor, for stuff like Yom Kippur."[43] In this, he may know that he's not Orthodox, but he knows little more than that, and it makes no apparent difference in his life. While

Richie the Catholic knows he's not supposed to eat meat on Fridays, he has no idea why. Indeed, only when he's confronted by his friends and placed in comparison with Stan's nominal Judaism does he begin to question his own religious socialization.

Second is the issue of religious illiteracy.

> "Do Catholics really go to hell if they eat meat on Fridays?" Eddie asked, fascinated, totally unaware that until two generations before, his own people had been devout Polish Catholics who would no more have eaten meat on Friday than they would have gone outside with no clothes on.[44]

While all this may seem a lot to pile onto three ten-year-old boys talking in the street, as we have seen, Stephen Prothero has argued that adults are rarely more informed about their own religion—let alone the religious beliefs of others—than are Eddie, Stan, and Richie.[45] Here, though, we get to the heart of the matter, just as we did with Jacky Torrance in Sister Beatrice's catechism class, and just as we will with Carrie White trapped in the walls of her mother's religious mania: Will it send me to hell? Will God punish me for it? For his part, Richie responds with a child's version of Pascal's famous wager: "I don't really think God would send me down to the Hot Place just for forgetting and having a baloney sandwich for lunch on a Friday, but why take a chance?"[46]

Why, indeed?

Like Jacky Torrance's catechism lessons, Eddie Kasprak's experience in Mrs. Portleigh's first-grade "Little Worshippers" class also involved a miracle—of sorts. Trying to impress on her young Methodists the importance of holy communion, which, mindful of their temperance heritage, they celebrated with "Welch's grape juice" and "cut-up cubes of fresh, springy Wonder Bread," Mrs. Portleigh told "her rapt Little Worshippers" about "a bad boy [who] had once stolen some of the communion-bread when the tray was passed and put it in his pocket. He took it home and threw it into the toilet-bowl to see what would happen."[47] Not surprisingly—this is Stephen King, after all—a horrific miracle took place. "The water in the toilet-bowl had turned a bright red. It was the Blood of Christ, she said, and it had appeared to that little boy because he had done a very bad act called a BLASPHEMY. . . . He had put his immortal soul in danger of Hell."[48]

Like many children, Eddie enjoyed the communion ritual. He got a bit of grape juice and a cube of Wonder Bread, sure, but more importantly it made him feel part of the community, part of grown-up church. That poor, misguided Mrs. Portleigh, whose name suggests nothing so much as a character from Dickens, only wanted to convey the importance of communion is more than likely. How King portrays her doing it once again speaks volumes to the power of religious socialization, and how much of it is rooted in fear. From that moment on, Eddie never looked at the ritual the same way. Rather than a welcome into the worshipping community, the sign and symbol of acceptance by both his church and his God, "his awe of the ritual darkened into something more potent, something rather dreadful."

> Simply reaching for the cubes of bread became an act which required courage, and he always feared an electrical shock . . . or worse, that the bread would suddenly change color in his hand, become a blood-clot, and a disembodied Voice would begin to thunder in the church, "*Not worthy! Not worthy! Damned to Hell! Damned to Hell!*"[49]

More than that, despite all his rationalization, his preadolescent attempts at explanation, Mrs. Portleigh's story "worried at him, gnawed at him, even caused him to lose sleep."[50] Decades before *Mythbusters* made science cool, he even imagined testing her claim: take some communion bread and throw it in the toilet bowl. After all, what's the worst that could happen? "But such an experiment was far beyond his courage," King tells us. "His rational mind could not stand against that sinister image of the blood spreading its cloud of accusation and potential damnation in the water."[51]

"I guess all religions are weird," Eddie decides, implicitly acknowledging that, while no necessary convergence exists between religion and rationality, religious belief is reinforced through the collusion of expectation and explanation.

Paul Edgecombe: Expectation and Explanation

As overtly religious as many people think *The Stand*, and though it contains an obvious diabolical character in Randall Flagg and ends with a somewhat anticlimactic *deus ex machina*, there is no real corresponding Christ-figure. Mother Abagail seems at best a prophetic voice crying out to kindred spirits from the depth of the post-contagion wilderness. *The Green Mile*'s John Coffey, on the other hand, a man capable of extraordinary acts of healing, though wrongly convicted of murdering two young girls and condemned to ride the lightning, is one of the very few Christ-figures we find in King's work. Even this interpretation, however, must be nuanced and restrained. Dreaming about Coffey years after the events at Cold Mountain Penitentiary, Paul Edgecombe, former head boss at the prison's capital punishment unit, makes the connection explicit.

> I dozed off and dreamed of Calvary Hill. Thunder in the west and a smell that might have been juniper berries. Brutal and Harry and Dean and I were standing around in robes and tin hats like in a Cecil B. DeMille movie. We were Centurions, I guess. There were three crosses, Percy Wetmore and Eduard Delacroix flanking John Coffey. I looked down at my hand and saw I was holding a bloody hammer.[52]

It is tempting to take the dream as King's word on the matter, to read John Coffey as a Christ-figure, Paul Edgecombe as the converted Roman officer, perhaps the one Christian legend remembers to us as Longinus, and let that be the end of the matter. After all, his initials are J.C., and that's been enough for some reviewers to misread science fiction characters such as Klaatu as a Christ-figure and *The Day the Earth Stood Still* as a Christian allegory.[53] Indeed, the search for Christ-figures in literature and film has become a popular pursuit among critics of all sorts.[54] To do so, though, once again gives the game away far too easily, and misses a number of the more important questions that King raises through the poignant story of John Coffey, Paul Edgecombe, and Mr. Jingles, the Miracle Mouse.

First, there is the problem of the "magical Negro." At some point in the past two decades, critics and commentators identified a recurring trope in literature and film: a selfless and self-effacing secondary character, usually black and often male, created explicitly to support and enable the primary characters, all of whom are white. Known variously as the "magical Negro" and "magical African-American friends,"[55] the trope was popularized by director Spike Lee as "the Super-Duper Magical Negro."[56] Identifying what she calls the "Five Points of the Magical Negro," fantasy author Nnedi Okorafor points out that he or she "is a person of color . . . in a story about predominantly white characters"; "seems to have nothing better to do than help the white protagonist"; "disappears, dies, or sacrifices something of great value" after the primary mission of helping the white character has been fulfilled; "is uneducated, mentally handicapped, at a low position in life"; but "is wise, patient and spiritually in touch."[57]

Although recognizing this as a deeply racist notion, Okorafor insists that King himself "is *not* a racist."[58] Some of his best-known novels from the first half of his career, however, do rely for their narrative momentum at least in part on the "magical Negro": Dick Hallorann, the Overlook chef in *The Shining* and Danny Torrance's spiritual guide in *Doctor Sleep*; *The Stand*'s Mother Abagail; and John Coffey, who patiently awaits execution on *The Green Mile* for crimes he did not commit. Though Okorafor does not consider her, the narrative obverse of the "magical Negro" is Sara Tidwell, whose brutal rape and murder created "the Sara-thing" in *Bag of Bones*. Though less obvious as a supernatural aid, Sara is still central to the entire story: her "sacrifice," unwilling and unwarranted, takes place generations in the past, but motivates events in the story's present. Without her, without her horrific death, there is no story.

Okorafor suggests that in the past, the "magical Negro" trope might have been an expression of the more culturally identifiable (and acceptable) racism we find in *Bag of Bones*: persons of color were slaves, then servants, then largely lower class. They certainly weren't treated as friends, neighbors, equals. "Like Asimov's robots," she writes, "black people had rules imprinted in their brains that made them so selfless."[59] As racism became both more prominent and more insidious as a social problem, however, the "magical Negro" went underground, as it were. Still deeply embedded in American cultural consciousness, people of color became the secondary supernatural allies in the classic hero's journey—which is always made by whites.[60] They are crucial to the plot, but not so crucial that they cannot be sacrificed to the main character's quest.

Second, in a narrative move that reinforces the "magical Negro" critique, the entire story is told as a reminiscence from Paul Edgecombe's end-of-life point of view. A prison guard in Depression-era Louisiana, Edgecombe was raised in a very particular religious milieu. Just like Jacky Torrance and the adolescent Losers from Derry, Edgecombe was socialized a certain way, and approaches the complexity of his experience on the green mile with the only vocabulary available to him.

> I had learned of matters eternal at my mother's pretty knee, and what I believed is what the Good Book says about murderers: that there is no eternal life in them. I think they go straight to hell, where they burn in torment until God finally gives Gabriel the nod to blow the Judgment Trump. When he does, they'll wink out . . . and probably glad to go they will be.[61]

Young Paul, however, hardly learned all that—what amounts to a complex yet simple-sounding theology—only at his "mother's pretty knee." Nor did his mother shape this manner of god-talk on her own. "As a boy," he continues, caught in the gauzy web of an old man's remembrance, "who'd grown up going to whatever Baptist or Pentecostal church my mother and her sisters happened to be in favor of any given month, I had heard plenty of Praise Jesus, The Lord Is Mighty miracle stories."[62] These unavoidable experiences gave Edgecombe the theological vocabulary—the god-talk—to interpret his experiences on Cold Mountain's death row unit so many years later. And, even decades after that, they still shape the contours of Old Paul's memory. "I knew—" he tells us, "believed at least—what I had learned about healing in those churches of Praise Jesus, The Lord Is Mighty, piney-woods amen corners much beloved by my twenty-two-year-old mother and my aunts."[63] Indeed, this is the principal lens, some would argue the *only* lens, through which he *can* understand his experience of John Coffey. Once again, it's easy simply to accept *The Green Mile* as a miracle tale, to take it as an uplifting story or gospel allegory that happens to contain a few scary bits—the execution of Eduard Delacroix and the death of Mr. Jingles chief among them—but doing so ignores other layers of meaning bred deep in the bones of the story.

Religious socialization not only prepares a believer to experience things in particular ways, but, as we saw with Mike Hanlon, it also excludes other ways of seeing the same thing. Part of the work of socialization is to restrict, even bound out alternative explanations. Edgecombe never considers that John Coffey might not be human, for example, that he might be a supernatural being of some sort—an angel or an alien. Even though science fiction pulps of the 1920s and 1930s had popularized the notion of extraterrestrials, usually in the context of an invasion from space, these remained firmly lodged in fiction. Popular culture was still decades away from considering the possibility of actual contact with an extraterrestrial intelligence. Yet, even as he writes as a centenarian well into the twenty-first century, Edgecombe's religious socialization will not permit him to imagine the possibility. And he could, for there are two Paul Edgecombes in *The Green Mile*. Besides Mr. Jingles the Miracle Mouse, he is the only character who exists both in 1932 and, decades later, in the moment of recollection. There is, as it were, Paul the *experient* and Paul the *remembrant*. The experient had no context to understand John Coffey, no vocabulary beyond that provided by the "Baptist or Pentecostal churches" he frequented with his mother and her sisters. The remembrant may well have, yet chooses not to. Even with the passage of so many years, the power of Paul Edgecombe's religious upbringing holds true.

"I grew up in a tradition of miracles and healings," he writes, but also a rural background of "stump-water for warts, moss under your pillow to ease the heartache of lost love."[64] When John Coffey brings Mr. Jingles back to life, when he heals Paul of a urinary tract infection, it never occurs to the prison guard to consider the giant convict as anything other than a conduit for a power not his own. "I helped it, didn't I?" John Coffey asks, to which Paul, the mirrored experient/remembrant, responds, "Except *he* hadn't. *God had*." Paul's socialization "in those churches of Praise Jesus, The Lord Is Mighty piney-woods amen corners" tells him that Coffey can only have misspoke, though through "ignorance rather than pride."[65] It is simply beyond the range of Paul's religious training that John Coffey could be anything other than a means for God to achieve divine ends. However mysterious those means may seem to us, what, then, are the ends? How does religious socialization train us to interpret what we understand as God's will? How do we not only explain the inexplicable, but give it meaning?

"Healing is never about the healed or the healer," Edgecombe tells us, remembering the myriad churches he attended as a child, "but about

God's will." More than that, rather than simply be grateful for the healing, "the person healed has an obligation to ask why—to meditate on God's will, and the extraordinary lengths to which God has gone to realize His will."[66]

What happens, though, when different visions of God's will, different versions of religious socialization compete for dominance? For this, we travel from Cold Mountain, Louisiana, to Castle Rock, Maine, from the terrible confines of *The Green Mile* to the inviting treasures of a little shop called Needful Things.

Steamboat Willie: Explanation and Reinforcement

"Churches in small towns," the narrator begins, "well, I guess I don't have to tell you how *that* is. They get along with each other—sort of—but they ain't never really *happy* with each other."[67] In this case, discontent has surfaced in the form of a Casino night intended to pay for roof repairs to Castle Rock's Roman Catholic church, a plan that "seems more than a wee bit wicked" to the Reverend William Rose and his congregation. In protest, the good folk of Rose's Baptist church have papered King's iconic Maine town with fliers condemning the event. "Hot damn! Just *look* at this thing, will you?" the narrator tells us, "DICE AND THE DEVIL printed right up at the top. In big red letters with *smoke* comin off em."[68]

A pleasant enough fellow, proud of his town in that wink-and-a-nod way common to places where everyone knows pretty much everything about everyone else, *Needful Things'* narrator catches us up on recent events in the Castle Rock storyworld. Frank Dodd, the sheriff's deputy and crossing guard who turned out to be a serial pedophile and child killer (*The Dark Half*); that poor old St. Bernard that went rabid and tore through a few more of the townsfolk, including the former sheriff, Alan Pangborn's predecessor (*Cujo*). We meet the locals, at least by name. Then the penny drops. Whatever squabbles the two groups of God's chosen have between them will seem petty indeed compared to what's coming, because, as the narrator warns us, "there's a storm on the way."[69]

"I thought I'd written a satire on Reaganomics in the eighties," King once told the *Paris Review*. "You know, people will buy anything and sell anything, even their souls. I always saw Leland Gaunt, the shop owner who buys souls, as the archetypal Ronald Reagan: charismatic, a little bit elderly, selling nothing but junk, but it looks bright and shiny."[70] Gaunt may be the allegorical embodiment of American life under the Great Communicator, but he is also the tempter, the trickster-god that shows up throughout our mythological imagination, setting people against each other, then sitting back to enjoy the show.

Rather than the apocalyptic scale and vast stakes of *The Stand*, *Needful Things* picks over the petty jealousies and everyday bigotry that mark so much of human behavior. Of all the ways King could have chosen to explore these behaviors—politics or race, for example, family bickering or the battle between the sexes—like so many other horror writers he draws once again from the well of religious conflict. In this case, the Catholics of Our Lady of Serene Waters and the Castle Rock Baptists led by the Reverend William Rose. Of Father Brigham we learn relatively little, while Rose, called "Steamboat Willie" behind his back, is the very portrait of fundamentalists such as Jerry Falwell, Jimmy Swaggart, and Pat Robertson. Indeed, *Needful Things* was written between October 1988 and January 1991, two years during which Falwell's Moral Majority movement was falling apart. Scandals dogged some of America's most well-known televangelists, including but hardly limited to Jimmy Swaggart and Jim Bakker. More than most of King's other works—*Under the Dome*, written nearly a decade and a half later, is another exception—*Needful Things* exposes what many horror writers consider the corruption of the organized church and the hypocrisy of her most devoted followers.

Throughout *Needful Things*, King weaves a history of the antipathy between Catholics and Protestants that has deep roots in American culture, and which many people believe continues to this day. Once again, he fills the stage with characters we recognize from daily life. Indeed, not only do we recognize them, we *know* them. More than occasionally, we *live* with them. "Never mind," says Myrtle Keeton, wife of the town's head selectman, after playing her "small prank" on the women gathered in the Daughters of Isabella Hall. "They're only Catholics."[71]

It's easy enough to dismiss these threads of prejudice as more callow, cynical set dressing, which, as missiologist Bryan Stone contends of horror in general, refuses to take "religious faith on its own terms or explain religious values or motivations with much complexity."[72] King, however, makes it clear that religious motivations and values are what drive the conflict in Castle Rock, the ways many religious believers are constantly socialized to regard the religiously different as the dangerous Other. Whatever America's dark theologian has to say about God in his stories, he leaves little to the imagination when it comes to God's followers— especially those who are convinced they have the inside scoop on the divine plan. As in the other examples we've considered, this conviction is the product of socialization and reinforcement.

For their part, the Castle Rock Catholics are almost a caricature of religious immigration in America: a congregation of second- and third-generation Polish immigrants led by a fiery Irish priest. Across town, the Baptists are the very picture of the Moral Majority, led by a preacher who sounds like no one so much as Jerry Falwell. It seems as though there ought to be big questions in play, weighty issues of good and evil on the table, but there just aren't. *Needful Things* is about perception, prejudice, and the precipice that yawns when those two come together.

Consider the Reverend William Rose. Steamboat Willie. Not only is he astonished to learn that there is nothing Sheriff Pangborn *can* do about "Casino Nite," there is nothing he appears *willing* to do. According to King, "the Rev. Rose was one of those deep-thicket Baptists who begin to twist the tails of their words when they are emotionally cranked up."[73] That is, he's from the same "Praise Jesus, The Lord Is Mighty, piney-woods amen corners much beloved" by Paul Edgecombe's mother and her sisters. When Pangborn tells him there's nothing illegal about the Catholic proposal, Rose responds, "'This-uh is not bingo! This is roulette-uh. This is playing cards for money. This is'—Rev. Rose's voice trembled—'*dice-uh!*'"[74] The sheriff tries to get him to see reason, but Rose is caught in the whirlwind of his own moral outrage, the self-righteous product of his "deep-thicket Baptist" heritage. "When-uh Jesus saw the whores and the moneylenders in-uh the Temple," he thunders, "He did not consult any written code of laws, Sheriff. When-uh Jesus saw those evil men and women defiling the House of the Lord-uh, He looked for no line of infringement. *Our Lord did what He-uh knew to be right!*"[75]

To which Pangborn can only reply, simply, "Yes, but you're not Him."

Certainly not, but Rose eagerly locates himself at the center of the battle between good and evil, or as many Protestant believers would have it, between Christians and Catholics. He is also, as King puts it, "a bigot of the first water; no question about it."[76] Indeed, as the two groups of God's faithful gather for the climactic battle in front of Leland Gaunt's little curiosity shop, fanning the flames of sectarian rivalry that go back five hundred years, we learn that it was precisely this prejudice that made Rose so popular in the first place.

Religious socialization is often as much about identifying the faults of others—pointing them out as "false believers"—as it is reinforcing the correctness of one's own beliefs.[77] The more stridently believers claim the exclusivity of their particular truths, the more anxious they are to point out the heretics in the woodpile. Indeed, among conservative Protestants, this has become something of a cottage industry. Consider Dave Hunt, for example, one of the most prominent and prolific of the late twentieth-century countercult apologists. "The only reason for becoming familiar with other religions and other religious writings" he wrote, "would be in order to show those who follow these false systems wherein the error lies and thereby to rescue them."[78] A virulent anti-Catholic, Hunt could have been the very model from which King drew the Reverend William Rose.

From pulpit-pounding sermons to home visits with parishioners, Rose reinforces the Baptist sense of moral and theological superiority, assuring his congregation of their salvation and their pride of place in God's plan. Rose's "first sermon as leader of the Baptist flock had been a sign of things to come. It was called 'Why the Catholics are Hellbound,'" and King's description is worth quoting at length.

> The Catholics, he informed them, were blasphemers, misguided creatures who worshipped not Jesus but the woman who had been chosen to bear Him. Was it any wonder they were so prone to error on other subjects as well? He explained to his flock that the Catholics had perfected the science of torture during the Inquisition; that the Inquisitors had burned the *true* faithful at what he called The Smoking-uh Stake right up until the end of the nineteenth century, when heroic Protestants (Baptists, mostly) had made them stop; that forty different Popes through history had known their own mothers and sisters, and even their illegitimate daughters in-uh unholy sexual congress-uh; that the Vatican was built on the gold of Protestant martyrs and plundered nations.[79]

"This sort of ignorant twaddle," the narrator tells us, "was hardly new to the Catholic Church, which had had to put up with similar heresies for hundreds of years."[80] Anti–Roman Catholic propaganda has appeared with some regularity and varying levels of vitriol since well before the Protestant Reformation. Geoffrey Chaucer lampooned the Church in *The Canterbury Tales*, while his Italian contemporary, Giovanni Boccaccio, did likewise in *The Decameron*. After the Reformation and across the Atlantic, anti-Catholicism became a minor publishing phenomenon in the colonies. Lurid accounts of "life behind the convent walls," written by putative victims such as Jane Dunbar Chaplin, Edith O'Gorman, and the pseudonymous Maria Monk were accompanied by alarmist cautionary tales such as Helen Dhu's novel *Stanhope Burleigh: The Jesuits in Our Homes*.[81] "The terrible Company of Jesus—," Dhu begins her note "To the Reader," "the deadliest foe Civil and Religious Liberty has ever had to contend with—after having been sooner or later driven from every civilized country, has at last fixed its stronghold in the United States."[82]

Together with stories of miraculous escapes from the clutches of Rome, atrocity narratives such as these contributed to a social undercurrent of anti-Catholicism that resulted in, among other tragedies, the 1834 Ursuline Convent riots and the torching of Mount Benedict, a convent and women's school in Charlestown, Massachusetts. Though some of King's readers might concede the anti-Catholic prejudice prevalent in earlier centuries, like racism a sad relic of a less-enlightened national past, how many would be surprised to learn that it is at least as virulent today? With titles such as *Reasoning from the Scriptures with Catholics*, *The Fatal Flaw*, and *A Woman Rides the Beast*, anti-Catholicism remains an important niche market for the ongoing religious socialization of fundamentalist Protestants.[83]

"Anti-Catholicism is the last refuge of acceptable bigotry in the United States," writes Robert Lockwood, former editor of the popular Catholic newspaper *Our Sunday Visitor*, while others contend that "as one of the few forms of bigotry socially acceptable in America, [it] is quite possibly the nation's original sin."[84] While many would suggest that America's enduring legacy of racism—whether directed at indigenous populations displaced and massacred during colonization and westward expansion, the blight of slavery on American history, or the various racial exclusion laws that either limited Asian immigration or allowed Asians in as little more than slave labor—is a more apt candidate for the nation's "original sin," or that since both these claims were made just prior to 9/11, any notion of "acceptable bigotry" in the United States has surely shifted to America's Muslim population (and those suspected of being Muslim), the anti-Catholicism underpinning the conflict in Castle Rock remains deeply rooted in American culture. For Steamboat Willie and his congregation, the stakes are much higher than simply whether the local Catholic parish uses "roulette-uh," "playing cards for money," and "dice-uh" to raise funds for a new church roof. For the Baptists, cosmic issues are in play, at the heart of which lies the all-important question of who is saved and who is not. Indeed, in the ongoing contest of the saved and the damned, the battle between our world and the unseen order, the trickster Leland Gaunt is almost incidental to the plot.

Telling the stories of our various faiths and reinforcing the lessons of our different religious teachers is the essence of socialization. It is in our nature to pass on what we have been taught, so that our stories inform the next generation, so that their values and principles reflect our own. Whether these are laudable ideals or not is beside the point. Few who bend their will in the name of God think themselves acting apart from his design. We share the vocabulary of our faith so that our children speak the same language as we and understand the world in the same way. Without this socialization process, religious views of the world would be considerably more tenuous and ephemeral than they are. But simply telling the stories is not enough. Equally important is how we embody our myths and legends in action, how we enact our ghost stories and god-talk in ritual.

5

Return to Ackerman's Field

Ritual and the Unseen Order

Although it's often a little thin on the *why* of things, religious socialization teaches us *what* we should believe about the relationship between
the seen and the unseen orders. Embedding those beliefs in the daily
round is the task of ritual. But what is ritual, and why do we continue the
rituals we do? Even when we're not sure whether they do anything for
us, even if we think that they may be futile in the face of life's implacabil-
ity, we continue them regardless. It's not so much that rituals reveal the
cracks in the world as that they disclose how we manage them. "Rainy
Season," from the *Nightmares and Dreamscapes* collection, showcases
another way Stephen King comments on our response to the thin spots
we encounter. We see this from the moment old Henry Eden says to
Laura Stanton, "Well, it's only once every seven years. And it has to be
done jus that way. Because—"

> "Because it's part of the ritual," she said glumly.
>   "Ayuh. It's the ritual."[1]

Indeed, we learn little more about it than that. Not where the ritual
came from, nor who started it or when, nor to whom it is dedicated. We
aren't sure whether it's intended to ward off some supernatural punishment or is simply a local artifact, a superstitious reaction to an extraordinary natural phenomenon. All we know is that every seven years, for
one terrifying night a torrent of carnivorous, demonic toads rains down
on the rural community of Willow, Maine, and woe betide the ones
caught out as ritual sacrifice.

Just prior to the horrific deluge, a young couple—a man and a woman,
always a man and a woman—arrives in town. Always. And, always, two
townsfolk warn these newcomers away, only for the one night, mind

you, assuring them that they will be warmly welcomed the following day. There's a very nice inn just down the road, they're told, and they'll be more than comfortable there. After all, it's only for one night. What's the harm? The choice to stay or go, though, is always theirs. The ritual requires the two Willow folk to encourage them to leave, but not to force them out of town. Never to force them. They must make the choice to stay, to go against the warning, *of their own free will*. This year, John Graham, a young academic, and his wife, Elise, choose to stay, unwilling to accommodate backwoods superstitions even for that one night.

Later, as the toads start falling—"*Thud-thud . . . Thud-CRASH!*"— John, who will be dead in a few minutes, begins to grasp the horror of their situation. "The thing hopping across the glass-littered floor toward him was a toad, but it was also not a toad. Its green-black body was too large, too lumpy. Its black-and-gold eyes bulged like freakish eggs. And bursting from its mouth, unhinging the jaw, was a bouquet of large, needle-sharp teeth."[2] By the time the end came, trapped in the coal cellar, Elise Graham had screamed herself hoarse and died in mute terror. "John Graham screamed quite adequately for both of them."[3]

As soon as the sun came up the next morning, "the living toads died; the dead ones simply rotted to that white fluid."

> It bubbled briefly and then sank slowly into the ground. The earth sent up ribands of steam, and for a little while every field in Willow looked like the site of a dying volcano. By quarter of seven, it was all over, except for the repairs, and the residents were used to them. It seemed a small price to pay for another seven years of quiet prosperity in this mostly forgotten Maine backwater.[4]

"Rainy Season" can be read as part allegory on the Garden of Eden, the warning to stay away from the Tree of the Knowledge of Good and Evil, and part meditation on humankind's free will choice to do otherwise. But it is considerably more than just a retelling of the original sin myth. It speaks also to the lack of understanding that so often accompanies religious ritual, as well as the fear that wells up in the face of our failure to fulfill ritual obligations.

Nothing in the story gives any hint that either Henry or Laura knows where the hideous toads come from, nor the genesis of the ritual that both of them are convinced keeps their town safe—but for the one septennial night known as "rainy season." They do know that, however distasteful, specific elements of the ritual process must be honored. A man and a woman will arrive and two members of the community warn them away. More than that, they must be told why. "I *hate* this," Laura says when they first meet John and Elise Graham, a "nice young couple" who now have less than twelve hours to live. "Got to be done," Henry tells her.[5]

> The woman looked back at John and Elise, appearing to steel herself, and said, "You see, folks, it rains toads here in Willow every seven years. There. Now you know." . . . "Toads, ayuh!" Henry Eden affirmed cheerfully.[6]

When the pleasant if somewhat confused young couple drive away, clearly not prepared to leave Willow, Laura tells Henry, "I *always* feel like a horse's ass when I see the way they look at us. At me." But it has to be done that way, and Laura knows it as well as Henry. Neither may know why, but neither is willing to risk the consequences. "'Because it's part of the ritual,' she said glumly."[7]

Later, after the toads, Henry wonders whether "we should have tried harder," but Laura responds simply, "It's the ritual."[8] She may have felt like a fool, but the Grahams are still dead, just like every other nice young couple who arrived in Willow, Maine, on the day of "rainy season" and refused to leave for just one night. "Well, sometimes I just feel like saying frig the ritual!"

"'*Henry!*' She drew her hand back, shocked in spite of herself."[9]

As much as she hates it, the thought of abandoning or even modifying the ritual terrifies Laura. A horrific version of Pascal's famous wager, the unknown consequences of forsaking what for generations they have been taught is their sacred responsibility are far more frightening than the gruesome but familiar cost of maintaining harmony between the seen and the unseen orders. The town is safe once again. That's what matters. "You know, Henry," she tells him, "we don't make ritual, we only follow it."[10]

"Ayuh," Henry agrees, because, after all, "seven years is a *hell* of a long time."[11]

Ritual comes in many forms and serves many purposes. From a quick "sign of the cross" before a college exam to the complexities of High

Mass, from a hasty offering made at a Shinto shrine as a Japanese salaryman heads home from work to the elaborate means by which Taoist priests battle *jiangshi* ("hopping ghosts" or "vampires"), ritual brings our beliefs about the unseen order into our daily lives. If religion is, as William James said, "the belief that there is an unseen order," then religious rituals are the means through which we maintain "harmonious adjustment" with that order. From rituals of propitiation, such as we find in "Rainy Season," to rites of protection and passage, these various machineries of "harmonious adjustment" tell us a lot about how we understand both the unseen order and our supreme good.

"I Know That Sounds Crazy": "N." and Ritual Understanding

We've been to Ackerman's Field before. It's that thin spot in rural Maine where the monstrous weight of the unseen order peeks through as a man known only as N. struggles both to retain personal sanity and maintain cosmological order. We return there as part of King's exploration of ritual, in this case, what we might call the *ritual progression*. Standing in Ackerman's Field, N. tells Dr. Bonsaint, is a circle of stones, some about five feet tall, others a bit more than half that. As he becomes increasingly invested in what's happening among the standing stones, also known as *menhir*, N. undergoes what anthropologist Tanya Luhrmann calls "interpretive drift": "the slow shift in someone's manner of interpreting events, making sense of experiences, and responding to the world."[12] What he at first takes to be little more than "a trick of the evening light" slowly shifts until he comes to see himself as a central character in the ritual drama represented by the standing stones.[13] His ritual prop, his object of power, is the camera he carries each time he goes to the remote field. To the naked eye, only seven stones stand there. The camera lens—the ritual eye that shifts perspective—brings the eighth menhir into focus. This is his role in the ritual: to return again and again to Ackerman's Field, to look through the lens and ensure that the final stone is there.

N. first sought out Dr. Bonsaint for help with obsessive-compulsive disorder, manifest, among other behaviors, in counting shoes on the way to and from work, and ensuring an even number of dishes in the dishwasher. His condition is also King's controlling metaphor for the ritual process. As N. opens up to Bonsaint, gradually disclosing the strange phenomenon of Ackerman's Field, his obsessive compulsions become an integral part of the ritual practice that he now believes keeps the world intact. No longer is the ritual of the camera something that simply keeps him sane or grounded; he now believes that it keeps reality as we know it stable and secure. Whole for the moment, if not completely safe. Now, far more than simply his state of mind is at stake.

The standing stones in Ackerman's Field, if that's what they are, are only one aspect of the problem. Arranged in a circle, the menhir mark the cardinal and ordinal points of the compass, and form a protective circle guarding this particular crack in the wall between the worlds. Whoever collected and arranged them had no interest in creating a gateway. Rather, recognizing the danger posed by the unseen order, they set the circle in place to keep out whatever might poke its head through. "Eight stones would keep them captive," N. continues, "—barely—but if there were only seven, they'd come flooding through from the darkness on the other side of reality and overwhelm the world."[14] That is, they will flood our world if the ritual is not performed correctly and consistently. Like the good folks from Willow, Maine, N. knows that if an element is omitted or done improperly, if only seven stones are allowed to remain, the fate of the world hangs in the balance.

Whatever it was that peered out from the thin spot at Ackerman's Field, N. is certain of one thing: "It saw me looking."[15] And, once N. saw—and was seen—like Jacky Torrance, he knew "you would always see it. You were damned to always see it."[16] More than that, this act of seeing has obligated him to a ritual duty of care; the fact of knowing has made N. a reluctant guardian on the watchtower of reality. "The conviction remained that I'd seen a face—worse, the suggestion of some huge reptilian body—in that circle of stones. I felt . . . *infected*. Infected by the thoughts in my own head."[17]

Although they present as a bit of a chicken-and-egg problem, superstitious behavior, magical thinking, and ritual process are intimately related to the evolution of the religious imagination. Put simply, at one end are the lucky charms we insist on carrying, despite no logical reason to suppose that they have any external effect in our lives. We simply *feel* better when we have them. From here, we move through superstitious behaviors, which we are convinced not only make us feel better about what we're doing, but often *affect* whether we can do it or not.

There is the sympathetic magic that assured a very frightened Trisha McFarland that if Tom Gordon got the save for the Red Sox, then she would be saved from the depths of the Maine forest. Finally, there are ritual practices so deeply rooted in our daily lives that to abandon them would call our entire view of the world into question. What changes as we move along the continuum from lucky pieces and rabbits' feet to sympathetic magic and religious rituals such as infant baptism are the stakes. We may do just as well on a history test without our lucky pen, but for devout Roman Catholics the eternal fate of a child actually turns on the proper performance of the ritual.[18] In this, the stakes could not be any higher.

Obsessive-compulsive disorders, which often manifest in counting, arranging, touching, or otherwise manipulating behaviors, are anxiety management techniques. When nervous, for example, many religious believers finger rosaries, malas, or prayer beads. While they may not actually *lessen* our anxiety, coping mechanisms like these allow us to function in its midst. N.'s daily obsessions—the shoes, the dishes—may seem like garden-variety coping strategies for everyday anxiety. What raises them to the level of religious compulsion are the stakes. Rather than the nervous tics of mundane life, as far as N. is concerned, Ackerman's Field has taken on cosmic proportions, and existence itself rests on his continued performance of the ritual.

"I understood other things, too," he tells his therapist. "One was that I had activated the place *just by looking at it*. Human eyes take away the eighth stone. A camera lens will put it back, but won't lock it in place. I had to keep renewing the protection with symbolic acts."[19] As much as any socially constructed world, whether benevolent or malevolent, acts of religious faith and devotion are matters of perception and reinforcement. We perceive something and interpret it in a certain way. We force a face onto a "jumble of whites and blacks." We "see" the body and blood in the bread and wine. Rather than the deepening shadows and shifting light at sunset, what landscape photographers call the "magic hour," N. sees monstrous, tormented faces in the cracks and fissures of the ancient menhir. Rather than the gloom of dusk in the Maine woods, he sees an unimaginable force, a primal malevolence leering at him from the circle, barely contained and anxious for release. And somehow, he has become its keeper. "I activated something. And in so doing, I became the latest baton carrier in a long, long line of them, maybe going all the way back to prehistoric times."[20] "I know that sounds crazy," he concludes, though the line between madness and prophetic devotion is often as thin as acceptance and as ephemeral as belief.

With its homage to Arthur Machen and his classic story "The Great God Pan," and with its undertones of H. P. Lovecraft and the primal reality that waits with infinite patience to press in on our own, more than many of King's stories "N." exemplifies both aspects of religion as William James defined it.

In *The Varieties of Religious Experience*, James actually proposes two interconnected ways of understanding religion, two ways of looking at our response to religious consciousness: belief and experience. First, as we have seen, James suggests that "the life of religion . . . consists of the *belief* that there is an unseen order, and that our supreme good lies in harmoniously adjusting ourselves thereto."[21] Elsewhere, though, he adds to that definition, pointing out that lived religion is the *experience* of this unseen order, and comprises "the feelings, acts, and experiences of [individuals] in their solitude, *so far as they apprehend themselves to stand in relation to whatever they may consider the divine.*"[22] That is, while his first definition can be interpreted as tending toward the social, religious experience is often a solitary experience, one for which we are rarely prepared and that can take us by complete surprise.

Consider a few of our well-known religious prophets—Jonah, Moses, Muhammad. When God's call came, when they found themselves "standing in relation to whatever they may consider the divine," they were more than a little surprised, and more than a little frightened. Jonah took flight rather than preach to the Ninevites; Moses insisted he was a nobody, unfit to return to Egypt under any circumstances; Muhammad told the angel three times, "But, I can't read!" Religious mythology may have framed their experiences as examples of prophetic obedience and sacrifice, but it's not hard to see their initial reluctance to the divine command. In the same way, N. goes to Ackerman's Field fully prepared to come away with a few nice photographs, one of which might find its way into the yearly calendar he has "printed at a little place in Freeport called The Windhaven Press."[23] He hardly expects to become a frontline soldier in the ageless war between light and dark. Because that *would* be crazy, wouldn't it?

What N. *feels* when he enters Ackerman's Field, what he *experiences* there, and how he *acts* in response may not seem much like "religion" as many of us understand it today. There are no churches, temples, or mosques; no prayer books or hymnals; no regular gathering of choir and congregation. Ancient evils rising from a fallow field in rural Maine, and one man called to keep the universe safe? The cosmic order poised on a razor's edge? It all seems a bit grandiose, doesn't it?

"I know that sounds crazy," N. repeats.

Most important to remember here is that "religion" does not mean simply "what we recognize as religion," even though this is a common way of looking at it. Moreover, "divine" does not necessarily mean "benevolent," even though in popular usage the two have become virtually synonymous. When something terrible or grotesque is done in the name of one's god, other followers of that deity are quick to distance themselves, often proclaiming loudly, "That's not *true* [insert religion here]!" "That's *not* what the [insert religious text here] *really* teaches!" However fervent these denunciations, though, we rarely if ever acknowledge that perpetrators of religiously motivated mayhem are often saying precisely the same thing. From terrorist attacks in major metropolitan areas to the bombing of abortion clinics to the murder of a mentally ill nun at a remote monastery, these believers look back at their putative co-religionists and offer the same defense. We have the "truth," not you.

What seems "crazy" is often little more than a shift in perspective.

We know nothing of N.'s religious life before he arrived at Ackerman's Field, but by the time he left he was well on his way to believing that "there is an unseen order" and "our supreme good" lies in managing our relationship to it. This is the essence of ritual. Once that perspectival shift happens, other things begin falling into place. Rather than just a tourist stop along the A303, a gathering place for aging hippies and wannabe Druids, what if Stonehenge is actually "a gigantic neurosis standing in a Salisbury field"?[24] More than that, though, King's story suggests, what if it's *not* a neurosis? What if it's all part of a much larger plan that we can no longer see? What if Stonehenge, Ville-ès-Nouveaux in Jersey, the Merry Maidens in West Penwith, Ackerman's Field in rural Maine, and the hundreds of other standing stone circles across western Europe, the Middle East, and North America are "protecting something as well as keeping track of hours and months. Locking out an insane universe that happens to be right next door to ours"?[25] What if it's not madness at all, but a line of watchtowers on the myriad thin spots where the seen and the unseen bump up against each other?

"I know that sounds crazy."

Managing this ongoing existential crisis, keeping insanity and instability at bay, is one way that Sigmund Freud understood the function of religion.[26] That is, religious belief and practice constitute a species-specific neurosis—no other species shares it, so far as we know—that keeps us from developing much larger and more dangerous mental illnesses. These "neurotic relics" keep the existential dread with which we live more or less locked in the closet.[27] Belief is only a part of this. The teachings of the faith are only a part of the cognitive framework that allows us to operate in spite of the fear and the potential for chaos. We ritualize our responses to these fears, and thereby raise the ritual stakes to cosmic proportions. What would happen if N. didn't return to Ackerman's Field, if he didn't use his camera to ensure that all eight stones are in place and that whatever nameless evil lurks behind the portal stays there? Certainly, as with other stories in the King canon, "N." can be read as a study in deepening psychosis. But in posing the "What if he's right?" question, it demonstrates how religious ritual emerges and evolves. This development is not linear, but organic, not circular, but rhizomatic, and consists of five self-reinforcing parts: explanation, rationalization, routinization, systematization, and expansion.

The appearance of the eighth standing stone in his Nikon's viewfinder, and the sense that a dark, malevolent entity is watching him from the circle, confronts N. with something he cannot explain. Not only has he no previous experience, he initially lacks even the vocabulary to frame his encounter. "It was turning very slowly," he tells Dr. Bonsaint, when he first seeks treatment for his obsessive-compulsive disorder,

but it never took its eyes off me. It *did* have eyes. Sick pink ones. I knew—my *rational* mind knew—that it was just light in the sky I was seeing. But at the same time I knew it was something more. That something was *using* that light. Something was using the sunset to see with, and what it was seeing was *me*.[28]

Faced with the inexplicable, his rational mind cannot resolve the contradictions in what he's convinced he sees: a breach in the wall between the seen and the unseen. Rather than a trick of the light, an illusion created at the confluence of shadow and sunset, he finds another *explanation*: whatever it is, the creature from the other side is using the dying light of day to see him, just as he uses his Nikkor lens to see the final stone that keeps the watchful entity in its own dimension.

Although it may not be rational, seeing the eighth stone allows N. to *rationalize* his experience: "Eight stones would keep them captive—barely—but if there were only seven, they'd come flooding through from the darkness on the other side of reality and overwhelm the world."[29] This expanded awareness gives N. a purpose, however unwanted. His life now has meaning, however unwelcome. Because, if he doesn't keep the thing contained, who will? From here, the ritual act becomes routine. In sociological terms, it is *routinized*. It becomes the way the world is, the new normal. In N.'s case it takes the form of obsessive behavior, which, in good psychological fashion, Dr. Bonsaint characterizes as a disorder. N., though, is desperate for his therapist to understand that, however it sounds, he is not crazy. This is not a disorder and he is not disordered. In fact, quite the opposite. It is life on the battlefield between our world and the other.

With routinization comes *systematization*: N. locates himself in the framework of a much larger conflict, one with set boundaries, a more or less agreed-upon rule structure, and a limited number of potential outcomes. He begins to see the causal links and relationships built into the system. "I understood other things, too," he tells the psychiatrist. "One was that I had activated the place *just by looking at it*." Another is that "human eyes take away the eighth stone. A camera lens will put it back, but won't lock it in place."[30] As he works out the organization of the system, he gradually establishes what works, what doesn't, what the system demands and what it will not tolerate. Demands that, by this point in the rhizomatic progression of ritual understanding, seem to N. entirely rational.

Although this is rarely pointed out, at its core, ritual is a correlation fallacy—which is both its weakness and its strength. On the one hand, N. has convinced himself that he is "the latest baton carrier in a long, long line of them, maybe going all the way back to prehistoric times."[31] If he doesn't continue the ritual, if he does not return to Ackerman's Field regularly and aim his lens at the standing stones, "an insane universe that happens to lie right next door to ours" will boil out and consume us. He has come to believe this, but that hardly means that it's true. It could simply be a trick of the light that he has interpreted through the lens of his own ego and obsession. On the other hand, with the systematization of the ritual, and N.'s understanding of it in such epic proportions, the stakes have simply become too high to chance being wrong. Here, then, resides one of the principal forces behind the power of religious ritual: non-falsifiability, the lack of "harmonious adjustment," and the fear of being on the wrong side of the unseen order. Churches, temples, and shrines of all types regularly perform religious rituals ranging from baptisms to burial rites for people who are, at best, only marginally connected to their faith and who have no devotional investment in it. They may not believe in the efficacy of the ritual, but in an ongoing nod to Pascal's Wager, they cannot avoid the implications of the question, *What if I'm wrong?*

Finally, with systematization come *expansion* and extension—more and more aspects of the experience must be integrated into the system. "I had to keep renewing the protection with symbolic acts," N. writes in the diary Bonsaint urges him to keep.[32] Gradually, as he becomes even more deeply invested in the ritual process—as his neurosis deepens, many would say—the stakes become greater still. As bad as whatever it was he saw that first evening in Ackerman's Field, "it was only the first and least of the abominations to be released from the other world" should he fail in his responsibility as the ritual guardian.[33] "I have come to like N.," Bonsaint writes in his annotation to the patient file, "and I don't want him to step into that ring of stones for good. It only exists in his mind, but that doesn't mean it's not real. [Final Session Ends]."[34] Ultimately, though, the responsibility is too much and N. takes his own life before his next meeting with Bonsaint. For N., at least, there are worse things than death.

"The Barrier Was Not Made to Be Broken": *Pet Sematary* and the Rite of Passage

In *The Forest of Symbols*, cultural anthropologist Victor Turner outlines what has become something of a standard model in ritual studies: the three-stage *ritual process*, comprising *separation*, *margin* (often called "liminality"), and *reincorporation* (also known as "communitas").[35] In the first stage, participants are separated "from an earlier fixed point in the social structure," "from a set of cultural conditions" with which they are familiar.[36] That is, they leave a particular way of thinking and being behind, and embark on a journey that may bring them back, but will leave them changed in significant ways. Next, "the intervening 'liminal' period" Turner describes as passage "through a cultural realm that has none of the attributes of the past or coming state."[37] This intermediate condition is unlike anything the participant has encountered before, but exists only in the passing moments of the ritual process. Finally, the journey ends, though the subject emerges, altered fundamentally, the same only different. Among other things, there are new "rights and obligations vis-à-vis others," and they are "expected to behave in accordance with certain customary norms and ethical standards" within the community.[38]

If "Rainy Season" describes the ritual of propitiation, and "N." the development of ritual as a practice, *Pet Sematary*, which we considered briefly earlier, explores Turner's concept of the ritual process, specifically the rite of passage.

Louis Creed is treating his first patient at the University of Maine infirmary, a student struck by a car while jogging and who now has only a few minutes to live. "Horror rolled through" the young doctor as Vic Pascow's blood and intracranial fluid soak the carpet of the small waiting room. His wounds are far too severe for Louis's limited resources and there's no time to get him to Eastern Maine Medical Center. As Vic's brain shuts down, though, and his body begins the convulsive slide into death, he speaks.

He speaks to Louis.

"'In the Pet Sematary,' the young man croaked" at Louis, and "a swooning mad terror struck him and his flesh began to creep avidly, seeming to actually *move* up and down his arms."[39] The helpless doctor might have been unsure what he heard the first time, but there was no mistaking the dying man's next words: "It's not the real cemetery."[40]

Despite his mother's intense religious faith, Louis was "a man with no deep religious training, no bent toward the superstitious or the occult."[41] Unlike Paul Edgecombe or Jack Torrance, he has no religious socialization upon which to draw, no way to frame his experience. However devout his mother may have been, she did not force her beliefs on her son, which left Louis "ill-prepared for this . . . whatever it was."[42] Indeed, how do we prepare for something for which there is no real preparation? If the origins of the religious imagination begin with our earliest awareness of death—a sudden, pin-hole confrontation with our own mortality—then a significant portion of religion's role in any society is preparing us for death, managing the transition from life to whatever follows, and in the wake of death ensuring the continuation of life for those left behind. It's no wonder that with "no deep religious training," however, Dr. Louis Creed was ill-prepared for what was to come. Not only did he lack the vocabulary for his experience, he lacked any ritual expression of it.

Anthropologists theorize that rituals for the dead, the notion of a "proper burial" in a "timely fashion," mark the early emergence of our religious consciousness. Grave sites tens of thousands of years old show evidence of careful arrangement of bodies and the inclusion of grave goods, presumably for use in the next life. While these began as rudimentary ritual practices, they evolved into the elaborate and extravagant burial ceremonies of the Egyptian pharaohs and Chinese emperors. Indeed, as Louis learns, the Egyptians "had gone that one better; they had slaughtered the pets of royalty so that the souls of the pets might go along to whatever afterlife there might be with the souls of their masters."[43]

Later that evening, Vic Pascow speaks to Louis once again, this time from the depths of a walking nightmare. As the doctor follows the dead man into the woods behind his house, Louis tries to convince himself it's only a dream. But it isn't. It's a message. A warning. "*I am following a dead man up to the Pet Sematary,*" Louis's mind tells him wildly, "*and this is no dream. God help me, this is no dream. This is happening.*"[44] As "the last of Louis's coherent mind began to slip away," the dead student, killed earlier that day while jogging, spoke to him: "Don't go beyond no matter how much you feel you need to, Doctor. The barrier was not made to be broken. Remember this: there is more power here than you know. *It* is old and always restless. Remember."[45] Evoking a standard warning trope in horror fiction, Vic reminds us that there are places we're not meant to go and things we were never intended to know.

Separation

In the history of religious evolution, the finer and finer divisions of what we are (or aren't) supposed to know are marked by two significant developments. First is the separation of religious knowledge into the *exoteric* and the *esoteric*, that which is intended for public consumption and available to any who would learn it, and that which is reserved for devotees, for those initiated into the mysteries of the faith. Second is the concept of initiation, and the gradual development of an initiate class— shamans and priests; ministers, pastors, and imams; rabbis, roshis, and religious professionals of all types. These are the ones to whom the various species of "things we're not supposed to know" have been revealed, and to whom subsequent revelation of the esoteric is entrusted. Up the trail behind Louis's house, on one side of the deadfall reside those things intended for everyone, exoteric knowledge, a little power, but not very much, enough to make us feel better about losing a dog or a cat. On the other side, though, it's a different story. "This place has power," Jud tells Louis later, as he leads him past the pet cemetery and prepares to initiate him into the mysteries of the Micmac burial ground. "Not so much here, but ... the place we're going" is vastly different.[46]

In terms of the evolution of religious consciousness, *Pet Sematary* has far more to tell us than novels such as *The Stand* or *Revival*—storyworlds that are often seen as more explicitly religious. Those works, however, are *exoteric*, their religious symbolism and plotlines on display and readily available to the public at large. In terms of the ritual process, *Pet Sematary* is more *esoteric*: the meaning is there, but reveals itself only to those willing to put in the effort, who dare to cross King's own narrative deadfall. The exoteric event, the superficial phenomenon, could not be more mundane. A family pet is killed in a busy roadway, and two men take the body into the woods to bury it. The esoteric, though, the deep meaning, is a horror fiction exploration of the ritual process. In anthropological terms, Louis's journey over the deadfall, through Little God Swamp, and up the hill to the Micmac burying ground is the classic ritual journey.

Initiation into the mysteries is, in many ways, a point of no return. It is a Rubicon moment; once we have passed it, we cannot go back. We may be able to return across the river, through the cavern, over the deadfall, but we are never really the same. We can never be as we were before. That is, we cannot recover ignorance and innocence, in the same way that once "the jumble of whites and blacks" reveals the face of God, we cannot ever not see it. Once N. discovers the truth of Ackerman's Field, he can never pretend he does not know. Once Louis follows Jud across the deadfall, he can never claim ignorance of what's on the other side.

Crossing the boundary, though, can be either an act of transgression or a moment of transcendence. In many traditions, the fundamental difference between these is the person of the *guide*, the one who has been there before and who initiates those who come after. This is Jud Crandall's role in Louis's initiation into the mysteries beyond the deadfall. Three of the guide's most important tasks are *evaluation, permission*, and *explanation*. First, a guide judges whether someone is ready, assesses whether they can handle what lies beyond. Earlier in the story, the young physician saved Jud's wife, Norma, from dying of a heart attack. Without hesitation, he stepped into the liminal space between life and death, and used his skill to coax the elderly woman into remaining on this side of the veil. Grateful beyond measure, the old farmer reckoned Louis fit for the journey beyond the deadfall—for transcendence, rather than transgression. Louis's willingness to help in that moment proved him worthy of initiation into the mysteries.

Second, serving as a guide implies that *permission* has been granted for the ritual; this becomes a journey of transcendence, not a momentary transgression. We are not trespassing. In the opening sequences of *Raiders of the Lost Ark*, bandits may have led Indiana Jones to the jungle temple, but they were transgressors, not guides, trespassing where they are not permitted and paying the price for their offense.

Third, and perhaps most importantly, the guide provides context for the ritual passage and *explains* the initiate's experience of the journey. One person literally guides the other. This is the traditional foundation on which the transmission of esoteric knowledge is built. Without a guide over the deadfall, Louis tells Jud as they approach the barrier, "we'll each break a leg and then probably freeze to death trying to get back."[47] Not everyone is judged worthy.

Liminality

"The steady ache in his muscles from carrying Church in one hand and the shovel in the other was a part of it. The wind, deadly cold, numbing exposed skin, was part of it."[48] But what, exactly, is *it*? A "feeling of contentment, odd under the circumstances but a pure fact."[49] Physical exertion, often far past the point of discomfort and pushing the edges of exhaustion, has for millennia been one of the ways by which initiates are prepared for the ritual journey. Fasting, pilgrimage, a vision quest—all are intended to invoke an altered state of consciousness, a magnified or clarified awareness of the relationship between the seen and the unseen orders. The "steady ache" and persistent wind not only numb muscles and skin, but blunt mundane awareness. They sharpen focus, forcing the initiate onward, one foot in front of the other until that's all the journey becomes. Space changes; time dilates. Louis's "feeling of contentment" marks the beginning of this altered state.

Like a repetitive chant or counting breaths during *zazen*, the fish drum's monotonous *thock thock thock* echoing in the meditation hall, for Louis "the bobbing light of Jud's flash was a part of it."[50] By leading, the guide provides assurance, allowing the initiate the freedom not to be constrained by fear or apprehension. "I have been here before," the moving flashlight implies, "and I returned, just as you will return." Many rites of passage, especially those related to coming of age and changes in marital state, separate initiates both by gender and from those too young to participate in the ritual. Here, Louis is isolated from his family: Rachel and the children have gone to visit her parents for the weekend. His normal support system is no longer in place. Once initiates are set apart, an older member of the tribe leads them toward the ritual ground, the secret place of initiation. Often, a boy's father or uncle takes a particular role in this. For girls about to become young women, it is the mother, an aunt, an older sister. Louis is already bound to Jud in ways few men ever are. He saved Norma Crandall's life. More than that, Louis, "who had lost his father at three and who had never known a grandfather," finds in eighty-three-year-old Judson Crandall "the man who should have been his father."[51] Consider the exoteric scene: a father and son go into the woods to bury a beloved pet. Not exactly a Hallmark moment, but these are the things over which we bond, and by which we are bound one to another. In this case, though, under the guidance of a surrogate father, a man already with children of his own begins a ritual process about which he knows nothing and of which he has only the dimmest awareness.

"He felt the pervasive, undeniable, magnetic presence of some secret," King tells us. "Some dark secret."[52] Since this *is* Stephen King, "dark secret" is reasonably read as "horrific mystery" or "terrifying enigma," but that need not be so. Just because our hominin ancestry gives us a healthy fear of the dark, doesn't mean that the dark is necessarily to be feared, or that fear is a bad thing. Popular songs may tell us that "love will keep us together," but for millennia fear has kept us alive. What Louis feels is the "magnetic" pull of the dark secret, the thing that must not be known or can't possibly be true. Like physical exertion or extended focus on a single object, emotional distress can be used to outwit the rational, discursive mind, the mind that's always chattering away about what can and can't happen. Fear and anxiety can allow for a more direct experience of the irrational, the unnatural. "King gets you to believe the unbelievable," reads the *Detroit News* blurb for *Pet Sematary*. But it's really not that difficult, since human beings have tens of thousands of years of practice believing the unbelievable.

We just call it "religion."

In the context of horror fiction, "dark" most obviously implies "fearful" or "to be feared," but can just as often mean "obscured," "hidden," "occluded"—that is to say, *occult*. And in many cases, the gap between "hidden" and "to be feared" can be measured in the difference between transcendence and trespass. Those who are not worthy or who are improperly prepared trespass, opening themselves up to the dangers of the "dark secret." Those who transcend the barrier in the company of a guide, who pass through the liminal phase as initiates rather than transgressors, learn to respect the power of the dark secrets, the esoteric, the hidden knowledge. Rites of passage demand process—preparation, approach, and initiation.

Rituals proceed by stages, waypoints beyond which only certain individuals may go. In first- and second-temple Judaism, for example, these barriers were marked by the Court of the Women and the Court of the Gentiles. Only Jewish men were permitted to enter the Temple's inner sancta, to draw near to the Holy of Holies. For nearly two millennia, the Roman Catholic sacrament of the Eucharist has been reserved for believers in good standing with the Church. Latter-day Saint temples allow only members in possession of a Temple Recommend to proceed beyond the visitors' center. When Jud suggests they rest at the pet cemetery the older man showed them months earlier when the Creed family moved in, the younger man is confused. "*Rest* here?" he thinks. "But they *were* here. He could see the markers in the moving, aimless sweep of Jud's light."[53] The deadfall on the trail by the tiny graveyard is the barrier separating the exoteric temple confines from the Holy of Holies, the place of dark secrets and the seat of true power. To pass through, you must trust your guide.

Experienced hikers know that deadfalls are among the most dangerous parts of any trail. The welter of fallen trees and broken branches, unpredictable footing, slippery bark, and hidden holes threaten everything from sprained ankles and twisted knees to fractured legs and broken necks. "'Just follow me,' Jud said. 'Follow me and don't look down. Don't hesitate and don't look down. I know the way through, but it has to be done quick and sure.'"[54]

Willingness to trust, in many cases to disregard the evidence of one's own senses, the warnings of the rational mind, is key to successful negotiation of the ritual process. "The one who hesitates is lost," says the proverbist. On a mundane level, this is simply good advice: I've been this way before; I know where to step and which spots to avoid. At the ritual level, though, it's about faith in one's guide, and the belief that whatever reward awaits is worth the risk of crossing over. Stepping "quick and sure" is the way we are taught to firewalk: "sure" in the sense that the entire foot comes down, spreading out the contact surface, "quick" movement ensuring that no part of the foot contacts the coals long enough to transmit heat. That's the intellectual, rational, discursive assessment. When you're faced with a forty-foot-long path filled with glowing coals, shimmering waves of heat, and the occasional tongue of flame licking at the air, it more often than not comes down to whether you trust the person who prepared you, the one who told you, "Just follow me. Follow me and don't look down. Don't hesitate and don't look down." When Jud Crandall begins to cross the deadfall, the initial barrier between the seen and the unseen, the known and the unknown, "he walked like a man who knows exactly where his next step is coming from."[55]

Each waypoint on the ritual journey presents its own challenges and dangers, but each brings its own sense of accomplishment—which is inevitably followed by a renewed feeling of trepidation. Louis "reached the bottom, and the exhilaration flared up in him like a shot of coal oil on embers. . . . He had not felt so young or so viscerally alive in twenty years or more."[56] The deadfall, however, marks only the first waypoint in his ritual journey, barely a quarter of the way to the place of dark secrets. Now, the more difficult work begins. Now, it becomes even more important to maintain focus. No longer is this a simple if unpleasant errand, a leisurely evening hike—if it ever was. Indeed, the proximate purpose, the reason they set out in the first place, has been subsumed to the more important ritual journey. "He switched the bag and the shovel more often," King writes, "but the ache in his shoulders was now constant. He fell into a rhythm of walking and became almost hypnotized with it."[57] Only as Louis moves deeper into the forest, only as, "almost hypnotized," he shifts into an altered state of consciousness, can he gain awareness of what historian of religions Mircea Eliade called a *kratophany*, a manifestation of power, the certainty of closely guarded secrets.[58] Indeed, "there was power here, yes, he felt it."[59] Not "he *could* feel it," or "he *thought* he felt it," as though there was some ambiguity in the experience. No, "he felt it." The ritual process gave him no choice.

The next three miles pass in this altered state. Time dilation or contraction, loss of time or losing track of time, are common elements in the mystical experience.[60] For King's readers, as for Louis Creed, these miles pass in the space of one brief paragraph.

"'We're almost where we're going now,' [Jud] said calmly. 'This next bit is like the deadfall—you got to walk steady and easy. Just follow me and don't look down.'" After the deadfall and the long, altered-state walk, "Little God Swamp"—"the fur traders who came through called it 'Dead Man's Bog'"—is the third ritual waypoint.[61]

At any moment in between, Louis could have chosen to turn around. He could have buried the cat in the bushes and simply gone home. Perseverance, though, the willingness not only to continue in the face of pain, discomfort, or exhaustion, but to accept them as companions on the journey, is often a necessary component of the ritual passage. With Jud as his guide, Louis has successfully navigated the first two ritual obstacles. Before he can enter the temple of the mysteries, however, before the "dark secret" can be revealed to him, he must pass the final barrier. He must move from one world to another.

Jud warns him of the various dangers and distractions in the swamp, things that will try to pull his attention away from the task at hand. Things like quicksand, though, as the older man described it, "for a moment Louis thought he saw something bright and not completely pleasant in the old man's eyes."[62] That is, this is no early evening jaunt, young one, don't ever forget that, and don't ever think otherwise. "There's a lot of funny things down this way, Louis. The air's heavier . . . more electrical . . . or somethin."[63]

But there's more.

> You might see St. Elmo's fire—what the sailors call foo-lights. It makes funny shapes, but it's nothing. If you should see some of these shapes and they bother you, just look the other way. You may hear sounds like voices, but they are loons down south toward Prospect. The sound carries. It's funny.[64]

However "terribly bland and totally unreadable" Judson Crandall appears to Louis at that moment, the closer we come to the mystery, the more careful we need to be, and the more we need to trust our guide.[65] At some point in the ritual process, however, doubt almost inevitably creeps in: "Jud, where are we going? What the hell are we doing out here in the back of beyond?"[66]

The ritual journey takes participants from one world to another, from the mundane to, as horror author Richard Matheson would put it, the supernormal.[67] However the space is set apart, it is *sacred* space.[68] It is not simply a change in location, but a shift in consciousness, a transformed state of perception that lets us peer behind the veil that ordinary reality places in front of us. In addition to the deadfall and the physical perils of Little God Swamp, the potential for visual and auditory hallucination marks the significance of this waypoint.

Although Louis sees no St. Elmo's fire as they traverse the boggy slough, "he looked down and saw his feet, calves, knees, and lower thighs had disappeared into a ground fog that was perfectly smooth, perfectly white, and perfectly opaque."[69] Almost immediately, anxiety mixes with excitement, as thoughts of his family drift in like discomfiting spirits.

Once again, focus is key to the process. Like a meditator, Louis must release these intrusive and distracting thoughts, allowing them to flow past him and disappear into the gloom of the swamp.

After the swamp, they reach a set of steps carved into a steep hillside. This is the final waypoint on the ritual journey. "We get to the top and we're there," Jud tells him. "The stone steps were wide enough, but the sense of the ground dropping away was unsettling."[70] By crossing the deadfall, following the path through the forest, passing through Little God Swamp, and climbing the precipitous stone stairs, Louis has traded the ordinary world for the liminal world of ritual space. In ritual, as historian of religions J. Z. Smith reminds us, "place directs attention," because "ritual is, first and foremost, a mode of paying attention."[71] Everything to this point has been about focusing Louis's attention in a new and distinct way. The ritual process convenes reality in a way that, as Victor Turner phrased it, "has none of the attributes of the past or coming state."[72]

Jud and Louis have arrived at the place of mystery, the holy of holies.

> He looked up and saw a billion stars, cold lights in the darkness. Never in his life had the stars made him feel so completely small, infinitesimal, without meaning. He asked himself the old question—*is there anything intelligent out there?*—and instead of wonder, the thought brought a horrid, cold feeling.[73]

They have arrived not at the pet cemetery, now miles behind and a world away, but at an ancient Micmac burial ground. Other local tribes avoided the area, Jud tells Louis, while European traders and trappers believed the whole region haunted. "I suppose some of them saw foofire in Little God Swamp," he says, relating the lore of the burial ground, reciting its history as part of the ritual, "and thought they were seeing ghosts."[74]

Because the old man insists that it's his job, Louis buries Church the cat. Throughout their walk, their ritual journey, he has moments of doubt—it may not be that Jud was lying to him, exactly, but he was certainly not telling him the whole truth. Louis has been initiated into the mysteries, but the fullness of their secrets is not yet his to know. Even here, now, only gradually does the burial ground become a *kratophany*, a place of ritual power.

"Jud smiled and Louis thought: *That isn't what you think at all.*"[75]

Church's grave finally dug, the unfortunate cat buried, and his plot marked with a stone cairn, Jud pronounces the ritual complete. "He clapped Louis on the shoulder. 'You did good, Louis. I knew you would. Let's go home.'"[76]

Reincorporation

In any ritual journey, the return home, the transition from supernormal back to mundane, is equally important. We cannot live our lives suspended between one world and the other. We must find our way back to the community. "*We just ran the film backward*, Louis thought tiredly as they emerged from the woods and into the field overlooking the house."[77] Recall that only pages before, just after crossing the deadfall, Louis "had not felt so young or so viscerally alive in twenty years or more."[78] Now, the weight of the ritual upon him, it has been decades since he has felt this tired. This is the envelope structure of the ritual process: enervation and exhilaration; elation and exhaustion.

As his ritual journey concludes, Louis "could not remember feeling so kicked-dog weary since his first day on Chicago's rubbish-disposal crew one high school summer sixteen or seventeen years ago."[79] All this to bury a housecat, some readers might think, setting the ritual process aside in favor of the supernatural mayhem that is surely to follow. This is Stephen King, after all. Yet even this line encompasses and extends the ritual, like a stone carefully selected and placed in the cairn of the story. In his teenage years, Louis didn't do odd jobs around the state trooper barracks, like Ned Wilcox in *From a Buick 8*. He didn't do road work, like *Christine*'s Arnie Cunningham. He was not an itinerant farmhand, like *The Stand*'s Stu Redman. He worked on a "rubbish-disposal crew." Of all the manual labor jobs King could have given him, he made Louis Creed a garbage man, someone familiar with the sweat-slick feel of greasy plastic bags. Because, consider: how many cats, dogs, gerbils and hamsters, ferrets, bunnies, and tropical fish, how many hundreds of thousands of beloved family pets did he unknowingly cart off and consign to the landfill, the ultimate place where memories go to die? The town dump is the opposite of the pet cemetery, and even further from the burial ground where Church rests in one of the most ritualistically memorialized places imaginable. Dr. Louis Creed, the physician, the materialist, the one more familiar than most with death, is about to learn more than he could have imagined—or ever wanted to know.

Inevitably, he is led to reflect on his experience, which has both a *noetic* and *ephemeral* quality. It taught him something he could not have known otherwise, and it happened in the transient space of the ritual journey. Back in the mundane world of screened-in porches and beers "of an evening," immensely, immeasurably far from the treacherous deadfall and the opaque ground fog of Little God Swamp, Louis's journey takes on a patina of unreality. What was so clear then is fading and he struggles to recall it. The experience becomes *ineffable*, hidden even from the one who made the trip.

"Jud, what did we do tonight?"

"Why, we buried your daughter's cat."

"Is that *all* we did?"

"Nothing but that," Jud said. "You're a good man, Louis, but you ask too many questions."[80]

That is, you've just begun your journey into the mysteries, youngster, don't press to understand it all at once. Here we see the difference between a simple graveyard for beloved animals and the site of enormous ritual power: the former closes a chapter in a family's life—the one entitled "Smucky the Cat," or "Biffer," or "Hannah the best dog that ever lived"—while the latter opens a new, much different chapter, one that leaves us irrevocably changed.[81] Once Louis crossed the deadfall, once he accepted initiation, knowingly or not, the forerunner, Vic Pascow, never visits him again. Although King is writing of sleep, the deeper meaning is more important: "He slept without even being aware he had gone over the edge."[82] You can cross the deadfall, but you can't ever go back. Not really.

Later, as Louis's memory of the ritual fades further, "like the conversation with the anesthetist just before he or she put you out like a light," Jud warns him not to talk about their activities the night before.[83] People wouldn't understand, though not only because "they don't like people they consider to be 'outsiders' to know about it."[84] That is, it's not simply that they don't want strangers thinking their rural customs quaint or silly, "not because some of those old superstitions go back three hun-dred years or more (although they do), but because they sort of believe in those superstitions."[85] In both the horror story and the ritual process, secrets revealed lead to even more secrets withheld.

"Your family is your family," Jud writes in a note to Louis, though it's not hard to read into that, "And you are part of *our* family now." Enjoin-ing Louis to silence binds him to the ritual of initiation: this is not for others to know. This is not for those who have not crossed the deadfall. Only those who have felt the world slip beneath the ground mist of Little God Swamp, and fall away below the stone steps leading to the site of ritual power, can understand.

For others, it's just the "Pet Sematary."

Crossing the deadfall ushered Louis beyond the safety and comfort of the familiar. It brought him in contact with realities he could not have imagined. Making his way through Little God Swamp, climbing the stairs to the Micmac burial ground took him further from the security of his medical practice and closer to the unseen order's darker, more closely guarded secrets. Though he could not know what would happen once they left the small cairn on the top of the hill, he knew that some-thing had changed and that nothing could ever be as it was before.

"Ritual," writes Victor Turner, "is transformative," and for millennia humankind has encoded its experience of the divine and the demonic, the agony and the ecstasy, in ritual practice.[86] Like Henry Eden and Laura Stanton, we may not understand why we perform the rituals we do, but we continue them regardless. We believe they are necessary. Like N., we come to accept that ritual practice allows us not only to control our experience of the unseen order, but to manage our interactions with it. We believe that ritual has power. And, like Louis Creed, we experi-ence the transformation that sets the ritual process apart from so many other aspects of human life. We believe that our rituals play a fundamen-tal role in shaping the varied contours of our religious experience.

6

Forty Years in Maine

Stephen King and the Varieties of Religious Experience

Forty years separate *Carrie* from *Revival*, from a young woman's psychokinetic rage to an old man's hubristic search for the secrets of the infinite. Between them, we find the microcosm of religious belief in *The Dead Zone* and its macrocosmic doppelgänger *Under the Dome*. Each in its own way demonstrates how what we're taught about religious belief and the ways those teachings are ritualized inevitably shape our perception of the unseen order and our relationship with it. They frame our tiny part of the story that is the human quest for meaning.

In this chapter, we explore four varieties of religious experience, four personal stories of the ways men and women understand and respond to the demands of the divine. We meet two mothers, Margaret White and Vera Smith, both of whom suffer these demands through their children, though meeting them in very different ways. We get to know two ministers, Piper Libby and Charlie Jacobs, both parents who have lost their families, and with them any sense of the divine—benevolent or otherwise. Their stories span four decades over which America's dark theologian returns both implicitly and explicitly to questions of what it means to believe—and of what we believe in.

Margaret's Story: Sinners in the Hands of an Angry God

Critics often note, though just as often in passing, that Carrie White's mother is a religious fundamentalist, a believer in some strict, intensely personal version of Christianity. Few seem to realize, however, that by the end of the novel we know far more about Margaret White than any other character, including Carrie herself. A species of hyper-Calvinist, Margaret has struggled her entire adult life to keep herself and her unwanted daughter separate and safe from the sins of the world. That

Carrie's religious upbringing retarded her social development is clear from the outset, given the abuse she suffers at home, the pranks pulled on her at Christian Youth Camp, and the bullying at school, including the novel's trigger event, her first menses. "When Carrie White realized that she was bleeding from the vaginal opening," King tells us, "she had no idea of what was taking place. She was innocent of the entire concept of menstruation."[1] As horrified as we may be by Carrie's treatment at the hands of her classmates (and her gym teacher, though there is at least some small measure of redemption there), as angered as we are by the assistant principal's impotence (after all, he can't even get her name right during their meeting), it's easy to miss the more obvious question: How did Carrie's life become what it is? How could she *not* know about menses? How did things go so horribly wrong for the young woman whose tragedy launched Stephen King's career?

Enter Margaret White.

King uses a mixed narrative approach in *Carrie*, a daring move for a beginning novelist, but one that allows for a certain omniscience, an ability to fill narrative gaps in ways that the story might not otherwise allow. Much of what we learn is presented as secondary source material, some more reliable than others, including books such as "*The Shadow Exploded: Documented Facts and Specific Conclusions Derived from the Case of Carrietta White*, by David R. Congress (Tulane University Press, 1981)."[2] These sources, however, tell readers only what they *should* think about the story rather than letting the story reveal itself. We do not learn about "the Whites' near-fanatical fundamentalist beliefs" as the story unfolds, but are told about them in retrospect, in academic commentaries, court records, and personal memoirs.[3] Likewise, we do not gradually experience Margaret White's abject horror of sex, the disgust she feels for her own body and that of her daughter, we learn about it from the eminent "David R. Congress." Scholars, he opines, "have made a more reasonable case for the hypothesis that the concept [of pregnancy], linked irrevocably in her mind with the 'sin' of intercourse had been blocked entirely from her mind."[4] That is, if King's putative intellectuals are to be believed, Margaret White no more knew she was pregnant with Carrie than nearly seventeen years later her daughter understood she was menstruating. Besides this fear of her own physical desires, which Margaret interprets as evidence of her separation from and rejection by

God, the Whites developed a variety of other "peculiar religious views," as Assistant Principal Morton says, "very peculiar."[5]

In terms of god-talk and the cosmic reality it represents, it's important to remember that this complex of beliefs doesn't exist *ex nihilo*; the beliefs don't stand on their own, like some strange, dark tower in the marketplace of ideas. They point to and are underpinned by a particular kind of God—a peculiar conception of who or what inhabits the unseen order. Margaret White believes in God no less fiercely than Vera Smith, whose story we will consider shortly, but where Vera sees every event as confirmation of God's plan for her, Margaret lives her life terrified that she has already lost divine favor. She is the quintessence of the Puritan Jonathan Edwards's "sinner in the hands of an angry God." For her, and by implication for her daughter, salvation hinges less on the relationship they have with God than on pointing out the shortcomings and sins of others, which both reinforces her own sense of righteousness and ensures that their influence does not corrupt the world she has built for herself and Carrie.[6] This is religion experienced as fear and loathing, sickening, intense, and overwhelming. Three concentric rings scribe the boundaries between Margaret's God and the rest of the world: the red-plague circle, the house, and the closet.

The Red-Plague Circle

Over the years, Carrie "had defied Momma in a hundred little ways, had tried to erase the red-plague circle that had been drawn around her."[7] As we saw with little Jacky Torrance and the "jumble of whites and blacks" that became the face of Jesus, this is the weight of religious socialization that becomes the young girl's only experience of religious belief. The first of these concentric rings is "the red-plague circle," and embodies her mother's most basic fear, a dread that she visits daily upon her daughter in the form of sexual ignorance and aversion. We never hear Margaret say it, but through Carrie we can hear her *saying* it: Beware the red plague. Beware the bleeding that marks you out as a woman.

Perhaps it's a reference to the onset of puberty, menstruation as the "red plague" that has haunted women since the Garden, the Fruit, and the Fall. Because once the red plague begins, other changes, other temptations, other threats to one's salvation inevitably follow. Breasts develop, for example, what Margaret called "dirty-pillows, as if it were all one word," attracting the attention of men, who come sniffing around after Only One Thing.[8] In this, she is practically Augustinian in her aversion to sex. In *The City of God*, the venerable bishop of Hippo allowed that within the conjugal relationship "lust is permitted for the duty of pro-creation," but he is clear that "the genital organs have become as it were the private property of lust."[9]

All Carrie knows of her own birth is that Momma "had been bad when she made her and that was why she had them"—the swollen breasts at which her infant daughter had nursed, but which served as a constant reminder of her sin.[10] Indeed, Carrie believed that if she was a "good girl," she wouldn't develop breasts at all. She would remain not only virginal, but prepubescent.

But the "red-plague circle" is also fear of spiritual taint, of faith-mixing, of a religious miscegenation that borders on xenophobia. More than anything, Carrie wants to be like other teenagers. She wants to have friends, go to parties and dances, maybe have a boyfriend one day. In short, like all kids, she longs to experience life beyond the do-main of parental control. The power of religious socialization, however, hardened by the force of a domineering mother, constantly brings her into conflict. Her life is the product of Margaret's conception of God and fear of losing salvation, and her overbearing fundamentalism is, in its own twisted way, a mother's desperate attempt to keep her daughter safe.[11]

For example, Carrie was not allowed contact with other Christians. "She had fought Momma tooth and nail over the Christian Youth Camp. . . . Momma told her darkly it was Sin, that it was Methodists and Baptists and Congregationalists and that it was Sin and Backsliding. She forbade Carrie to swim at the camp."[12] Perhaps, in a bathing suit no matter how modest, someone would see her budding "dirty-pillows"—the same reason Momma "forbade her to shower with the other girls at school."[13] Even at camp, though, Carrie was the butt of "a thousand prac-tical jokes." When she went home early, shattered by her treatment at the hands of fellow believers, "Momma had told her grimly that she should treasure the memory of her scourging as proof that Momma knew, that Momma was right, that the only hope of safety and salvation was inside the red circle," beyond the reach of sexual development and temptation, sheltered from the lure of "sin and backsliding."[14] Although King does not quote the passage, it's difficult not to hear in Margaret's words echoes of the Sermon on the Mount: "Blessed are ye, when men shall revile you, and persecute you, and shall say all manner of evil against you falsely, for my sake," Jesus tells the assembled multitudes. "Rejoice, and be exceeding glad: for great is your reward in heaven" (Mt. 5:11–12).

Inside the red circle Margaret White has created, fear and loathing are the touchstone of religious belief: fear of the God she worships and who she is convinced keeps close watch on everything she does, and a deeply rooted self-loathing that is itself a function of the revulsion she knows her God must feel for all humankind. The house in which she and her daughter live, but which could hardly be called a "home," reflects this austere and terrifying god-talk.

The House

Early in their marriage, Margaret and Ralph White had been Baptists, but "left the church when they became convinced that the Baptists were doing the work of the Antichrist."[15] From that point, "all worship had taken place at home. Momma held worship on Sundays, Tuesdays, and Fridays. These were called Holy Days. Momma was the minister, Carrie the congregation. Services lasted from two to three hours."[16] To experience this chilling home-church separatism, consider the gauntlet the rare visitor endures as she makes her way through the house, which is nothing more nor less than the architectural reflection of Margaret's desperate faith.[17]

Coming into the front hallway, we are greeted by "a luminous picture above the coathooks," whose image "limned a ghostly Jesus hovering grimly over a family seated at the kitchen table. Beneath was the caption (also luminous): *The Unseen Guest.*"[18] Just as God is always watching Margaret, noting her failures, scowling at her sins, anyone entering the White house is immediately aware of this divine surveillance. Remember, we are told, *He* is watching—at any time, at all times. Unlike Vera Smith's God, who looks for her to fulfill her role as a believer, Margaret's God watches, waiting only to punish the sinner and the backslider.

Save for a small sewing table, "two chairs with straight arms" are the living room's only furniture. Any more than that would be pride, ostentation—in short, the sins of indulgence, of vanity and the comforts of the flesh. Carrie may have liked some of the religious pictures on the walls—the less judgmental ones—but most ran to Margaret's theological taste: "Jesus turning the moneychangers from the temple; Moses throwing the Tablets down upon the worshipers of the golden calf. . . . Noah's ark floating above the agonized, drowning sinners, Lot and his family fleeing the great burning of Sodom and Gomorrah."[19] If our god-talk is the representation of our worldview, there is little in the White house save for the punishment a jealous and vengeful God metes out upon those deserving of his wrath.

"Mass-produced items of religious devotion," writes sociologist David Halle in his study of class and domestic décor in America, "statuettes, inexpensive pictures, crucifixes, and so on—surely place near the bottom of any ranking, by status, of the artistic and cultural motifs in the home."[20] Indeed, Halle's study, which was conducted in a variety of neighborhoods in and around New York City, found that even people who were religious—including a group of priests living together in a Manhattan rectory—were unlikely to display religious art or iconography openly, and those who did tended to limit or offset its placement. It was never the central fixture in the home, nor the dominant decorative theme. That said, when religious art or iconography is present, it is carefully chosen to project a particular religious identity—but never too much of it. What we put on display both tells the world and reinforces for us who we think we are and who we aspire to be. Faculty offices hung with a staggered row of sheepskins say, "I have all these degrees. You should take what I say very seriously." A lawyer who wants several linear feet of leather-bound books for his office pretends to a professional importance he may not feel. A home adorned with nothing but family pictures and portraits tells anyone with eyes to see about the centrality of clan and kinfolk. Like the clothes we choose day-to-day—or which, in many cases, are chosen for us—our homes tattoo the skin of our lives with meaning. "In general," Halle concludes, "the audience selects (consciously or not) those images, and attributes to them those meanings that resonate with their current lives and beliefs, especially as these relate to house, neighborhood, and domestic social relations."[21] In short, home is the place we hope to be most ourselves, the place that reflects most clearly who we are and what we consider important.

As we pass through into the White living room, the only other piece of furniture is "a small deal table," holding "a lamp and a pile of tracts. The top pamphlet showed a sinner (this spiritual state was obvious from the agonized expression on his face) trying to crawl beneath a large boulder. The title blared: *Neither shall the rock hide him ON THAT DAY!*"[22] Obviously one of the odious Chick tracts,[23] the meaning with which Margaret has marked the skin of their lives is clear: those who screamed at Noah and clawed in vain at the rain-slicked sides of his enormous boat thought that God had not seen their wickedness; the men, women, and children who ended their lives consumed in the fire and fear of Sodom at one time believed themselves beyond the reach of the stranger's god; the Hebrew people, freed from Pharaoh's tyranny, quickly abandoned the God of Moses and set themselves to worship the golden calf; the moneychangers in the Jerusalem Temple thought they were safe. They were wrong, Momma knew. They were all wrong, and everything in her home testifies to the omniscience of her terrifying God.

The living room itself "was actually dominated by a huge plaster crucifix"—unusual for a fundamentalist Protestant who considered Catholics only one step removed from outright heathens. It hung "on the far wall, fully four feet high. Momma had mail-ordered it special from St. Louis."[24] That is, from a wide range of options she considered and compared, Margaret had selected this expensive piece of statuary because, as Halle would say, it resonated with—indeed, embodied—her life and beliefs. "The Jesus impaled upon it was frozen in a grotesque, muscle-straining rictus of pain, mouth drawn down in a groaning curve. His crown of thorns bled scarlet streams down temples and forehead. The eyes were turned up in a medieval expression of slanted agony."[25]

As we move deeper into the house, further from the relative normality of the street outside, we encounter the innermost circle of separation. Off the living room, with its relentless images of sinners punished, past the corpus of the "mutilated Christ," in the small bedroom Margaret had turned into their chapel is the most terrifying place of all.[26]

The Closet

"When thou prayest," Jesus tells his followers in the Gospel of Matthew, "enter into thy closet, and when thou hast shut thy door, pray to thy Father which is in secret; and thy Father which seeth in secret shall reward thee openly" (Mt. 6:5–6). Margaret's world is a set of overlapping enclosures, increasingly intense zones of ardent piety and fragile safety. Only within "the red-plague circle" are they secure in their salvation—however tenuous that security. If something breaches the circle, if something invades their house and threatens their standing in the eyes of Margaret's grim and humorless deity, there is, finally, the closet.

Far more than a place of prayer and meditation, the closet represents the harshest form of religious socialization, ritual reinforcement, and pious experience of the unseen order. If the "red circle" establishes the contours of Margaret's fundamentalism, and the path through their house marks the vigilance of her god, the closet is the site of the divine punishment she knows she deserves. "'For strait is the gate,' Momma said grimly," and this is what awaits those who stray from the path.[27] For Carrie, this "was the worst place of all, the home of terror, the cave where all hope, all resistance to God's will—and Momma's—was extinguished. The closet door leered open. Inside, below a hideous blue bulb that was always lit, was Derrault's conception of Jonathan Edwards's famous sermon, *Sinners in the Hands of an Angry God*."[28] Cast in there for hours at a time, occasionally as long as a day, "she was alone with Momma's angry God."

> The blue light glared on a picture of a huge and bearded Yahweh who was casting screaming multitudes of humans down through cloudy depths into an abyss of fire. Below them, black horrid figures struggled through the flames of perdition while the Black Man sat on a huge flame-colored throne with a trident in one hand. His body was that of a man, but he had a spiked tail and the head of a jackal.[29]

Though more than once Carrie swore to herself she would not break, of course she did. She called and called, pounding on the door, screaming for her mother to release her from the purgatory that "leered" mere feet from their crude, homemade altar. When Momma finally unlocked the closet and "Carrie scrabbled madly for the bathroom," "the Black Man grinned at her with his jackal mouth, and his scarlet eyes knew all the secrets of woman-blood."[30]

For Margaret, the closet is where her peculiar god-talk begins and ends. As the story opens, when Carrie arrives home from school, terrified and humiliated by the incident in the changing room, her mother's reaction exemplifies the most rigid and desperate religious experience. She demands that they "pray to Jesus for our woman-weak, wicked, sinning souls."[31] Nothing Carrie has done could be even remotely construed as wrong, but Margaret knows in the depths of her soul that they are, as Christopher Hitchens never tired of pointing out, "created sick, then commanded to be well." Dragging and beating Carrie through the house, the hallway, the living room, and finally the closet forms a kind of *via dolorosa*, a Way of Suffering that instantiates the self-loathing misogyny at the heart of Margaret's fundamentalist theology.

Though she would likely not know who wrote it, Margaret's fears reflect those that have framed a significant portion of Christian theology for nearly two thousand years. "You are the Devil's gateway," wrote the early apologist Tertullian in his tract "On the Apparel of Women." "You are the unsealer of that (forbidden) tree: you are the first deserter of the Divine law: you are she who persuaded him whom the Devil was not valiant enough to attack."[32] For Margaret, this is anything but a story. "Eve was weak," she shrieks, kicking her daughter as she crawls across the living room floor, "and loosed the raven on the world . . . and the raven was called Sin, and the first Sin was Intercourse."[33] For her seduction of Adam, "the Lord visited Eve with a Curse, and the Curse was the Curse of Blood."[34]

But in the midst of it all, we learn that somehow "Momma had torn the Something out of herself and was pure."[35] It's difficult to know just what King means here. Does Margaret's abject fear of God and horror of her own sexuality cause her menstrual cycle to cease? Emotional stress is one possible cause of secondary amenorrhea. Was there another child before Carrie, one Margaret aborted, either spontaneously in terror or deliberately in disgust? The constant state of religiously induced fear is only exacerbated in Margaret by the knowledge that no matter how hard she prays, no matter how many tracts she hands out or sinners she scolds, no matter how many barriers she erects between Carrie and the rest of the world, it will never be enough. "And still Eve did not repent," she tells her weeping, screaming daughter, "nor all the daughters of Eve, and upon Eve did the Crafty Serpent found a kingdom of whoredoms and pestilences."[36]

"Perhaps a complete survey of Carrie's mother will be undertaken someday," writes the eminent "David Congress" in *The Shadow Exploded*, which, according to one of the few townspeople to survive Carrie's telekinetic rage, is "probably the only half-decent book written on the subject."[37] The Constant Reader knows, though, that Margaret's godtalk has already been surveyed. She's just another sinner dangling above the flames, caught forever in the hands of her angry God.

Not so Vera Smith.

Vera's Story: You Are a Chosen People

As pattern-seeking creatures, we look relentlessly for meaning and purpose in "the jumble of whites and blacks," anything that will convince us that all *this* isn't all in vain. More than anything we want to know that we matter. Both Margaret White and *The Dead Zone*'s Vera Smith teach us something about belief and certainty. Where the former lives in terrified certainty of damnation, the latter's faith is anchored in her unwavering confidence in God's love and God's plan. Reinforced through ritual expression, our religious experience relies on socialization and conviction. Because what, really, are the alternatives? Religious belief comes with precious little in the way of empirical evidence, though few believers will admit that rather unremarkable fact. In its place, we tell each other, "Well, you just have to have faith," a spiritual commodity that is, as often as not, a singular function of circumstance.

The Dead Zone's plot is quintessential fifth business. Everything is normal until one thing changes, and then nothing can ever be the same. A young man out on a date has a terrible accident on the way home. Left in a coma for years, he wakes with two extraordinary abilities: paracognition and precognition. Just by touching them, Johnny Smith can tell things about people even they didn't know, and, more significantly, he knows what's going to happen in their future. It is not Johnny's story, however, that reveals another of the varieties of religious experience in Stephen King's world, but his mother's. Through Vera, King explores two interconnected ways of understanding our relationship to the unseen order and what many believers consider their place in the divine plan: hubris and plasticity.

Hubris

When Vera and her husband, Herb, first learn of Johnny's accident, the scene has a familiar register. Trying to remain calm in the face of rising panic, Herb wants to find out what, exactly, has happened. Vera, on the other hand, just as desperate for news of her son, "clawed for the phone like a tigress. 'What is it? What's happened to my Johnny?'"[38] Hardly surprising. A loving mother imagines the worst. Who wouldn't? And who could blame her?

> "He's dead?" Vera asked. "He's dead? Johnny's *dead*?"
>
> He covered the mouthpiece. "No," he said. "Not dead."
>
> "Not dead! Not dead!" she cried and fell on her knees in the phone nook with an audible thud. "O God we most heartily thank Thee and ask that You show Thy tender care and loving mercy to our son and shelter him with Your loving hand we ask it in the name of Thy only begotten Son Jesus and . . ."
>
> "*Vera, shut up!*"[39]

King records this first, impassioned prayer with no punctuation and no sentence break. It's easy to imagine the gasping haste with which Vera approached her God, barely taking a breath, never doubting his ear cocked her way from heaven. Without knowing Johnny's condition, merely that he's "Not dead!"—note that she does not proclaim that her son's "Alive! Alive!" but repeats that he's "Not dead!"—Vera falls back on the simple belief that grounds her simple faith: God's hand is in everything.

For decades, from tent revivals in the cornfields of Nebraska to megachurch pulpits in places like Chester's Mill, Maine, Protestant evangelists have proclaimed this promise to the unsaved and backslidden alike: "God loves you and has a plan for your life." This is the "blessed assurance" to which Vera has moored her beliefs. Like Civilia Martin's famous gospel hymn "His Eye Is on the Sparrow," Vera locates every action, every event within the purview of God's omniscience and omnipotence. Which is to say, the resilience of her faith tells her that there are no accidents. Everything happens for a reason. And, in a certain sense, this is true.

Gravely injured, her son lies comatose in Eastern Maine Medical Center because "Johnny's cab and the Charger met head-on and Johnny felt himself being lifted up and out."[40] Two teenagers racing muscle cars down a winding road in the middle of the night. What could possibly go wrong? Ego, fearlessness, and speed—the physics of foolhardiness— are the *reason* for the crash. What Vera's faith requires, though, is its *purpose*, the *meaning* behind the reason. As soon as she learns Johnny's "Not dead!" she prayerfully assumes that he survived because God wants him alive. For Vera, this is the straightforward calculus of her religious experience. If God had not intervened, if it had not been in God's plan, her son would be dead—like Johnny's cabbie and the driver of the other car.

Both of them were crushed to death when the impact slammed their steering columns back with catastrophic force. Both had scant seconds to realize it was already too late. "*Jeeesus!*" is all the cab driver had time to say.[41] When survivors emerge from any harrowing situation— whether natural disaster or human conflict—they often relate how they prayed that God would keep them safe, they tell hungry news cameras how grateful they are that God was watching over them until they were rescued. The media sound bite is simple: God saved me. God wanted me to live.

Which means God wanted other people to die.

If they're aware of it at all, few believers willingly admit this necessary corollary. While Vera Smith is on her knees thanking God for saving her son, somewhere else in eastern Maine another mother has just begun the horror of burying her child. In the taxi driver's home, a son learns that he has to face the prospect of growing up without his dad, a father who told Johnny that "every week, no matter how thin that week was, I put five bucks away for his college."[42] A father who, until that night, "never had a major crash, for which I thank Mary Mother of Jesus, Saint Christopher, and God the Father Almighty, know what I mean?"[43]

But what *does* that mean? King wonders. How does God choose? And what is the plan?

Johnny may be alive, but he's critically injured and will lie in a coma for nearly five years before resuming anything like his life. He's alive, but what message are we to take from his injuries? Surely, if God has a plan, those injuries must be part of it. Sounding "like some nutty Greek chorus in the background," in the space of one brief phone call Vera goes from abject terror at the thought of losing her child, to rapturous gratitude when she learns he's "not dead," to the hubristic search for meaning in his grievous injuries.[44] As Herb hangs up the phone, "Vera uttered another shriek, and he saw with some alarm that she had grabbed her hair, rollers and all, and was pulling it. 'It's a judgment! A judgment on the way we live, on sin, on something! Herb, get down on your knees with me.'"[45]

On the one hand, it would be easy enough to dismiss her reaction as a side effect of the shock. On the other, though—and this is another reason King's work provides us opportunity to think about the nature of popular religiosity—responses such as Vera's do not exist in a vacuum. Like Margaret White's fearful separatism, they do not appear *ex nihilo*. They have a history, a bedrock of god-talk upon which they are founded.

In what is often the arrogant self-centeredness of popular evangelicalism, Vera assumes that Johnny's injuries must be a punishment of some kind, "a judgment on the way we live." This is Vera's tacit nod to Margaret's angry god. What must this say, then, about the families of those who died in the accident? What skeletons rattle in *their* closets? Vera concludes that it must be a judgment "on sin," the tendency of the religious to blame the victim because of the unimpeachable righteousness of God. For her, the logic of faith is unassailable: since God is perfect, we must be to blame, because things don't just happen for no reason, do they? That is, and most telling in terms of religious experience and the search for meaning, an accident cannot be simply an accident, there must be a higher purpose. It must be a judgment "on something."

Many religious believers live as though they are lead actors commanding center stage in God's grand cosmic drama. Whatever happens is *about* them, *intended* for them, and God help them if they don't get the message. Nowhere does it occur to Vera that if God is punishing anyone it might be Johnny, or one of the other crash victims. Nowhere does it occur to her that his injuries and her grief might be little more than collateral damage in the divine plan to teach somebody else a lesson. Nowhere does it occur even to ask *what kind of a god* would kill a teenager and a father, who would grievously injure two other people, who would ruin countless lives, all to convey a life lesson to Vera Smith, a middle-aged housewife in Pownal, Maine.

In 2007 sociologists at Baylor University asked survey respondents to rate the attributes of God according to two broadly conceived orientations: "a more benevolent and engaged God," by which they mean more merciful and compassionate, and a more "severe God of judgment," something closer to Margaret White's understanding.[46] When they investigated the relationship between these perspectives and various measures of religiosity—frequency of prayer, for example, church attendance, Bible reading, and public identification as a person of faith—the results were striking. "It isn't even close," they report.[47] Those who believe in a loving God, one who cares about them and has some sort of plan for their lives, were twice, often three times as likely to engage in these activities. That said, the notion of a vengeful, punishing God remains deeply embedded in American evangelicalism.[48] Vera fits right in with these results: knowing that God loves her and cares about her, but more than a little wary that he's keeping tabs somewhere.

"I, the Lord your God, am a jealous God," writes the unknown author of Exodus (20:5) as he describes Moses bringing the commandments of Yahweh to the Hebrew people, "punishing the children for the sins of the parents to the third and fourth generation of those who hate me." Although the author is talking about the danger of worshipping gods other than Yahweh, it's not difficult to see how a simple Baptist believer like Vera would make the connection between her sins and her son's accident. Much of popular evangelicalism posits that anything that takes our attention away from God is, by definition, a form of idolatry. Any sin, then, anything regarded *as* sin can become a golden calf.

"We'll pray for him," Vera says, looking wild-eyed at her husband, grasping at whatever will help make sense of the situation and afford her some measure of control over it. "We'll pray for him . . . promise to do better," she tells him.[49] Like so many ardent believers, though, Vera quickly decides that *she* isn't to blame; God isn't angry with *her*. He didn't choose to punish their son because of something *she* did. This refraction of hubris is the enduring resilience of religion, its ability to manufacture order in the midst of chaos.

"If you'd only come to church more often with me," she accuses Herb, "I know. . . ."[50] She knows what? That God wouldn't have brought the taxi and the Charger together on that lonely mountain road? "Maybe it's your cigars, drinking beer with those men after work . . . cursing . . . taking the name of the Lord in vain . . . a judgment . . . it's a judgment."[51] It's someone's *fault*, it's *Herb's* fault—all so that Vera can maintain certainty in the whirlwind of chance. Whatever happens, her one pillar of faith is that meaning and purpose can be found so long as she holds tight to God's plan. It wasn't God's plan that Johnny should die that night out on Route 6—because he didn't die. It was God's plan that he remain comatose for nearly half a decade—because he did. Just as it was God's plan that he come out of his coma—because on January 12, 1975, he began to speak. This may be circular logic, but it's the logic of Vera's faith. It's the world her theology demands.

Early on in Johnny's coma, Herb suggests that they might have to prepare for the inevitable, the heart-rending reality that he may simply slip away. Vera turns on him fiercely. "Don't you *ever* say that. Don't you *ever* say that Johnny isn't going to wake up. . . . It's God's plan for him. Oh yes. Don't you think I *know*? I *know*, believe me. God has great things in store for my Johnny. I have heard him in my heart."[52] Inner certainty, an ineffable sense of knowing, is common to many religious traditions. Latter-day Saints look for a "burning in the bosom" when praying about the truth of the Mormon Church. Personal gnosticism, the belief that if it feels right to you then it must be right, is all but an article of faith among many modern Pagans. Inner certainty is a powerful motivator, but it doesn't make any of it true.

When, against all medical odds, Johnny does wake up, for Vera it's less a profound moment of joy and relief than a vindication of her religious belief, her faith in God, and her priority in God's plans. Indeed, her reaction to news that Johnny might be recovering mirrors her initial response to the accident. There is purpose, meaning, order in her universe—however unseen these may be by others.

Once again, we can almost hear the words spilling out like a flood. "'O my God I thank you for your will be done my Johnny You brought me my I knew You would, my Johnny, o dear God I will bring You my thanksgiving every day of my life for my Johnny *Johnny JOHNNY—*' Her voice was rising to a hysterical, triumphant scream."[53] When Herb tries to calm her down, she reveals the sense of persecution felt by many devout believers when their faith is challenged. Accusing her husband of telling people she was crazy, she throws her vindication in his face. "'You *told them with your eyes!*' she shouted at him. 'But my God wasn't mocked. Was he, Herbert? *Was he?* . . . I told you. I told you God had a plan for my Johnny. Now you see his hand beginning to work.'"[54]

King presents Vera Smith's religious belief as an airtight circular argument, a closed system of god-talk to which nothing untoward is ever admitted. In this sense, it is the theological version of Margaret White's house. Because everything is under God's control and part of God's plan, anything that happens reinforces the believer's faith. If Johnny had died in the accident, that would have been proof positive that Vera and Herb were being punished for something. That he was not killed is evidence of God's mercy and plans for him—and by extension a reward for Vera's faith. Had he died in the coma, slipping away to the other side as his body gradually returned to a fetal position, this would have been evidence that his parents had not sufficiently atoned for whatever sins brought God's wrath down in the first place. His recovery justifies Vera's faith, especially in the face of those who doubted her and, by doing so, mocked her God. As King points out later in the novel, "It was a seamless argument."[55] The non-falsifiability of religious belief—that is, its plasticity in the face of change and challenge—is key to religion's durability and resilience.

Plasticity

When Sarah Bracknell, the young woman Johnny should have married, but who lost him in the accident just as surely as he lost himself, calls to check on his parents, Herb tells her that Vera has left, unable to face the daily pain of her son's condition. "The truth is," he said, "she's up in Vermont. On a farm. Waiting for the end of the world."[56] Vera has joined a group King calls "The American Society of the Last Times," a Christian-inspired UFO contactee group similar to groups dating back to the 1950s.[57] King's brief description, written with almost journalistic flatness, is worth quoting in full.

> Mr. and Mrs. Stonkers clamed to have been picked up by a flying saucer while they were on a camping trip. They had been taken away to heaven,

which was not in the constellation Orion [as another group with whom Vera corresponded believed] but on an earth-type planet that circled Arcturus. There they had communed with the society of angels and had seen Paradise. The Stonkerses had been informed that the Last Times were at hand. They were given the power of telepathy and had been sent back to Earth to gather a few faithful together—for the first shuttle to heaven, as it were.[58]

Non-falsifiable experience, claims of supernormal abilities, a special message for the chosen few, and the opportunity to be at the center of events—all are stock-in-trade of end-times prophets, and powerful incentives for those believers willing to commit to God's plan. "The farm had no furnace," King continues, "and when the saucers had still not come by late October, Vera came home."[59] Important here, though, is that she did not return dispirited—disappointed, perhaps, but not deterred. It was all simply one more aspect of God's unfolding plan, one more test for the faithful.

> The saucer had not come, she said, because they were not yet perfect—they had not burned away the nonessential and sinful dross of their lives. But she was uplifted and spiritually exalted. She had had a sign in a dream. She was perhaps not meant to go to heaven in a saucer.[60]

As King charts Vera's deepening religious mania, which includes, among other things, a conviction "that Christ would return from below the earth at the South Pole," he tacitly invokes decades of research into the durability and resilience of religion, its *plasticity*, not in spite of discouragement and disappointment, but precisely because of it.[61]

It's easy to read characters such as Margaret White and Vera Smith as straw personae written into the story almost as comic relief. Their willingness to believe—and to maintain belief with the tenacity of a well-anchored weather vane—is solidly grounded in the sociology and psychology of religion. The need for a scapegoat—whether as a propitiatory sacrifice to appease the monsters in King's novella "The Mist," or a distraught, confused father and husband in *The Dead Zone*—has deep roots in religious history.[62] It's easy to write these characters off as little more than set dressing meant to mock religion and ridicule believers, but this would be a mistake. In the same way he presents the ordinariness of life disrupted by the extraordinary, King illustrates the nature of religious experience in response to these incursions. Hard to believe for many, but hard to relinquish for others. Because, consider the alternative for Vera Smith: the possibility that everything cannot be contained within God's plan calls into question not only the plan, but God himself. Her entire worldview, her identity, her sense of self-worth, what psychologists would call her ego structure—all are entirely bound up in her devotion to that plan and her conviction that she is an important part of it. Without that dubious, shifting certainty, she faces only the abyss.

What happens, though, when the abyss stares back?

Piper's Story: *Deus Absconditus*

Both Margaret White and Vera Smith are principal, if secondary characters. Piper Libby is not. A minor character in *Under the Dome*, she's the Congregationalist minister in Chester's Mill, Maine, a woman trying like everyone else to survive their strange imprisonment. As they are in many American small towns, religious believers are more common than not in Chester's Mill. Some of these King draws more colorfully than others. Duke Perkins, for example, the chief of police, doesn't last long in the story, but he casts a lengthy shadow. We meet him on Dome Day, less than an hour before his pacemaker explodes as he approaches the mysterious barrier. Like most of his fellow citizens, Perkins is a committed Christian. While the details King gives us may seem trivial, they are anything but. We learn that Perkins prefers listening to "sacred music on WCIK (call letters standing for *Christ Is King* and known by the town's younger denizens as Jesus Radio)."[63] We know that when he's teased about his name, "he tried to be a Christian about it—he *was* a Christian about it"—which means, presumably, that Duke simply turned the other cheek.[64] When he learns of the accidents heralding the advent of the Dome, he's mowing the lawn while listening to the Norman Luboff Choir singing "What a Friend We Have in Jesus" and "singing along with 'How Great Thou Art.'"[65]

These are the markers of Duke Perkins's cosmology, his understanding of how the world works and why. Although he doesn't live to realize it, the Dome's appearance invokes one of our most potent fears, that of a change in the sacred order.[66] "It is not the physical or mental aberration itself which horrifies us," King writes in *Danse Macabre*, "but rather the lack of order these things imply."[67] God-talk set to music, hymns are an important way many believers express their understanding of who God is and what their relationship with God looks like. The Dome threatens precisely the theology underpinning the hymns King chooses for this scene. Of the hundreds, perhaps thousands, of popular Christian hymns, why choose "What a Friend We Have in Jesus"—which speaks explicitly to the salvation aspect of the Christ story—and "How Great Thou Art"—which proclaims as few others do the majesty and sovereignty of the Christian God? Because both of these fundamental principles are challenged by the arrival of the invisible, impenetrable barrier. Perhaps it doesn't matter if we have a friend in Jesus. Perhaps Duke's God is not so much great as simply . . . not.

Enter the Reverend Piper Libby.

Piper is who Vera Smith might have become had Johnny died that night on the mountain road: someone whose faith did not so much evaporate in the face of personal tragedy as simply slip away. The minister at First Congregational Church, Piper "no longer believed in God, although this was a fact she had not shared with her congregation."[68] Three years before the Dome came down, Piper's husband and two young sons were killed in an accident. In one terrible instant, her entire family was taken from her. In this, she's like Paula Robeson in "The Things They Left Behind," whose experience of 9/11 stripped her of belief in God, like *The Stand's* Frannie Goldsmith, who screams, "Killer God! *Killer* God! . . . He's no god. He's a demon," like Mrs. Ross, crying out in *Desperation*, "What sort of God lets a man forget killing a little boy?"[69] All of this brings us to the stone-cold question of theodicy: the presence (or absence) of God in the face of suffering. How do we understand our pain if our faith insists that God loves us? For some people, despite their pain God's presence is never in doubt, while for others doubt becomes the order of the day. If Vera Smith's cry of faith is *Christus victor*, the God who reigns in spite of tragedy, Piper Libby lives quietly in the shadow of *Deus absconditus*, the god who is not there. Piper's faith melted away in the long, lonely nights with no one beside her in bed and no gentle snoring from down the hall. Any belief she had in the Divine faded over time, going from "The Omnipotent Could-Be" to "The Great

Maybe" to the one she called, simply, "Not-There."[70] Because her god is no longer there, however, does not mean that the unseen order is empty.

The Dome that came down over Chester's Mill, eventually killing all but a handful of the residents, did not appear out of nowhere. Something created it. Something put it in place. Something was watching. When Dale Barbara touches the Dome's power supply, he connects momentarily to "the creatures who were holding them prisoner. Holding them and torturing them for pleasure."[71] They are the "leatherheads," because no other word can describe the experience. He doesn't know what they are, where they came from, or what they want. All Dale knows is that "they inspired a deep sense of loathing in him, perhaps because they were so alien he could not really perceive them at all."[72] Maybe, suggests King, this is what it must be like to look upon the face of what we have for millennia called "God," remembering that the word, the concept, is little more than a placeholder for an encounter that is so *outside* our realm of experience that it beggars description. Even were we to credence the pale metaphors we share among ourselves and call "creation stories," can we really begin to imagine the experience of meeting something so different, so *totally other*, so alien as "God"?

When Piper reaches in and touches the power source, like N. in Ackerman's Field or Louis Creed as he makes his way through Little God Swamp, she too experiences a profound shift in perspective. "She was thinking," King writes, "of all those late-night prayers to The Not-There. Now she knew that had been nothing but a silly, sophomoric joke, and the joke, it turned out, was on her. There *was* a There there. It just wasn't God."[73] In the same way we learn so little of It or the Tommyknockers, so little of *Desperation*'s Tak or *Duma Key*'s Perse, we learn little more of the leatherheads than *that* they are, nothing of *what* they are. We are confronted, though, with the brute fact that none of the myriad prayers for salvation flung aloft in the firestorm that destroys Chester's Mill were answered. In terms of the dueling cosmologies *Under the Dome*, there is no contest. It isn't even a horse race. Thirteen-year-old riot grrrl Norrie Calvert thinks she understands why. She is convinced the aliens are like her.

"Kids," she tells Piper.

"When you asked them why," the atheist minister responds, "what did they say?"

"Nothing."

"Did they hear you, do you think?"

"They heard. They just didn't care."[74]

For years before the accident that took her family, Piper Libby had preached the love of God to her congregants. She had celebrated with them and wept with them. She had baptized their babies, joined their children in marriage, and buried the dead. Before the accident she had done all these things secure in her belief that the God they worshipped really was there and really did care about them. It took a fatal car crash to challenge the former and the coming of the invisible, impenetrable, and implacable Dome to undermine the latter.

Which brings us, finally, to Charlie's story.

Charlie's Story: The Day of the Terrible Sermon

If *'Salem's Lot* is Stephen King's revisiting of *Dracula*, *Revival* is his homage to Mary Shelley's classic, *Frankenstein*, which many consider the first science fiction novel. The book has never been out of print and its story has been retold countless times, but what's often forgotten is Shelley's subtitle: *The Modern Prometheus*. This may not have been what the Reverend Charlie Jacobs set out to be in *Revival*, but it's what he becomes—the one who steals the secrets of the gods and pays for it in ways he can't begin to imagine.

Like Piper Libby, the young Methodist minister in rural Harlow, Maine, wants nothing more than to do the best he can for his small congregation. And when, like her, Charlie loses his wife and young son in a car accident, King guides his readers through yet another kind of religious experience, another exploration of what our world looks like when faith is pressed beyond its limits. Believers are fond of telling each other that God never gives us more than we can handle, to which Stephen King responds: Really? Tell Brian Ross's mother that, or Frannie Goldsmith, or Paula Robeson. Tell Piper Libby.

Tell Charlie Jacobs.

Stories, writes literary scholar Jonathan Gottschall, are at least in part extended thought experiments that invite readers to consider how they might respond in similar circumstances. Our species-wide addiction to story not only encourages us to read ourselves into this tale or that, taking the perspective of one character or another, it provides a culturally understood stockpile of examples against which real-life situations may be tested. Gottschall's favorite metaphor for this is the flight simulator. "Fiction," he writes, "is a powerful and ancient virtual reality technology that simulates the big dilemmas of human life." That is, storytelling "allows our brains to practice reacting to the kinds of challenges that are, and always were, most crucial to our survival as a species."[75] Through story, we can test our reactions, compare them to those of the various characters, and wonder, "What would I do if that happened to me?" "How would I react?" "Could I survive?"

Charlie returns to the pulpit just a few weeks after the loss of his family, on "the Day of the Terrible Sermon." Struggling to put what's happened into some kind of meaningful perspective, he recounts to his congregation a number of stories gleaned from the newspapers, stories of people just like them. A father and his two young sons drown when their dog falls out of the boat and they try to save him. They died "because they tried to rescue the family pet—did they ask God what was going on? What the deal was? And did He answer, 'Tell you in a few minutes, guys,' as the water choked their lungs and death darkened their minds?"[76] Hardly the sort of thought experiment one can propose at the dinner table without drawing horrified looks and exclamations of "That's so morbid!" In much of our society we are so frightened of death, so unaccustomed to its rock-solid reality, that we lack the willingness even to discuss it. Just the suggestion that we should keep an up-to-date will is often met with horror—as though through some kind of sympathetic magic, preparing for death actually invites it.

That morning Charlie confronts this reality, and from the honest pain of his loss asks real questions about why God allows the kind of suffering he's so recently experienced. In doing so, though, Reverend Jacobs breaks one of the unwritten rules of parish ministry: Thou shalt not tell them things they do not want to hear.

What did the good folks in West Harlow want to hear that day? What did they want their poor, grief-stricken minister to tell them? Simple. That everything's okay. That their faith is justified. That their God is in control. They want to hear that Patsy and Morrie Jacobs are "in a better place now," eating roast beef and mashed potatoes with Jesus. They want to hear how their spiritual leader had "walked through the valley of the shadow of death" and come out the other side stronger for it, sure of God's love and certain of his faith. What they wanted more than anything was to be comforted *by him*. What he learns, though, is the corollary of rural ministry's first commandment: If you can't tell us what we want to hear, then we don't want you to tell us anything at all.

In one brief homily, Charlie Jacobs wrestles with the angels of his own doubt, and proclaims the four arguments most often made to challenge the reasonableness of religious belief: *theodicy* and the problem of suffering; *theological conflict* and the problem of contradictory god-talk; *evangelism* and the problem of religious violence; and *hell*, the problem of eternal punishment at the hands of a loving God.

He begins the Terrible Sermon pointedly reiterating what we so often steadfastly avoid: bad things happen; prayers go up, often on the wings of our screams; tragedy continues; heaven is silent. A small Baptist congregation somewhere along Oklahoma's tornado alley gathers to thank God that the three twisters that touched down that afternoon claimed no lives. While they were praying, while they were perhaps singing "What a Friend We Have in Jesus," "a fourth tornado—a monster F5—swept down and demolished the church."[77] A hurricane strikes North Carolina, killing six "children at a church day-care center. A seventh was reported missing. His body was found a week later, in a tree."[78] A missionary family is murdered in central Africa, and their "killers may have been of a cannibalistic bent."[79] The dog and his humans we already know.

The point is that Charlie Jacobs isn't wrong. As Jamie Morton recalls years later, he had spoken nothing but "the exact, unvarnished truth."[80] And that truth is that we are surrounded by transcendent suffering, tragedy surpassing the boundaries of our ability to understand. "All too often," Charlie tells his stunned congregation, many of whom are already grumbling with disapproval, "we poor mortals here on earth are left with ugly heaps of maimed meat and that constant, reverberating question: Why? Why? *Why?*"[81] A question permissible to ask, it seems, only if it can be answered with some pious, vile platitude. God works in mysterious ways.

Like Piper Libby, Charlie is not satisfied. He wants to *know*. But "nowhere in scripture is that question directly addressed."[82] The best St. Paul can do is tell us that it's *all* dark glass, that "we wouldn't understand, anyway . . . as if life were a joke, and heaven the place where the cosmic

punchline is finally explained to us."[83] Job, he tells them, theodicy's para-
digmatic example, is even less help. In the midst of his unimaginable
loss—all part of a Divine game, it seems—God's response to him "trans-
lates, in the language of our younger parishioners, to 'Buzz off, Bunky.'"[84]

Even at this point, no one has walked out. They remain sitting in their
hard wooden benches, hoping that "the Rev'run" can walk his way back
to the comfortable pew. People only start leaving, slamming hymn books
shut and making for the door, when he questions not what they believe,
but whether what they believe is correct. Naming more than a dozen different denominations and knowing he could list "half a hundred more,"
Charlie raises the one question many religious believers do not want to
hear: How do we know we got it right? How do we know we didn't *all*
get it wrong? "And do you know what I find fascinating?" he asks. "Each
and every church dedicated to Christ's teaching thinks it's the only one
that actually has a *private* line to the Almighty."[85]

"Some of these various sects and denominations," he continues, as
congregation members begin walking out, "are peaceful, but the largest
of them—the most *successful* of them—have been built on the blood,
bones, and screams of those who have the effrontery not to bow to their
idea of God."[86] Not to mention believers who will not sit in church and
listen to the effrontery of those who challenge their comfortable notions
of the Divine.

More than that, we continue to visit this theological chauvinism on
our children. Echoing antitheists such as Richard Dawkins and Christopher Hitchens—*Revival's* opening chapters may have been set in the early
1960s, but the novel was written in the era of the new atheist movement—
Charlie implicitly equates the teaching of eternal punishment with child
abuse.[87] "The stick we're beaten with is hell, hell, hell! A Sheol of eternal
damnation and torment. We tell children as young as my dear lost son that
they stand in danger of eternal fire if they steal a piece of penny candy or
lie about how they got their new shoes wet."[88] Or, perhaps, eat something
other than fish on a Friday, or fail to find the face of the Savior in a "jumble
of whites and blacks." Having considered all this, in a sermon that lasts no
more than a few minutes, he tells them, "I had a revelation."

> Religion is the theological equivalent of a quick-buck insurance scam,
> where you pay in your premium year after year, and then, when you need

the benefits you paid for—pardon the pun—so religiously, you discover the company that took your money does not, in fact, exist.[89]

However those who seek sanctuary in religion arrive at this same conclusion, churches and temples, synagogues and mosques, houses of worship of all types shelter men and women who are shuffling somewhere along the path to a place of unbelief. Millions of people understand Charlie Jacobs and Piper Libby far more than they do Vera Smith or Margaret White. For Charlie, the moment of leaving God behind came after only a few weeks and in a flash of insight, while for Piper the journey from "The Omnipotent Could-Be" to "The Great Maybe" to "The Not-There" took a few years, fading like an echo until she wondered whether she ever really heard it at all. Both, though, reach the point of *Deus absconditus*. While one lived her life in quiet desperation, the other continued his search for the secret reality of an unseen order in which he never stopped believing. When Jamie meets Charlie many years later, he observes, "You went from preaching to huckstering."

"No difference," the former Reverend Charlie Jacobs replies. "They're both just a matter of convincing the rubes."[90]

Often, when those who profess religious belief act differently than we expect—consider *Needful Things'* Steamboat Willie or *Under the Dome's* Big Jim Rennie—we are quick to accuse them of hypocrisy. Any number of editorial cartoons, for instance, depict believers piously praying together, then ranting, raving, even coming to blows over a fender bender in the church parking lot. Inconsistency is seen as hypocrisy, a sign that these are not "true" believers, when it seems far more a part of what we might call "human nature" than not.

Because of this, it would be a mistake to look for consistency in the religious beliefs of King's characters, any more than we should expect to find it among those who ply their faith outside his storyworlds. Indeed, if there is a consistent theme to the various ways he explores religious experience, it is that religion and religious believers appear anything but consistent. For millions of people, religious faith is about trying to hold their beliefs in tension with their experience—a process that for many seems contradictory. Martha White's fear of God, and her need to reconcile her beliefs and her behavior, eventually drove her to an insular faith, one in which she alone was the arbiter of consistency. Vera Smith, on the other hand, was blown hither and yon, guided only by her conviction that God loved her and had a plan for her life. Piper Libby and Charlie Jacobs experienced similar losses, but responded in different ways. Not because they were inconsistent, but because they are human. What is constant, though, what we share with each of these characters, is our experience of suffering and the challenge it sets to our understanding of the Divine. This is the question to which we turn now.

If It Be Your Will

Theodicy, Morality, and the Nature of God

Stephen King enjoyed a banner year in 1996, which saw the release of three very different novels: *The Green Mile, The Regulators*, which he published as Richard Bachman, and its mirror story, *Desperation*.[1] On the surface, *Desperation's* plot is relatively simple, a staple of last-person-standing horror stories: a psychotic killer abducts passersby along a deserted stretch of highway and murders them in sundry unspeakable ways. Some fight back; most die. A few survive, and unless there's a sequel in sight, we safely believe the killer dispatched. The stuff of B-movie horror for decades, it's no more complicated than that. Since this was also how Viking marketed the book, we might be surprised to learn that *Desperation* is one of King's most candidly religious novels and contains some of his most carefully elaborated dark theology. As always, though, he raises more questions than he answers.

Although developed from very different perspectives, *Desperation* and *The Green Mile* both present the Constant Reader with explicit conceptions of the unseen order. In the latter, God is a reflection of Paul Edgecombe's religious socialization, the numerous childhood churches of "Praise Jesus, The Lord Is Mighty," while the former's concept of God derives from the immediacy of religious experience. In *The Green Mile*, events are made to fit an established framework of understanding, while *Desperation* continually wrestles with the process of belief in the face of horrific challenge. Both novels also contain characters that come as close to Christ-figures as we find in King's massive canon: the condemned John Coffey and a twelve-year-old boy named David Carver.

Described by his spiritual mentor as "a perfect late twentieth-century religious illiterate" and "the only honest convert he had ever seen," David embarks on a journey of faith divided roughly into three acts—conversion, acceptance, and sacrifice—each marked by the tragic and the miraculous.[2] Each stage recognizes the reality of the Divine, but also probes who or what the Divine really is. Put differently, acknowledging the existence of God inevitably leads us to question God's nature, character, and behavior.

David's conversion begins the day his best friend, Brian Ross, is "struck by a car while riding his bike to school," and is not expected to survive.[3] As David wanders aimlessly around the neighborhood, revisiting their favorite haunts and hangouts, he struggles with what life will look like without his friend. Tears sting his eyes and, despite having no formal religious training, his child's mind reaches out for the unseen order.

> *Why am I here?*
> No answer.
> *Why did I come? Did something make me come?*
> No answer.
> *If anyone's there, please answer!*
> No answer for a long time . . . and then one *did* come. . . .
> *Yes*, this voice had said. *I'm here.*
> *Who are you?*
> *Who I am*, the voice said, and then fell silent, as if that actually explained something.[4]

God's cryptic words to Moses—"I AM WHO I AM"—were surely as surprising to the former prince of Egypt as they are to a small boy in suburban Ohio. But, as it was for Moses, for David the divine self-disclosure marks only the beginning of a conversion process. Influenced by American televangelism and its pop culture representations, many people think that conversion is a kind of singular event, an instant of decision during a crisis or in response to some evangelistic invitation. It is a Rubicon moment that changes one's life forever. This may certainly be the case for some, and it has been the model for Christian conversion narratives dating back to Saul of Tarsus and Augustine of Hippo. For most people, though, while conversion may begin there, it's more of a gradual awakening as they explore new conceptions of the seen and the unseen, new understandings of what "our supreme good" means, and new ways to manage "harmonious adjustment." We develop belief and grasp its nuances over time, gradually adjusting our life course to conform to the waypoints our new faith provides.

For David Carver, the first of these waypoints is a simple response. "*Tell me what you want,* he asked the voice."[5] When the voice doesn't answer, he presses. "*Do you want me to pray?* he asked the voice. *I'll try if you want me to, but I don't know how*."[6] Still the voice is silent, and we begin to see how the novel's title becomes the controlling metaphor for everything that happens in its nearly seven hundred pages. Not only is it the name of the derelict mining town where the malevolent entity, Tak, takes its victims, not only is it the essence of their situation, it is the driving force behind David's religious conversion. He is, quite simply, desperate not to lose his friend. Finally, the voice replies, "*You're praying already,*" and challenges David to ask "for what none of them dare to ask for."[7]

> "Make him better," he said. "God, make him better. If you do, I'll do something for you. I'll listen for what you want, and then I'll do it. I promise."[8]

That evening, the telephone rings in the Carver household: "Brian's awake."[9] Although he is unlike Vera Smith in many ways, for David these words confirm, as they did for Vera, the reality of the voice and the truth of his experience. He had prayed, the voice had answered, Brian was awake. What the young boy dared ask for, though, came with a warning: "*If you take the credit, it stops here*."[10] David needs to understand that he is no more the author of the miracle than was John Coffey, decades ago and thousands of miles away in another storyworld. At best he is a conduit for a power far greater than he can imagine.

Months later, tragedy has overtaken David again. While on a holiday road trip, he and his family are seized by Tak and trapped in Desperation, Nevada. Kirsten, his seven-year-old sister, is already dead, callously hurled down the stairs like so much trash. Indeed, when she hit the bottom "there had been this *sound*, this awful sound like a branch breaking under a weight of ice, and suddenly everything about her had changed."[11] Now, having used up the gigantic body of police officer Collie Entragen, the demonic being has taken David's mother as its new host. For the moment, David, his father, and the rest of the survivors huddle in Desperation's abandoned theater, uncertain what to do, unsure whether they will even survive.

They share a simple meal together, everything they've been able to scrounge, including Ritz crackers and a tin of sardines. Before they begin, David asks if he can say a prayer.

> Then he closed his eyes and put his hands together again before his face, finger to finger. Johnny was struck by the kid's lack of pretension. There was a simplicity about the gesture that had been honed by use into beauty.
> "God, please bless this food we are about to eat," David began.[12]

Though exhausted, terrified, and starving, some still insist that others eat ahead of them. There's plenty to go around, they say, all the while certain there isn't. Most know that their meager supplies can't possibly feed them all, but the empathy-based altruism that marks so many primate species, including our own, overrides even this wretched situation.[13] Surprisingly, at the end of the meal everyone has had more than enough to eat, and Cynthia, the original cynic, announces, "This settles it once and for all. . . . Food is *way* better than sex."[14] The box of Ritz crackers lies forgotten on the grimy floor.

> It had gone all the way around the group, everyone had at least half a dozen crackers. . . . But that cylinder of wax paper was still in there, and Johnny could have sworn it was half-full; that the number of crackers in it had not changed at all.[15]

Few places in King's work make such an obvious biblical allusion, this to the loaves and fishes, one of the few miracles recorded in all four canonical gospels. It's almost quaint, this miraculous flowering in the midst of desperate circumstance. Sharing a meal together inscribes the scene with a fleeting sense of normality, a feeling that everything is going to be all right.

Almost.

"Bless our fellowship," David had said, continuing his prayer, "and deliver us from evil. Please take care of my mom, too, *if it's your will.*"[16] Consider those last words carefully: "if it's your will." For millennia, in countless ways and numberless languages, we have prayed but pretended not to presume on the nature of God. *Inshallah . . . B'ezrat HaShem . . .* Lord willin' and the creek don't rise—we're careful always to phrase our supplication in "harmonious adjustment" to the presumed will of the unseen order. After all, our sense of natural justice wonders, why wouldn't God want to save Ellen Carver? He saved Brian. But then why didn't he save Kirsten? Or Peter Jackson, shot three times in the stomach by Tak/Collie just moments after their arrival in Desperation? Why won't he save David's father, Ralph, who at this point has only hours to live? Because, we are so often and so blithely told, "God moves in a mysterious way, his wonders to perform." Arguably among the most common responses to the problem of theodicy, the words of William Cowper's famous hymn are an answer without an explanation. For many people, they do little more than keep God in the picture and at least nominally in control, because the alternative, the abyss of Piper Libby's *Deus absconditus*, is simply too terrible to contemplate.

Almost.

In the middle of his prayer over the ersatz loaves and fishes, David "paused, then said in a lower voice, 'It's probably not, but *please*, if it's your will. Jesus' sake. Amen.' He opened his eyes again."[17] That is, it's probably not in God's will that Ellen Carver survive. But if not, why not?

Near the end of the novel, at "the ragged yawn that was China Shaft," the survivors again pause to pray before David leads them into the mine tunnels to face Tak.[18] "Remember who's in charge," Johnny Marinville tells him. When the young boy mutters about the kind of god that would put them in this situation at all, the aging writer responds, "That's right. He's cruel. But you knew that. And you have no control over the nature of God anyway. None of us do."[19] If Desperation's theater is the spot in the desert where Jesus fed the multitudes, the slope below the opening into the China Pit is David's Garden of Gethsemane. "Will you light us on our way?" Johnny asks.

> "I don't want to," David whispered. Then, pulling in a deep breath, he looked up at a sky in which the stars were just beginning to pale and screamed: "*I don't want to! Haven't I done enough? Everything you asked? This isn't fair! THIS ISN'T FAIR AND I DON'T WANT TO!*"[20]

But he does. He is the dutiful servant and, minutes later, his father lies dead on the tunnel floor. In that instant, David knows he will live the rest of his life in terrible, desperate loneliness. Believing that he's the only one who can defeat the enemy, he sets out to finish Tak once and for all. But Johnny, who has had his own religious awakening—more Saul on the road to Damascus than the still small voice on the wind—holds him back. "*Let go!*" David screamed. "*It's my job! MINE!*"[21]

> "*He can't take them all and then not let me finish! He can't do that! He can't!*" . . . "*No!*" David whipped his head from side to side in a frenzy. "*No, it's my job! It's mine! He can't take them all and leave me! Do you hear? HE CAN'T TAKE THEM ALL AND—*"[22]

Having accepted the reality of sacrifice and his role as the sacrificial victim, David is now unwilling to let it go. With the unbridled fury of a young child and the righteous anger of a prophet, he spits in Johnny's face. Wiping away the spittle, the old man responds,

> "Listen to me, David. I'm going to tell you something you didn't learn from your minister or your Bible. For all I know it's a message from God himself. Are you listening? . . . You said, 'God is cruel' the way a person who's lived his whole life on Tahiti might say 'Snow is cold.' You knew, but you didn't understand." He stepped closer to David and put his hands on the boy's cold cheeks. "Do you know how cruel your God can be, David? How fantastically cruel? . . . Sometimes he makes us live."[23]

Sitting in our comfortable pews week after week, we listen to pastors, priests, and preachers drone on about the duty of faith, the demand for sacrifice, the need to submit to God's will. We hear the words, nodding and perhaps offering up an "Amen, brother!"—yet all the while grateful that the cup of suffering will almost certainly pass from us. How many believers, King wonders through Johnny Marinville, are ever really faced with the cruelty of God in the face of sacrifice? And what would we do if the call came?

For twelve-year-old David Carver, the real sacrifice is *not* to give his life for others. The hollow miracle is that he will survive the battle in Desperation, and he will move on with his life, doomed to relive those events every time he closes his eyes. Despite everything that's happened, as the survivors leave their dead behind, David still clings to the only thing that can bring meaning to the chaos, the belief against all evidence to the contrary that "God is love."

Believers regularly react with scorn and indignation when someone like Stephen King suggests that religion and fear are not only connected, but intimately related. "That's not the kind of God I worship," they say, despite the fact that no more credible proof may exist for their deity than for Tak. "My God is loving and compassionate," they declare, despite having to ignore tremendous swaths of religious history and theology that beg the contrary. Through the religious experiences of Margaret White, Vera Smith, Piper Libby, and Charlie Jacobs, we saw some of the ways believers interpret—and more importantly reinterpret—aspects of the Divine by which they are confronted. Perhaps we withdraw within the red circle of domestic faith or we abandon our everyday lives for the hope of apocalyptic rapture. Perhaps we lose our faith, either gradually or in the space between one heartbeat and the next. Regardless of the particular response, each of these reactions is driven by the same question: How could this possibly happen? In *Desperation*, America's dark theologian confronts us with two of the most important challenges we can face in terms of how we understand the unseen order and negotiate our relationship to it. These are (a) theodicy and the possibility that God just doesn't seem to give a damn, and (b) morality and the problem of our limited perspective in the face of divine indifference.

Theodicy: Cries of Pain and Suffering

While "The Things They Left Behind" is many things—part ghost story, revenant tale, meditation on survivor guilt, and miracle play—it is also part *theodicy*. For those who question either the goodness of a supreme being, someone in benevolent control of the unseen order, or that being's very existence, theodicy has been one of the hardest nuts to crack. As an exercise in theodicy, King's short story is a cry of indignation against a god who could allow events such as 9/11—and the myriad horrors that both preceded it around the world and have followed in its wake.

Literally, "theodicy" means the "justification of God," specifically a defense of the divine in the face of evil and suffering. Different religious traditions have worked the problem in different ways. For karmic/samsaric traditions such as Hinduism and many streams of Buddhism, for example, suffering is the inevitable result of cause and effect, repercussions and consequences acted out on the timeless stage of endless rebirth. How we play our role in one life determines what role we will play when we return to the stage in our next. Thus, for these believers David Carver's furious cry, "This isn't fair!" is simply a non sequitur. If something bad happens in this life, it means you must have done something to deserve it in a previous life. Not only does this explain the reality of suffering, it legitimates it in the context of the relationship between the seen and the unseen orders. As sociologist Peter Berger writes, "It is not happiness that theodicy primarily provides, but meaning."[24] It offers us an explanation. We may not like what's happening, but at least we understand why, and why there's no sense bitching about it.

Millenarian religions, on the other hand, those that look forward to some manner of glorious future once the struggles of life are done, often understand suffering as the necessary precursor to the reward that follows for the faithful. Fundamentalist Christians for whom apocalyptic fiction provides such comfort are, at least in theory, content to endure whatever comes their way because they trust in the promise of a wondrous eternity. It's not difficult to find the genesis of this perspective. "Blessed are you when people insult you and persecute you," Jesus told the multitudes gathered for the Sermon on the Mount. "Rejoice and be glad, for your reward in heaven is great" (Mt. 5:11, 12). Once again, we may not like what's happening, but at least we know things will get better in the end. Sinners will be punished, the faithful rewarded, our sense of cosmic justice ratified.

Whether believers admit it or not, these putative explanations actually confound our basic (if often self-interested) instinct for fairness, and have been used for centuries to contest the very existence of any god whom believers claim is both loving and just. For monotheistic religions such as Christianity, Judaism, and Islam, the classic argument is simple: billions of believers insist that God is all-powerful, all-knowing, and all-good, yet unimaginable, unwarranted suffering occurs, and has for the entirety of our existence. For critics, this leaves the religious with few options.

Perhaps God is not omnipotent, but limited in such fundamental ways that it begs whether we should call such a being "God" at all. Perhaps God is not omniscient, and exists largely unaware of our suffering. Perhaps God is not omnibenevolent, which so challenges colloquial notions of the Divine that it questions why anyone would want to worship such a god—even if it does exist. Or, as Piper Libby and Charlie Jacobs remind us, perhaps God simply does not exist, that whatever we have called "god" has never been more than a soothing fiction intended to keep our existential night terrors at bay. Stories of this god put the monstrous in its place and continue to tell us that everything will be all right.

"When we discuss monstrosity," writes King in *Danse Macabre*, "we are expressing our faith and belief in the norm and watching for the mutant. The writer of horror fiction is neither more nor less than an agent of the status quo."[25] As much as anything else, this is what makes horror religion's literary and cultural sibling. Religions, broadly speaking, are the *sine qua non* of normative agents, in part because they raise questions of the status quo in cosmic terms—salvation is at stake, the universe hangs in the balance—but also because they operate so deeply embedded in our cultural background. They are the "taken-for-granted" mental furniture of our lives, the stealth program running in the background and monitoring our relationship between the seen and the unseen.

The question of theodicy calls our confidence in the essential goodness of religion—the good, moral, and decent fallacy—out onto the stage and unmasks it for all to see. The comforting if superficial and insubstantial belief that the universe is a friendly place and that God is on our side is exposed through needless suffering. Asking, in his author's notes to *Just after Sunset*, "why some people live and some die," King questions the very concept of "God—in any of his supposed forms," and, more than that, "the will of God—who, if He is there at all, may have no more interest in us than I do in the microbes now living on my skin."[26]

Return to Cold Mountain

When *The Green Mile*'s Paul Edgecombe tells us that "healing is never about the healed or the healer," but that "the person healed has an obligation to ask why—to meditate on God's will," we enter theodicy's arena and face off against *The Dead Zone*'s Vera Smith.[27] Recall that no matter what happened, it is beyond the reach of Vera's religious vocabulary even to ask whether God had been asleep at the switch the night a Dodge

Charger roared out of the blackness and changed her family's lives forever. Whether he has the vocabulary or not, though, decades after the events on Cold Mountain's death row, Paul Edgecombe does ask.

Unlike Johnny Smith, Paul's wife, Janice, did not survive the accident between the Greyhound bus and a fertilizer truck. On the highway somewhere "outside Birmingham in a driving rain," he cradled his wife as she died. She was "fifty-nine, and as beautiful as ever."[28] There was no plan, no divine drama, no reason. It was no one's fault and there was no one to blame. "'Help me!' I screamed. 'Help me, someone, help me!' No one helped, no one ever came."[29] Nearly thirty years before, he'd watched, dumbstruck, as John Coffey cured him of a crippling urinary infection, and, later, removed a brain tumor from the prison warden's wife. When the sadistic Cold Mountain Prison guard Percy Wetmore callously stomped Mr. Jingles to death, Paul bore witness as the giant inmate cradled the tiny creature's broken body and breathed life into him again. And, many years later, as "the rain pounded down," in his panic and fear Paul is convinced he sees the long-dead John Coffey. "'*John!*' I screamed. '*Oh John, please help me! Please help Janice!*' Rain fell into my eyes."[30]

At this point, Paul metaphorically leaves his mother and her sisters behind. In the pouring rain, he steps away from "the churches of Praise Jesus, The Lord Is Mighty," and shrieks the question that looms in the background for so many of us, but to which so few give voice. "*John! JOHN COFFEY! WHERE ARE YOU, BIG BOY? . . . You saved Hal's wife, why not my wife? Why not Janice? WHY NOT MY JANICE?*"[31] Indeed, why not?

Of course, there is no answer. There is only the rain falling in his eyes and onto the face of his dead wife. There is "only the smell of burning diesel and burning bodies, only the rain falling ceaselessly out of the gray sky."[32] In terms of theodicy, what those skilled in the ways of god-talk call the logical arguments for the justification of God, Paul's final reflections are worth quoting at length.

> I look back on these pages, leafing through them with my trembling, spotted hands, and I wonder if there is some meaning here, as in those books that are supposed to be uplifting and ennobling. I think back to the sermons of my childhood, booming affirmations in the church of Praise Jesus, The Lord Is Mighty, and I recall how the preachers used to say that

IF IT BE YOUR WILL | 175

God's eye is on the sparrow, that He sees and marks even the least of His creations. When I think of Mr. Jingles and the tiny scraps of wood we found in that hole in the beam, I think that it is so. Yet this same God sacrificed John Coffey, who tried only to do good in his blind way, as savagely as any Old Testament prophet ever sacrificed a defenseless lamb.[33]

If what Paul writes is true, then this same God let Janice die on a rain-swept highway somewhere outside Birmingham, just as he let nearly three thousand men and women perish on a bright, sunny morning in September 2001.

Return to New York

When "the things they left behind" start appearing in Scott Staley's apartment, we have to wonder whether he is simply delusional, an unfortunate if understandable side effect of his survivor guilt. That's what Paula Robeson believes when she agrees to keep one of the items locked in her apartment safe. That way, the small Lucite cube with the steel penny inside can't return to his apartment—as it has every time Staley has tried to throw it away. A simple test for truth, dispassionate, third-party observation and verification will prove—as much to Paula as to Scott—that "the things they left behind" are nothing more than the ephemera of sadness and fantasy. Touching the cube, though, she, too, glimpses the horror in the Twin Towers that morning: a man, his hair already on fire, hides beneath his desk, while the air around him fills with the screams of his coworkers and the stench of burning jet fuel. "He was crying," she said, shaken to the core by her experience, "because in that instant he understood he was never going to own a catamaran or ever mow his lawn again."[34] For Paula, who wants nothing more than to live her life in relative obscurity, this is all too much. After seeing these things, life can never be the same and hers is the cry that has haunted our god-talk for millennia.

> They did it in the name of God, but there is no God. If there was a God, Mr. Staley, He would have struck all eighteen [sic] of them dead in their boarding lounges with their boarding passes in their hands, but no God did. They called for passengers to get on and those fucks just got on.[35]

Indeed, what Paula considers the unmitigated evil of the 9/11 hijackers is actually easier to understand than a god who let them prepare and allowed them to carry out their attacks—let alone a deity in whose name the attacks were carried out. It is impossible for her to reconcile the reality of God with the fact of that particular species of evil. For if God watched as "those fucks just got on," then what can that possibly say about God?

Apple farmer George Banning agrees. In King's short story "My Pretty Pony," as George is walking one of his orchards in upstate New York, a few hundred miles from Manhattan's Ground Zero, he offers his grandson Clivey an essential life lesson—the lesson of time. Rather, he says, the three kinds of time. First, there's time that moves so slowly you'd swear the clock itself had stopped. "When May comes," he rumbles, "you think school's never gonna let out, that mid-month June will just never come."[36] When the small boy grows into a young man, though, he'll realize that time has changed. It shifts and "starts to be *real* time," what George calls Clivey's "pretty pony."[37] Which is to say, this is the "second time," the time we should value the most, the time of which we should take most advantage. Finally, in our sunset years, especially when we're in pain like "poor old Johnny Brinkmayer, who went so slowly with the bone cancer last year," time once again slows down.[38] As we pray for death to take us, time itself becomes an agony, which brings George to the theological heart of the lesson.

"I think God must be one mean old son of a bitch," he tells his grandson, echoing concerns about the divine that reach back at least to the plays of Aeschylus and Euripides. That is, regardless what "that Reverend Chadbrand the wife sets such store by" preaches,

> To make the only long times a grownup has the times when he is hurt bad. . . . A God like that, why, He makes a kid who sticks pins in flies look like a saint who was so good the birds'd come and roost all over him. . . .
> I wonder why God wanted to make living thinking creatures in the first place. If He needed something to piss on, why couldn't He have just made Him some sumac bushes and left it at that?[39]

Notwithstanding the complicated landscape of global geopolitics, Paula Robeson has no trouble pointing to the proximate cause of the 9/11 tragedy: nineteen young men in the "boarding lounges with their board-ing passes in their hands." What had "poor old Johnny Brinkmayer" ever done, George Banning wonders, that he finished his days wrapped in the agony of bone cancer? What kind of a god allows such unwarranted suffering? This question, placed by an American horror writer in the mouth of a cantankerous old farmer, is the same one asked millennia ago by a prosperous man who lost everything he had in what we are told was nothing more than a wager between God and Satan. It's the same question posed by every person who has ever wondered what they did to deserve what's happening to them at that particular moment.

"Why me?" is the singular cry of the heart in pain and confusion.

Critics often disparage horror stories for not treating religion "se-riously," for using religious themes and imagery merely "for effect." Although he's writing specifically about horror movies, we can eas-ily imagine Bryan Stone's comments applied to horror culture more broadly:

> Because it offends, disgusts, frightens, and features the profane, often in gruesome and ghastly proportions, other than pornography, horror is the film genre least amenable to religious sensibilities. . . . The mere fact that horror films rely on symbols and stories as mere conventions to scare the hell out of us does not make a case for religious vitality in our culture; in fact, their persistence eviscerated of any deeper connection to our lived questions may be a good example of the decline of the religious in our culture.[40]

Stone was writing at a time when it was still academically fashion-able to dismiss popular culture as a legitimate vehicle for understanding society in general, and religion in particular. Moreover, as an evangeli-cal Christian, he approaches the question of horror culture from the limited perspective of his own faith, as though "religious sensibilities" are not and have not been implicated in many of the most offensive, disgusting, and gruesome aspects of human history. In terms of horror culture writ large, and Stephen King's work in particular, suggesting that a scary story "uses symbols and stories as mere conventions" or that the "persistence" of such stories and symbols "eviscerated of any deeper con-nection to our lived questions" speaks to a "decline of the religious" in our culture misses the mark by as wide a margin as possible. Certainly, we could find examples where this is the case. But the reality is that few issues cut closer to the bone of lived religion than when George Banning mutters, "God must be one mean son of a bitch," and wonders why we were even created in the first place. If all we are born into is, as Clive Barker so masterfully put it in *The Hellbound Heart*, "a world of rain and failure," then what's the bloody point?[41]

This is the very problem of Job: Why do people suffer? More to the point, given our propensity to seek patterns in the tides of life, why do *good* people suffer, often for no apparent reason? Where is the natural justice in that? For George, the answer Job receives from the heart of the whirlwind—essentially, "Because I'm God and you're not, so shut up"—is one of the most deeply unsatisfying possible. Indeed, it is unworthy of any being who claims worship as a loving God. As physicist and Nobel laureate Richard Feynman wrote with admirable understatement, to think that the universe "is all arranged as a stage for God to watch man's struggles for good and evil seems inadequate."[42] What question could be *more* deeply connected to our lived religion?

It's important to note that George Banning is not so much commenting on a religious answer to the question as asking the question from the same place as religious traditions have claimed to answer it. The problem is that religion, as a cultural and social convention, has laid claim to questions that more properly belong to human beings as a function of their humanity, not the belief system to which they adhere or into which they were born. Questions of meaning and purpose, suffering and justice, even truth and beauty—we have tended to call these *religious* questions. They are, however, more properly *human* questions. Without doubt, religion and myth are two of the ways humans have explored questions of existence. But they are not the only ways, nor are they necessarily the best ways—if for no other reason than that so many of their adherents think they are the only ways.

For critics such as Stone, however, the problem is not *that* horror culture handles religion, but *how*. "Rarely," he continues, "have [horror] films treated religious faith on its own terms or explored religious values and motivations with much complexity."[43] But what does "on its own terms" even mean? While we might also question the sophistication

with which an average church service proceeds, a deeper problem underpins this one: the assumption that religion is somehow the foundation for such stories and that they are intended only to explore religious
beliefs, practices, and conventions. In many cases, of course, this is true.
Fictional storyworlds ranging from the *Narnia* novels of C. S. Lewis to
Philip Pullman's *His Dark Materials* are explicit commentaries on particular religious traditions. Some, like Lewis, serve as comfort food for
believers, while others, like Pullman, question why we continue to eat at
religion's table at all. Indeed, in one of the most trenchant criticisms of
theodicy, Feynman's fellow Nobel laureate Steven Weinberg notes, "With
or without religion, good people can behave well and bad people can do
evil; but for good people to do evil—that takes religion."[44]

Morality: From Black and White to Blue and Orange

We all know someone like *The Tommyknockers*' Anne Anderson, Bobbi's
sister, someone so convinced of her own self-importance, the absolute
rightness of her opinion, that she seems less a person than a force of
nature. A family member, perhaps, a particularly galling colleague, a
friend we regard with a smile but a jaundiced eye—people who make
us wonder, "How can they possibly be like that?" Among other things,
for example, Anne illustrates why church attendance is rarely a reliable
measure of religiosity or depth of religious conviction. A little more
than a week before her visit to Bobbi's cabin, we learn, their father has
"died a miserable death."[45] The fact is that while Anne drove him to it,
"she would no more admit that she knew this than she would admit the
fact that though she had attended St. Bart's in Utica ever since earliest
childhood and was one of the leading laywomen in that fine church, she
believed the concept of God was a crock of shit."[46]

We've met men and women like Anne before. Mama Sweet, who
cruelly sought to comfort a grieving young mother in "The Man in the
Black Suit." The Methodists gathered in their sanctuary on the shores
of Dark Score Lake, singing hymns as a young woman and her son are
murdered in their midst. The Baptists and Catholics coming together
for one final battle in front of a little curio shop called Needful Things.
Indeed, in terms of the "Great Casino Nite Controversy," for the believ-

ers of Castle Rock, "a couple of murders could not hold a candle to the prospect of a really good holy grudge match. After all, other things had to take a back seat when it came to questions of religion."[47]

Theirs is the *performance of belief*, the public recitation of piety and morality. That people such as Anne, characters with no redeeming qualities whatsoever, are cast so rarely in King's vast *dramatis personae* testifies to his faith in the basic goodness of people—minor warts and blemishes notwithstanding. Anne Anderson is not Margaret White or Vera Smith, driven all but mad by the intensity of their religious devotion. Nor is she *Misery*'s Annie Wilkes, who managed the façade of sanity until the night Paul Sheldon flipped his '74 Camaro right into the world of someone who was "dangerously crazy."[48] She is not even the unfortunate Emily Sidley, she of "Suffer the Little Children," who, at the end of a long career teaching children without number, may or may not have seen monsters. No. Anne Anderson is a character who only rarely walks the boards of King's storybook theater, just often enough that we recognize her and shiver as though a goose walked over our grave. Jim Gardner, however, the alcoholic poet and one of the few people immune to the Tommyknockers' influence, sees through her right away. He recognizes the "heavy freight of evil that was simultaneously wearing her out and eating her up."[49] If the presence (or absence) of God in the face of suffering prods the question of theodicy, people such as Anne Anderson force us to ponder the related issue of morality.

Morality is subjective, and any claim to an "objective morality" inevitably founders on the rocks of hypocrisy, inconsistency, and stupidity. We may repeat to ourselves the pious phrase "Thou shalt not kill," but we still find all manner of justification for killing. We may tell ourselves we take the Golden Rule seriously, that we really do want to treat others as we would have them treat us, but like *Needful Things*' Myrtle Keeton we know that doesn't really apply to everyone. After all, "they're only Catholics."[50]

However we might wish it otherwise, morality comes to us not so much in black and white as in the myriad shades of gray that lie between. Behavior we value and reward exists along one end of a continuum bounded at the other by actions we despise and condemn. But few among us can agree on where particular actions should rest on the range. More than that, our moral compass is not fixed, but swings according to time, circumstance, and context. We do not all value the same behavior the same way. In Roman Catholicism, for example, the prohibition against suicide remains a theological absolute, while in medieval Japan it was a moral imperative under certain conditions. Indeed, for a member of the samurai class, one of the most shameful experiences was to be forbidden to take his own life when honor demanded it. In many religious traditions, homosexuality is all but the unpardonable sin, yet other communions within the same faith welcome gay men and lesbians not only as members, but as ministers, preachers, rabbis, and roshis.

As we've seen, though, our pattern-making brains not only allow us to make sense of the data around us, they try to force those data into patterns—whether what we see fits or not. We often view the behavior of others only through the chauvinism of our own behavioral filters. Catholic missionaries encountering ritual suicide for the first time in Japan must have thought it bizarre—immoral at best, blasphemous at worst. Because suicide is a mortal sin, but they so willingly embrace it, the Japanese must be heathens in desperate need of salvation. On the other hand, because Westerners did not conduct themselves with the same strict decorum (or hygiene) required by medieval Japanese social convention and cultural codes, they must therefore be *gaijin*, barbarians.

But consider this: however different they appear at first blush, these are not two species, but merely two cultures. They share the same biology—human; they can learn to share a common language—take your pick; they have the ability to think in common categories—"food" means the same thing, whether we eat the same meals or not. Yet, for all this, their understanding of death and their appreciation for its mystery and meaning could not be more different. However abhorrent someone like Anne Anderson might seem, she and her sister, Bobbi, grew up in the same home and hugged the same father, but each emerged with a moral compass boxed in very different ways. Imagine for a moment two completely different species, each competing for dominance, each acting according to its own codes and conventions, each bringing its own sense of morality to the encounter.

Midway through James Cameron's classic science fiction film *Aliens*, Ellen Ripley realizes that it's unlikely that she or any of the other humans will leave the small planetoid LV-426 alive. The terrifying xenomorphs are coming and there's little even the Marines can do. Once again, Ripley and her companions have been sold out by the Company. "You know, Burke," she says, slamming the corporate fixer against the steel bulkhead, "I don't know which species is worse. You don't see them fucking each other over for a goddamn percentage!" In the end, Ripley will fight for survival; she will defeat the alien queen; she will protect her surrogate daughter, Newt, in the same way the queen fights to protect her eggs. But nowhere does she condemn the aliens for being what they are. They're supremely dangerous, to be sure, they're an imminent threat, but nowhere do we get the sense that they are morally evil. Ripley recognizes that things aren't always black and white.

Sometimes, they're blue and orange.

"Blue-and-orange morality" is a recent narrative trope that acknowledges the difficulty of imagining different cultures, let alone different species, through the prejudiced lenses of our own morality, our own shades of black and white. It suggests that, not only can we not understand their actions in the context of our moral frameworks, we often barely appreciate that different frameworks are at work. Indeed, there are moral codes and compasses so utterly alien we scarcely recognize them as morality at all.

When Dale Barbara touches the control unit powering the Dome that has trapped Chester's Mill, it connects him to the leatherheads, "the creatures who were holding them prisoner. Holding them and torturing them for pleasure."[51] As we saw earlier, they "inspired a deep sense of loathing in him, perhaps because they were so alien that he could not really perceive them at all."[52] More than that, though, Barbie, as the townsfolk knew him, has no frame of reference—moral or otherwise—for understanding his experience of the leatherheads. "The part of his brain tasked with interpreting sensory input could not decode the messages his eyes were sending."[53] If he cannot describe what they look like, nor even determine how many there are, how could he possibly begin to understand their motivations? How could words and concepts like "justice" or "morality," "compassion" and "empathy" even apply?

Compare the questions King raises in *Under the Dome* to the hubris of human theology, displayed, for example, in the work of Sjoerd Bonting, a Dutch biochemist and Anglican priest. Writing for the journal *Zygon*, the "journal of religion and science" named for the shapeshifting extraterrestrials in *Dr. Who*, Bonting confidently asserts that alien "life forms would resemble earthly life (biochemistry, genetic systems, neuronal processes), and also develop a religious and moral life. As creatures with free will they would be prone to sin and in need of salvation." Furthermore, Bonting argues, their salvation "would not require multiple incarnations, since Jesus is the cosmic Christ."[54]

Even if we concede Bonting's dubious point about the biological parameters of life, it's not long before the hem of his cassock slips from beneath the lab coat. Whether they look like us or not, that extraterrestrial lifeforms would "also develop a religious and moral life" is an extraordinary claim. While there may be some intuitive evidence for the latter—some kind of other-directed altruism seems necessary for the long-term survival and development of any complex organism—the former is hardly demonstrable.[55] Religion and morality are neither coequal nor consequent phenomena. One neither necessarily flows from nor leads to the other. Bonting's speculative leap from general biological similarity to particular soteriological necessity is breathtaking in its arrogance and shortsightedness.

On the other hand, implies Stephen King, perhaps Barbie's experience is closer to what it must be like to look upon the face of anything we might call "God," remembering that the word, the concept, is simply a placeholder for an encounter so far *outside* our experience that we all but lack the vocabulary to describe it. At first, the characters trapped under the dome try to understand the leatherheads as children, less-developed versions of beings who would eventually outgrow their need to dispassionately torture defenseless creatures. But even that interpretation is exposed as little more than a vaguely comforting fiction. Does the concept of "suffering" have any meaning for them? And if so, do they see us as worthy of consideration in that context? Would it matter if they did?

With It, with Tak, with the Tommyknockers and the leatherheads, with *Duma Key*'s Perse, we are in the domain of blue-and-orange morality, frames of moral reference as alien from ours as the technology powering the Dome is from your average car battery. Indeed, in these cases, wonders King, do questions of moral reference even apply? When newspaper writer Julia Shumway asks Barbie, "What kind of intelligent race would allow their children to do such a thing to another intelligent race?"—which seems a profoundly naïve question for one human to ask another, given the history of violence that marks our species apart from all others with whom we share this "pale blue dot"—he answers, simply, "*We* think we're intelligent, but do they?"[56] Julia counters, again naïvely, that if we found life on other planets "we wouldn't destroy them. Because life in the universe is such a precious commodity."[57] While the latter may be true, and we can only hope that it is, precious little in humankind's long history of warfare and conquest suggests the former.

Something happens between the deserted mining town of Desperation, Nevada, and Chester's Mill, Maine; something happens in the dozen or so years between one storyworld and the other. However cruel he may have appeared to David Carver, the God who was there in Desperation was *there*, and displaced Tak in the end. For all those believers crying out to Heaven in Chester's Mill, their God was nowhere to be found when the Dome fell or when it was lifted. Implacable pity from the leatherheads, beings whose thought processes and moral compass we cannot even begin to comprehend, cannot be mistaken for mercy, much less for grace. All of those calling upon their God learn in their penultimate moments that God will not, or cannot, or is not there to save them.

Those who insist on putting themselves at the center of the universe—men and women like *Under the Dome*'s Lester Coggins, the methamphetamine-addicted pastor—will always see tragedy as a divine message in a bottle meant especially for them. Like Vera Smith, he believes that God communicates grace through the suffering of others, especially the innocent, and survival is the vindication of faith, confirmation of one's worth in God's eyes and one's place in his design. Not for a moment do they wonder about the blue-and-orange morality of such a being, nor why it should be worthy of our respect, let alone our reverence. The few who survive when the Dome lifts may be grateful to be alive, but there is no one and nothing to thank. Teenaged Ollie Dinsmore, for example, will have to live the rest of his life with the memory of his brother's death, and the suicides of both his parents—mother and father who, in desperation, chose to leave him in Chester's Mill. In this, *Under the Dome* may be one of Stephen King's bleakest storyworlds. Although a few people survive, no one really escapes.

When Piper Libby learns more about the leatherheads, her revelation is staggering in its implications for human religious thought. What if, she suggests, all our pretentious theologizing is little more than a by-product of alien baby-talk? Or we've mistaken extraterrestrial adolescents for the divine. "They're kids," she tells Barbie flatly. When he asks how she knows, she smiles and says, "I just do. . . . They're the God I stopped believing in about three years ago. God turned out to be a bunch of bad little kids playing Interstellar X-Box."[58] Surviving *Under the Dome*, Piper Libby answers the question of suffering in terms of the third option in the classic statement. It wasn't that God had no power to change things or lacked the will to do it. God, as she knew him, simply wasn't there.

There is, however, a fourth option.

Return to Desperation: The Fourth Option

At the end of Paul Edgecombe's long green mile, he comes to an understanding that is not an explanation, an answer that leads inexorably to more questions. "If it happens," he writes, "God *lets* it happen, and when we say, 'I don't understand,' God replies, 'I don't care.'"[59] In *Desperation*, as aging writer Johnny Marinville and twelve-year-old David Carver struggle to understand the death of David's mother, caught in Tak's awful grip, the young boy points out,

> "She wasn't a bad person, you know. What happened to her was kind of like being caught in a landslide or a flood, something like that."
> "An act of God."
> "Right."
> "*Our* God. Yours and mine."
> "Right."
> "And God is cruel."
> "Right again."[60]

In the end, David looks at the man old enough to be his grandfather and asks, "You know what God finally told Job when he got tired of listening to all Job's complaints?" Johnny looks at him and nods. "Pretty much told him to fuck off, didn't he?"[61] A few minutes later, Johnny says it again, "God is cruel." This time, though, the boy replies, "He sure is. Better than Tak, maybe, but pretty mean, just the same."[62]

Better than Tak. Maybe.

"David," asks yet another of King's long line of alcoholic writers, "this thing out there—Tak—what is it? Do you have any idea? An Indian spirit? Something like a manitou, or a wendigo?"[63]

> I don't think so. I think it's more like a disease than a spirit, or even a demon. The Indians may not have even known it was here, and it was here before they were. *Long* before. Tak is the ancient one, the unformed heart. And the place where it really is, on the other side of the throat at the bottom of the well . . . I'm not sure that place is on earth at all, or even in normal space. Tak is a complete outsider, so different from us that we can't even get our minds around him.[64]

This is the fourth option: that the being David Carver calls God is merely one player among many on the cosmic chessboard. "Because there were other gods in Desperation. He was sure of it."[65]

Religious belief traffics in certainties, if for no other reason than that for believers the stakes are often so high. Salvation balances on the razor's edge of faith. But what happens when our certainties collapse in the face of new and terrible convictions? To a young boy, the cosmic forces contending for dominance in that small Nevada mining town must have seemed like gods. What other vocabulary did he have? What other language had his religious socialization provided? In the end, David is certain of only one thing: We are not alone. There are other forces waiting in the wings, anxious to tread the boards and play their part on humanity's stage. Perhaps they are the Lovecraftian "elder gods," delighting in nothing but chaos and destruction. Perhaps they are alien adolescents, children of a race so far advanced as to seem like deities, but whose apparent cruelty is nothing but the expression of their own boredom. Perhaps they are "horrors beyond comprehension," beings and forces so different from us that we can only imagine them in our nightmares and dreamscapes.[66]

8

The Land Beyond

Cosmology and the Never-Ending Questions

"Vintage King" is how *USA Today* described *From a Buick 8*, the story of an old car that shows up one day at a Pennsylvania state trooper barracks. The car, however, like the derelict station wagon in "Mile 81," is anything but what it seems. Stored in a shed behind the barracks, it is a portal to another world, a vastly different place where nothing is quite the way it seems. When the Buick 8 has one of its "episodes," when the trunk pops open and the other realm peers in on ours, no one is sure what will come through or what will happen when it does. It is another intrusion from the unseen order, another crack in the world we think we understand.

Characterizing anything as "vintage King" risks consigning him to the dustbin of readers' perceptions—a serious mistake with one of the most versatile writers of late modern genre fiction. On the other hand, as King's work has done for more than forty years, *From a Buick 8* asks one of horror fiction's classic questions: What happens when we're confronted with something that can't possibly happen? Something that can't possibly exist—but does? Part of the answer comes as Troopers Curtis Wilcox and Sandy Dearborn prepare to dissect one of the strange, frightening creatures that seem to have simply appeared in Shed B, courtesy of the Buick 8 that is anything but just an old car. They want what we all want in the stories we have told for millennia. They want to know. They want to understand. They want the answer. But "'what if that's a lie?' Sandy asked. . . . 'What if there's no satisfaction? What if you're never able to solve for *x*?'"[1] That is, what if there are no answers, and all we're left with are the questions?

Answers are contingent and ephemeral, King tells us again and again. Questions are forever.

The two state troopers never get their answers. Not really. They never solve the puzzle of the Buick 8. Dearborn, the barracks commander, sees more than anyone what the car-that-is-not-a-car represents: an alien landscape with, as Lovecraft might have put it, "colors out of space," bats that are not *quite* bats, and an atmosphere as toxic to us as ours is to whatever crosses over from *there* into *here*.[2] But he still doesn't understand it. That brief glimpse doesn't solve for *x*. Was the Buick 8 a portal between alternate dimensions or a parallel universe, between *here* and *not-here*? Was it a probe, or some kind of transporter, plying the unimaginable light-years between Earth and another world? Was it a trap, like the muddy, battered station wagon in "Mile 81"? "Not much different from a Venus flytrap or a pitcher plant," Sandy says to Curtis's son, Ned. "Don't you see that?"[3]

At the beginning of the novel, as eighteen-year-old Ned struggles to come to terms with the death of his father, who was killed in the line of duty, he echoes Piper Libby and Charlie Jacobs as he tells Sandy, "If there was a God, there'd be a reason. . . . If there was a God, there'd be some kind of thread running through it. But there isn't. Not that I can see."[4] We search for meaning, we pattern seekers, and are deeply uncomfortable when things don't easily fit the familiar. Events that have "that odd, flat, declamatory quality which is the sole property of Polaroid photographs" disturb us. "*I see a world where there's only cause and effect*, they seem to say. *A world where every object is an avatar and no gods move behind the scenes*."[5] No purpose, no meaning, no plan.

The Buick 8 is Stephen King's reverse rabbit hole. Rather than conducting Alice to Wonderland, it is another thin spot, letting creatures from a different *somewhere* come here. Rather than talking rabbits and a mad hatter's tea party, however, these strange beings expire screaming and terrified in an environment for which they were never intended and cannot themselves understand. King's novel makes a single, oblique reference to Lewis Carroll's iconic nonsense fantasy. When the Buick 8 has one of its "events" and its trunk spews a cloud of what the troopers decide are leaves, one of the younger staties draws a picture. "'It looks kind of like a smile,' the kid said. 'Like a goddam grin,' I said."[6] Indeed, King includes the drawing in the text—a rare moment in his storyworlds. When the leaves disappear, it is as though they vanish just like Carroll's Cheshire Cat, "ending with a grin, which remained some time after the rest of it had gone."[7]

As we have seen, throughout King's work cracks in the world get wedged open in a variety of ways: the enormous spacecraft Bobbi Anderson uncovers in *The Tommyknockers*, or the alien ship that crash-lands in *Dreamcatcher*; the flytrap station wagon in "Mile 81," the standing stones in Ackerman's Field, or the yawning chasm of the China Pit. Now, we have the mysterious car-that-is-not-a-car. *From a Buick 8* is not a "religious" story in any conventional sense. Certainly, it lacks *Desperation*'s explicitly religious storyline and there are no readily identifiable religious characters such as we find in *The Stand*, *Needful Things*, or *Under the Dome*. But, like many other entries into the King canon, it raises profoundly religious questions, or, more accurately, profound questions about the nature of reality, questions that purport to have been answered by religious doctrine and dogma. If much of what we think we know about reality is, at best, incomplete, at worst, dead wrong, why entertain the notion that what we conjecture, what we imagine about the nature of things, must be true? In this, King confronts us directly with the question of cosmology.

Confronting Cosmology

Edgar Freemantle was a successful contractor until a horrific accident at a job site. "When a pickup truck, even a Dodge Ram with all the bells and whistles," Edgar tells us, "argues with a twelve-story crane, the pickup is going to lose every time."[8] For Edgar, this meant losing his right arm, much of the sight in his right eye, a significant portion of memory and emotional control, and, as far as he could tell, his entire life. "*At first you were afraid you'd die*," his friend Wireman tells him much later, "*then you were afraid you wouldn't*."[9] On the advice of his psychiatrist, Edgar takes a "geographical," a yearlong period of recuperation in an entirely different place. For him, this means traveling from the bleak cold of St. Paul, Minnesota, to a small islet in southern Florida called Duma Key. There, as part of his recovery, he decides he's got the time and he wants to learn to paint. He discovers a ferocious talent for the work and his paintings quickly become wildly popular in the local art community. His almost supernatural ability, however, manifests on canvas as both a window into and a vehicle for a dark and malevolent aspect of the unseen order. This is, after all, Stephen King.

Duma Key takes a while to build, though always with the assurance that Something Terrible will come to pass. Unlike writers who avoid foreshadowing, King is happy to let his Constant Reader know just how bad things are going to get, then dare them to follow. At the opening of Edgar Freemantle's first and last art show, three forerunners grace the text like the derelict barque crossing the cover of the *Duma Key* Pocket Books edition. First, when it's clear that the show is a "sell," that Edgar's paintings have sold out, the gallery owner toasts the success of his newest artist. "We raised our glasses and drank," Edgar tells us, "not knowing that my brilliant career was, for all practical purposes, at an end."[10] Second, scant minutes later, Elizabeth Eastlake, the dowager of Duma Key and former doyenne of the Sarasota art scene, flamboyantly lights a cigarette in defiance of local ordinance and twenty-first-century propriety. In retrospect, Edgar wonders "if she would have smoked more of it if she had known it was to be her last."[11] And, third, as the rest of the guests are leaving for home, Edgar says goodbye to his daughter, Ilse. Looking at her through the hazy, polarized glass of the departure lounge, he tells us, "I wish with all my heart that I could have seen her better, because I never saw her again."[12]

These forerunners, these moments of precognitive storytelling, remind us that far fewer things are under our control than we imagine, that far less than we presume is as we think it is. "Not only is the universe queerer than we suppose," wrote geneticist and evolutionary biologist J. B. S. Haldane, "it is queerer than we *can* suppose."[13] A significant part of religion's function as a principal guardian of the status quo is to reduce the tension implicit in Haldane's statement, to render the universe less strange, less frightening, more familiar. But what if all our various religious imaginings got it wrong? In storyworlds ranging from Derry, Maine, to Wentworth, Ohio, and from Florida's Duma Key to a lonely peak in western New England, Stephen King challenges us to question everything we think we know about the nature of reality. "I didn't want to write about answers," the dark theologian reminds us. "I wanted to write about questions."[14]

Derry, Maine: "Before the Universe . . ."

In 1997 the United Nations sponsored a literary anthology to celebrate the advent of the six-billionth child, who was to be born that year. Novelist Salman Rushdie, best known for *The Satanic Verses* and for the death sentence pronounced on him by the Ayatollah Khomeini, contributed a short essay. "Dear Little Six Billionth Person," Rushdie begins, telling his tiny, unknown brother or sister about some of the various ways "the other 5,999,999 of us" have answered the question, Where did we come from?[15] "As human knowledge has grown," he writes, "it has also become quite plain that every religious story ever told about how we got here is quite simply wrong. This, finally, is what all religions have in common. They didn't get it right. . . . But here's something genuinely odd. The wrongness of the sacred tales has not lessened the zeal of the devout."[16] Indeed, for Rushdie's friend and fellow secularist Christopher Hitchens, that religion "wholly misrepresents the origins of man and the cosmos" and "that because of this original error it manages to combine the maximum of servility with the maximum of solipsism" are two of "the four irreducible objections to religious faith."[17]

In their own ways, the scientist, the novelist, and the pundit point us toward the cosmology of *It*, rehearsed in a mere two pages out of a book that spans more than a thousand. There, King posits an alternate vision of reality, one that is no less rational for being part of his novel than any of the other fictions taken as historical truth by those who come to the question with "the zeal of the devout." In these two pages, King implies what Rushdie states: when it comes to knowing what reality is *really* about, theologically speaking, all bets are off.

"Something new had happened," It thinks to Itself. Hiding deep in the sewers beneath Derry, Maine, It waits in the dank and the dark as the members of the Losers Club hunt It down. "For the first time in forever, something new. Before the universe there had been only two things. One was Itself and the other was the Turtle."[18] Forget about the Turtle for the moment. Set it aside, and consider instead those three simple words: *Before the universe.* Few phrases could make the religious imaginings of a primitive bipedal species on a backwater planet seem more provincial, more pedestrian than this. *Before the universe.* Before there was anything, there was It. It was—already. The Turtle may have "vomited the universe out whole," but that doesn't change anything.[19] It was and It is. And It is there in Derry. With, as it were, this lapse into form and substance, came something new, something unexpected in a being, a creature, a force for which the concepts of "expected" and "unexpected" heretofore held no meaning.

For the first time, It knew fear, and it did so "because the only thing It had in common with the Stupid Old Turtle and the cosmology of the Macroverse outside the puny egg of this universe was just this: all living things must abide by the laws of the shape they inhabit."[20] Once again, forget the Turtle. Forget the law of shapes and forms. Consider just this: "the cosmology of the Macroverse outside the *puny egg of this universe*." This, finally, is what Haldane and Rushdie and Hitchens mean: that what we think we know can never match the unutterable strangeness of what is, and the more dogmatically we proclaim to know, the more likely we are to have it wrong.

None of this is to say, of course, that King has it *right*, or that *It* proposes a cosmology meant to be taken as anything other than a device for a horror novel. *It* is not a stealth ontology, Stephen King's vision of the way the world *actually* is—Macroverse and all. Bearing in mind the counsel of the scientist and the novelist and the pundit, though, we may say that in the context of our varied religious imaginings, the vast panoply of creation stories we've told ourselves, *It* makes no more or less sense than any other. *It* doesn't provide an answer, but it's not meant to. *It* points us once again to a question misattributed to Albert Einstein, but no less important for that: "Is the universe a friendly place or not?"

Certainly, in this storyworld it isn't. As Jennifer Hecht writes in her introduction to *Doubt: A History*, "We live in a meaning-rupture because we are human and the universe is not."[21] That is, hawkers of intelligent design can tell us all they want that a benevolent God created the universe just the way it is and just for us, but our terrible fragility in the face of that creation continually pushes back against this claim. From the cold vacuum of space to the dark and unimaginable pressure at the bottom of the ocean, from Tennyson's "Nature, red in tooth and claw" to the myriad horrors we daily visit on each other, the world seems anything but designed for our benefit. Which takes us nearly a thousand miles west of Maine, to a quiet street in a small town in Ohio.

Wentworth, Ohio: "It Has No Religion"

To ask what "religion" means in a storyworld, what it adds to the narrative, is in part to ask what happens if we take it away. How differently would America's dark theologian read without the religious themes, plotlines, and subtexts we've discussed throughout this book? Although a cataclysmic battle between "good and evil" is hardly limited to the religious imagination, without it *The Stand* would be a very different story. Likewise, the kind of psychological control *Carrie*'s Margaret White wields over her daughter could easily be imagined without her extreme fundamentalism, but it would take the story in an entirely different direction. Although it's conceivable that both *The Shining* and *The Dead Zone* could work as horror fiction without their religious subtexts or background, *Pet Sematary* or *Needful Things* could not. With that in mind, how differently would *Desperation* read without the religious journeys of David Carver and Johnny Marinville?

As it happens, in *Desperation* and its mirror novel, *The Regulators*, Stephen King offers us a rare paired example through which we can explore the work of religion in one storyworld in terms of its absence in another. We can ask *why* include such a prominent religious theme in one, and *what* that theme adds. Both *Desperation* and *The Regulators* were published in 1996, the former under King's own name, the latter as Richard Bachman—more than a decade after a Washington, D.C., bookstore clerk outed the pseudonym. Both novels involve essentially the same characters, but each follows an altogether different plot and tells the story of Tak in an almost-but-not-quite-our-universe way.

Unlike *Desperation, The Regulators* takes place along one block of a quiet street in suburban Ohio—a setting well off King's usual beaten path, but which stands in as his literary Middletown.[22] Here in Wentworth, David Carver is not a twelve-year-old boy, nor is he the hero of the story that he is in *Desperation*. Certainly, he is no Christ-figure. In the Bachman universe, he's the Carver husband and father, and he dies in the initial supernatural attack that sets the novel's events in motion. Similarly, *The Regulators'* Johnny Marinville is not a well-respected but dissolute man of letters on a road trip to recover former glory, but a promising novelist whose first book provoked comparisons with Hemingway, Faulkner, and Steinbeck. Unwilling to assume the weight of such a prestigious literary mantle, however, this version of Johnny Marinville is content to live quietly on Poplar Street and write children's books for a living. In *Desperation*, Collie Entragen is a gigantic highway patrolman possessed by the entity Tak, while in *The Regulators* he is a disgraced former police officer who has been falsely accused and dismissed from the force.

Tak, as well, is different in the two storyworlds. In *Desperation*, we have the sense of vast, contending cosmologies, a universal conflict only the latest skirmish of which plays itself out in a near-deserted Nevada mining town. David's God against the primal malevolence. There, Tak's energy is too much for humans to contain and its hosts gradually balloon in size until they literally split. The entity then sloughs off the used meat-suit like a snake shedding its skin, and takes control of another temporary host. In the end, Tak is banished from our world, but not destroyed, and any relief we feel can only be temporary.

On Poplar Street, Tak works through Seth Garin, a four-year-old autistic boy who is the sole survivor of his family's earlier encounter with the strange being. Unlike *Desperation* and the China Pit mine, here there is no cosmological conflict, and the novel, including Tak, could easily be read as an extended psychokinesis story—not unlike *Carrie* or *Firestarter*. Indeed, in *The Regulators* Tak could be interpreted as a metaphor for the latent abilities of the human mind, the undiscovered mental country that is the mind in the grip of autism. Because Tak's assault manifests in the form of Seth's favorite television shows, and much of the action to defeat the entity is intrapsychic, it's entirely reasonable to interpret the storyworld's logic metaphorically. As the residents grasp at language to describe their plight, Old Doc asks, "Is it a demon, Aud? Some kind of demon?" "No," Seth's aunt and guardian, Audrey Wyler, answers. "It has no . . . no religion, I suppose you'd say. Unless TV counts. It's more like a tumor, I think. One that's conscious and enjoys cruelty."[23]

Once again, we are faced with an unseen order so alien, so outside our frame of reference, that we struggle even for language to describe it. For thousands of years, the heart of our search for meaning has been the quest for a cause. Why did *this* happen and not *that*? Why did this happen to *me*? What have I done wrong or, more importantly, whom have I displeased? Malevolent beings from brownies, sprites, and leprechauns to demons, demigods, and angry ghosts have borne the brunt of our constant need for a pattern. Inequity aversion, our instinctual reaction to perceptions of unfairness—a trait we share with a number of other animal species—tells us, rightly or wrongly, that there must be a reason for what is happening. Nocturnal emissions are the result of spiritual attack by *succubi*. What we would today call psychomotor epilepsy our ancestors understood as demonic possession. An epidemic is not the result of contaminated drinking water, but our failure to honor the proper gods—or to honor the gods properly.

Absent its implicit and explicit religious components, *Desperation* would be an entirely different novel—a road-slasher story like so many others. The only "religious" aspect in *The Regulators* is a brief scene through which King highlights the hypocrisy and powerlessness of fundamentalist Christianity. Indeed, more than anything and like so many of King's major works, *The Regulators* demonstrates our *lack of understanding* about the universe and the frightening speed with which any pretense to civilized behavior falls away in the face of the threatening and inexplicable. When the residents of Poplar Street are confronted with challenge and chaos, little remains to bind them together except a shared postal code and the occasional waved hello or goodbye.

So we return to the question of difference: why include "religion" if stories can be told as well without it? *The Regulators* is no less a horror story for its lack of religion than *Desperation* is for its inclusion. Whether his Constant Readers have the ability to articulate their religious beliefs or not, King recognizes how deeply embedded are their various understandings of the unseen order. America remains both profoundly religious and acutely conflicted about that. The storied predictions of secularists and anti-theists notwithstanding, religion is not going away anytime soon, but how we think about it, and what we think it is, will continue to evolve. We will continue to ask what the heck is going on.

Duma Key, Florida: "What the Fuck Is That Thing?"

Duma Key is a story on par with *Bag of Bones*. Instead of a blocked writer escaping to his summer house in the wake of his wife's death and finding there the ghosts of a buried past, a badly injured man comes to a lonely Florida islet to recover from his accident, and discovers an extraordinary talent for painting, and a disturbing supernatural ability. Edgar Freemantle's artwork has the power both to heal and to kill, a force connected to the epicenter of tragedy that is Duma Key. For nearly five hundred pages, King follows Edgar's journey into what amounts to "psychic artwork," a kind of "spirit painting" akin to automatic writing. Then, like the *Perse*, the death ship that appears on the horizon, the story takes a much darker turn, one King has warned us about many times.

On Duma Key, Edgar and his two friends, Jack and Wireman, come to believe in ghosts—and much worse. Ghosts, they discover, can indeed interact with our world. They can "write on canvas," they can "move Ouija board planchettes and write on window-frost."[24] When the *Perse* first appears in Edgar's artwork, she's obviously a ship of the dead, perhaps even the damned. As the "three-masted corpse" emerges from the sea mist, and we catch our first glimpse behind "the *Perse*'s disguise," "hundreds of skeleton arms arose from the water in a dripping salute. And standing on the foredeck was a baggy, pallid thing, vaguely female, wearing a decayed something that might have been a cloak, a winding shroud."[25] However frightening the apparition, though, the reality is far more horrific than Edgar might have imagined. "*This is everything awful*, it said. *This is everything you feared to find waiting in the dark.*"[26]

Edgar's rule of thumb is that "If one person sees a thing, it could be a hallucination. If two people see it, chances of reality improve exponentially."[27] When the first "sailor" from the death ship comes for him, we know already that it's not a phantasm. Someone else saw it too. "'What the *fuck* is that thing?' Wireman whispered."[28] Perhaps it's a vampire, Edgar wonders, grasping desperately for something even vaguely familiar. There "are no such things as vampires, Edgar!" Jack insists. "There could be ghosts. I'll give you that much—I think almost everyone believes there could be ghosts—but there's no such thing as a vampire."[29] Edgar points out, though, that "maybe vampires aren't the only things that come back from the dead."[30] When Jack suggests zombies, pop culture's other low-hanging fruit, Jack waves him off. "I thought of the *Perse* with her rotting sails," he writes. "Let's say deserters."[31]

King tells us the conditions for this *not* to be a hallucination, then promptly fulfills them. Perhaps Edgar was not *meant* to survive the accident that awakened his paranormal artistic ability. Perhaps he cheated death on the job site and the Grim Reaper has come ashore on Duma Key to collect. If only it were that simple; if only it were that . . . ordinary. "'Okay, it's a ship of the dead,' Jack said. . . . 'If that's what's coming for me in the end, I sort of wish I'd never been born in the first place.'"[32]

This is not merely a "ghost story as god-talk." On Duma Key, King confronts us with another cosmology completely alien to our more comfortable imaginings, one that answers any question about the friendliness of the universe with a sour laugh fading to a desolate, despairing chuckle. As the novel slips from simply spooky to something else altogether, King once again sets out to parse the nature of the unseen order, and goes from a ghost story to a vision of something much more threatening, much more malevolent, something . . . Other.

More like It. More like Tak.

Almost without noticing, we leave the realm of the familiar—even the hauntingly familiar, such as ghosts, spirits, and spooks. Then, King raises the question of what Perse really *is*. Even when Edgar is attacked by the first of the death ship "deserters," the "one-man press gang" that would take him to become "part of the crew," even then we sense that this is merely an opening gambit.[33] The horror to come is nothing so prosaic as a long-drowned sailor dragging some poor unfortunate down to Davy Jones's Locker. Things could not possibly be that easy. "Perse," Edgar wonders. "What exactly was she?"[34]

And that's the question, isn't it?

"Where would a thing like that have come from to begin with, Edgar?" asks Jack, as they struggle to grasp what they have encountered. "A phrase rose to my lips, from where I don't know, only that it wasn't my own: *There were elder gods in those days; kings and queens they were.*"[35] *Duma Key* contains a number of these Lovecraftian references, Stephen King's tip of the gimme cap to the old master. Edgar's doomed daughter, Ilse, for example, was writing an English Lit paper on the weird fiction of the strange Rhode Islander. As soon as Lovecraft is invoked, and the possibility of an alternate vision of reality introduced, we learn more about the "Perse-thing."

The three friends recognize that the ship that consistently appears in Edgar's psychic paintings is "a ship of the dead," but that still leaves them groping in the dark for an explanation. "A ship called . . . what?" Wireman wonders. "*Persephone?*"[36] King's subtext, though, whispers, *Call her that if you want, if it brings you comfort and gives the experience meaning.* After all, what's in a name? What is "Yahweh" or "Allah" or "Jehovah," or any of the countless names by which we have tried to fathom the depths of difference between the seen and the unseen orders?[37] They are nothing more than our limited attempts to label the inexplicable. "It doesn't matter," Edgar replies, "we're not thinking Greek mythology here. We're talking about something much older and more monstrous."[38]

Daughter of Zeus and Demeter, Persephone is the Greek goddess of the underworld and with her mother a central figure in the mystery religion that flourished in the town of Eleusis, a few miles outside Athens. In Book XI of *The Odyssey*, which contains one of the earliest descriptions of Hades, Homer relates how Odysseus, having departed the island of Circe and sailed to the very edge of the world, sees and speaks with the honored dead. Finally, as the shade of the divine hero Heracles departs, Odysseus looks around, "in case any other heroes who had previously died might still come."[39] He hoped particularly to see Theseus and his friend Pirithous; instead "countless hordes of the dead swarmed together with frightening shrieks."[40] Now terrified "that dread Persephone might send from Hades a Gorgon head of terrible portent," Odysseus returns to his ship and orders the crew to cast off.[41]

While this may be King's classical source, he explicitly reimagines Persephone not so much as a goddess, but as the "Perse-thing," "baggy, pallid" and only "vaguely female," standing at the death ship's prow. I don't want to make too much of the connection—ghostly conveyances for the dead or those about to die are common in many cultures—but more important here is King's suggestion that this is not Persephone, but "Persephone." That is, the goddess of the Eleusinian mysteries was simply one more mask worn by something inconceivably older and more alien, something we came over time to regard as entirely malevolent. The Greeks did not invent the gods, King tells us, not in this storyworld. They may have given them names, put the primal forces in familiar bib-and-tucker, but those forces were alive—if "alive" is even the right word—numberless eons before the children of Zeus crawled from their caves. Like *It*, *Desperation*, *Insomnia*, and *Revival*, *Duma Key* raises questions of cosmology, and posits an alternate, altogether darker "Once upon a time . . ."

Something is here on Duma Key, something terrible. But not ghosts, something *far worse* than ghosts. Something like Perse.

"She's been playing the game for a long time," Edgar writes. "I had an idea she'd been old when the Children of Israel were still grubbing in the gardens of Egypt. Sometimes, she slept, but now she was awake."[42] Think of the scroll discovered at the beginning of Universal Pictures' classic *The Mummy*, the one mocked by the Western rationalist, but eyed warily by the one who knows that the ancient gods are not dead, but merely sleeping.[43] Consider the ancient evil that is the demon Pazuzu, awakened from millennia-long slumber when *The Exorcist*'s Father Merrin unearths its likeness in an all-but-forgotten Iraqi dig site. Like these, once again King ushers us into the realm of *what if?* What if reality is not only "queerer than we suppose, but queerer than we *can* suppose"? Indeed, as they prepare for the final battle, not unlike those trapped *Under the Dome*, Edgar admits that he "had a queer sense of being part of a prepared slide. Soon I would be placed under a microscope and studied."[44] In *Duma Key*, Perse is one of the Old Ones, though even to call her an "elder god" in the Lovecraftian sense may limit our understanding of what King is suggesting. These are the names we give to forces so different from us that masks are all we have.

Stephen King has said often that horror fiction is about the status quo—the reinscription of normality—but storyworlds such as *Duma Key* challenge what we think the status quo is. Perhaps that's what's been fooling us all along. As Wireman and Edgar send the ancient being into the depths one more time, "I had an idea that Perse was good at finding her way back to the surface. That she had done it before, and would again."[45]

Like the Losers Club chasing It into Derry's labyrinthine drainage system, the men on Duma Key descend into a derelict cistern to confront Perse. Were Edgar the only one to see, we could easily read *Duma Key* as a kind of Jungian allegory. The wounded hero seeks closure by descending into the earth, facing terrible trials, and returning to the surface—the same but changed. If it were only Edgar, this could be the classic hero's journey. But others see, others know, others tell us that something *else* is going on.

As with It and Tak, as with the unnamed horrors of Ackerman's Field and Skytop, Maine, Perse is not eliminated in the end, but merely contained. Defeated for the moment, she is not destroyed and the threat remains. Indeed, in terms of cosmology, stories such as these question whether something so ancient, so primevally Other, can actually be destroyed. Against such forces, says King, we win the battle only for a time, but we do not win the war. It is as though the war is not ours to win. We are not at the center of the universe.

All of King's varied cosmologies remind us that "religion" does not describe the way the world is. For all our god-talk, our systematic theology, our sacred stories, we can only represent the world as we believe it is or would like it to be. Through a variety of social, cultural, and psychological mechanisms, though, religion chief among them, we tend to forget this not-insignificant fact.[46] In this respect, *Duma Key* is an important book in King's canon, not because of what Edgar and the others see—the reality of the entity they call "Perse" overlaid with the myth of Persephone—but because of the ways that primal force might have been imagined by those who encountered it in the past. Perhaps those ancient "Children of Israel" met Perse in the guise of Moloch, to whom the sacred texts suggest children without number were sacrificed. Perhaps, deep in the Mesoamerican jungle, the Aztecs masked their experience of her as the god Huitzilopochtli, the one who required blood sacrifice to maintain its version of balance in the unseen order. Perhaps to medieval Catholics, Perse appeared as the Devil, the central villain in the horrid morality play that was the *Malleus Maleficarum*.

In this regard it's easy to write off Carson Jones, Ilse's insufferably Baptist boyfriend, wannabe pastor, and lead singer for the gospel group the Hummingbirds. For much of the novel, Edgar's rather unsubtle dislike for Carson looks as though it could foreshadow a final showdown between father and fiancé, or that he could in some way be the source of the conflict around Edgar's supernatural gift. When Edgar, Wireman, and Jack battle Perse and her minions, it seems as though Carson might even appear as a proxy *deus ex machina*, a slightly more odious version of David Carver. He turns out to be none of these. Indeed, we never actually meet him. Ilse breaks up with him when she learns that he's slept with his Hummingbird duet partner. After that, he disappears from *Duma Key*. We could dismiss him as a red herring, perhaps a character King included early in the novel, but couldn't figure out how to use, so he was benched, as it were.

But that would be *too* easy. At a couple of places in the final battle, Edgar wonders aloud whether there might be some kind of positive force working on their behalf, but these are never more than slight rhetorical hints. Compared to the magnitude of the danger Perse represents, the entirely Other order of reality her very existence signifies, Carson the "good Christian" is King's way of highlighting the pettiness and banality of human religious consciousness. Put differently, if people *really* knew what was going on out there, would anyone care in the least about the

Hummingbirds or the God they want to proclaim? When faced with the great blue heron that serves as Perse's eye in the sky over Duma Key, one tends to see the Hummingbirds as little more than the inconsequential avatars of a meaningless religion.

In terms of the metataxis of horror, this is the shift in the sacred order through insignificance: "the fear that the gods to whom we pray or make offerings, whose altars we adorn with service and sacrifice, whose rules we follow and to whose promises we cling, simply don't matter."[47]

De Vermis Mysterii: "We're Not Meant to See"

In terms of *Revival*, if the God of Motton's little Methodist congregation is a fraud, "a profitable and self-sustaining construct of the world's churches," then what *is* the unseen order into which Charlie Jacobs taps at the end of the novel?[48] What is the cosmology of Skytop, the thunderstruck mountain peak in rural Maine where he hopes to unlock the mysteries of the universe?

Since leaving Motton in the wake of the Terrible Sermon, Charlie has earned his keep in carnival sideshows, making "Portraits in Lightning" and offering electric snake oil along the way. As Jamie says, "You went from preaching to huckstering," though it's clear the older man never abandoned his quest to understand the nature of reality.[49] He still believes that the truth of life and death lies hidden in what he calls the "secret electricity." Indeed, he counters archly when Jamie confronts him, of more than three thousand "verified cures" through this "secret electricity," less than 3 percent of his "patients" experienced permanent side effects of one kind or another. So it seems that *something has happened*—the only question is *what*? When Charlie cures Astrid, Jamie's teenage sweetheart who is now dying of lung cancer, he tells them, "The energy I intend to tap—energy present in this room, all around us at this very moment—can't be measured by ordinary instruments. It is essentially unknowable"—a thought that does little to lower Jamie's anxiety.[50]

As we noted earlier, if *'Salem's Lot* is King's nod to *Dracula*, then *Revival*, the title of which is at least a triple entendre, is his homage to the first great classic of horror fiction, Mary Shelley's *Frankenstein*. As we have seen before, though, in the race to find out what *happens* in one of King's novels, many readers might well miss what's *happening*, specifically, the revival of a young woman who could have been named "Mary Shelley," and who had borne a son she named Victor.[51] While King's debt to Lovecraft is also apparent in *Revival*, this is *Frankenstein*, even to the remote laboratory at Skytop—though this aspect of the story owes more to James Whale's classic 1931 film than Shelley's original text. Nonetheless, this is where Charlie hopes to harness the power of natural lightning to solve the enigma of "secret electricity." Peering through death's keyhole, he demands to glimpse the unseen that lies beyond the door of the seen. To accomplish this, Charlie dares to revive the woman who might have been called Mary Shelley, and who at this point in the novel has been dead for about fifteen minutes.

"We're not meant to see," Jamie protests, as the real horror of what Charlie intends finally seeps in. Yet, while we might not be meant to see, religious believers without number have felt sufficiently competent to conjecture, to proclaim, and to condemn based on what they believe. Charlie does not want to believe; he wants to know. As a young Reverend Charles Jacobs told his rural congregation nearly half a century earlier, "There's no proof of these after-life destinations; no backbone of science; there is only the bald assurance, coupled with our powerful need to believe *that it all makes sense*."[52] And that, for the Charlie Jacobs who is nearing the end of his own life, is one of the lies he wants to expose on Skytop.

"I intend to bring Mary Fay back to some form of life," he tells an increasingly terrified Jamie. "I intend to learn the truth of what's on the other side of the door that leads into the Kingdom of Death. I'll learn it from the lips of someone who's been there."[53] Once again, King returns to the question that has animated our religious imagination from the beginning. "I want to know what the universe has in store for all of us once this life is over," Charlie tells Jamie, "and I intend to find out."[54] As much as he wants to know, however, he wants even more to throw that knowledge in the face of religious believers—all the Myra Harringtons, Reggie Keltons, and Ray Easterbrooks who walked out on his pain and abandoned him on the Day of the Terrible Sermon. At all of them—and their anemic God—Charlie wants nothing more than to hurl his contempt: "*Here it is! What all your crusades and murder in the name of God were for! Here it is, and how do you like it?*"[55]

What comes through the door following the woman's brief revival recalls not only Shelley's *Frankenstein*, but King's short story "N.," which was written just a few years before *Revival*, and H. P. Lovecraft's "From Beyond." Indeed, the resuscitation sequence at the end of the book is reminiscent of the cautionary, admonitory tones adopted by many of Lovecraft's fictional narrators. As difficult as it is for Jamie Morton to record his experiences later, "I must," he tells King's Constant Reader, "if only as a warning for anyone else who contemplates some similar experiment in damnation, and may read these words, and turn back because of them."[56] That is, through Jamie, Charlie, and the woman he brought back momentarily, King reminds us that whatever we think we know about the unseen order is speculation at best. Our Sunday morning stories may keep the worst of our existential dread in check, *Revival* says, but they serve little more purpose than that. What may lie on the other side, what may come from beyond when cracks appear in the wall between the worlds, should cause us to be afraid. Be very afraid.

What the two men learn is that our world, as solid and real as it appears to us in life, is the real illusion, "nothing but a scrim, as flimsy as an old nylon stocking. The *true* world was behind it."[57] Contra secularists such as Rushdie and Hitchens, though, just because human religious imaginings got it wrong, doesn't mean there's nothing there. In fact, as Jamie discovers, it's "an insane netherworld I now know is so close to our own."[58]

> The foolish mirage of earthly life had been torn away and instead of the heaven preachers of all persuasions promised, what awaited them was a dead city of cyclopean stone blocks below a sky that was itself a scrim. . . . Beyond the sky were *entities*. They were alive, and all-powerful, and totally insane.[59]

"One idea saved my sanity," Jamie concludes, "and I still cling to it: the possibility that this nightmare landscape was itself a mirage."[60] As his youthful psychiatrist tells him years later, in tones reminiscent of N.'s Dr. Bonsaint, even with everything Jamie experienced that terrifying day, the day of Charlie Jacobs's truly Terrible Sermon, "it still wouldn't follow that the vision you saw of the hellish afterlife was a *true* vision."[61]

He may hold tight to the thought that more near-death or revival experiences describe positive afterlife events and outcomes than negative, but that doesn't banish the sheer horror of what reveals itself at Skytop. He knows what he saw. King closes with a passage worthy of Lovecraft himself, words in which the puny imaginings of human religions are drowned.

> Horrors beyond comprehension wait on the other side of that door. Not just the land of death, but the land *beyond* death, a place full of insane colors, mad geometry, and bottomless chasms where the Great Ones live their endless, alien lives and think their endless, malevolent thoughts.[62]

One Last Trip to Derry: "There Are Yet Other Levels"

"Some of horror's current popularity," Stephen King told audiences in the early 1980s, "has to do with the failure of religion."[63] As "a fallen-away Methodist," if he fell away, he wasn't alone. In the late 1960s and throughout the 1970s, a number of mainline denominations witnessed such precipitous membership decline that the phenomenon spawned a sociological specialty known as secularization theory—the (mistaken) belief that religion itself was on the decline.[64] Millions of people like King went on to describe themselves, somewhat vaguely, as "spiritual but not religious," which was their way of retaining connection with a measure of belief in the unseen order, without having to maintain allegiance to any organized religious community. Belief in the gods had not disappeared, however ambiguous and ambivalent our relationships with them have become.

And, as King points out, through it all, our burning questions remain. Scary stories and sacred myths address the same key issues. "Horror fiction," he told fans gathered at the public library in Billerica, Maine, "supernatural horror fiction, suggests that we go on. All those supernatural possibilities are there, good or bad, black or white, they suggest that we go on."[65] Which is to say, once we pass the deadfall that awaits each of us, there is a There *there*. Of all the things he said that evening, the last reason King gave for reading horror fiction is that "it's a rehearsal for death. . . . We know it's going to happen," and "we have to do something about that awareness."[66]

"Religion" is the principal way we talk about these possibilities, the dominant means by which we give our hopes and fears shape and texture. Indeed, part of the appeal of both horror stories and religious myth is not simply *that* we still believe in the supernatural, the unseen order, but *why* we continue to believe. In many ways, especially in terms of the evolutionary timescale, we are not so very far from the caves of our hominin ancestors. We may know different things, but we don't think with different brains. However locked away they may be, their fears remain our fears, their pattern-seeking and meaning-making equipment the same as ours: *Homo sapiens* standard-issue.

As we have seen, although his myriad stories cross paths in a few extended storyworlds—notably the Castle Rock novels and the stories set in the dark spaces of Derry, Maine—unlike H. P. Lovecraft, King offers little in the way of a coherent or consistent vision of the unseen order, and fans would be hard-pressed to generate anything like Lovecraft's Cthulhu mythos, a single dark theology. Put differently, what remains consistent in King's horror fiction is the *seen order*. It's the *unseen* he changes up in different stories and myriad ways. Once again, rather than proposing answers, he poses questions. He imagines how these seen and unseen orders interact, occasionally collide, but always influence each other.

In conclusion, let's make one last trip to Derry.

As a couple of pages do near the end of *It*, a dozen or so pages tucked into the middle of King's 1994 novel *Insomnia* raise once again questions of being and cosmology. For retirees Ralph Roberts and Lois Chasse, who grew up and grew old in Derry, the way the universe works must have seemed as limited as the narrow band of visible light that illuminates all we think we know about the world. That is, until a strange bout of insomnia altered their perception, and enabled them to see three small, strange creatures they came to call the "little bald doctors."

Initially dismissing the beings as a side effect of sleep deprivation, Ralph thought that they "looked like aliens in a movie about UFO abductions—*Communion*, perhaps, or *Fire in the Sky*."[67] Both films, however, are based on real events and what those involved claim are real experiences. The former is adapted from fellow horror writer Whitley Strieber's novel of the same name. Strieber insists that the events he has fictionalized actually happened to him and his family at their

cabin in upstate New York.[68] After one particularly frightening experience, Strieber's son, Andrew, dubbed the aliens the "little blue doctors."
"That was what *they* called them," King writes in *Insomnia*, "the folks
who claim to have been abducted by them . . . examined by them . . .
operated on by them in some cases. They were physicians from space,
proctologists from the great beyond."[69] If we have encountered these
beings in the past, King implies, they have been written into our myths
as gods, and into popular culture as extraterrestrials. What Ralph and
Lois quickly learn, though, is that the truth may be much stranger still.

Two of these beings allow the perplexed humans to watch as they perform their appointed task in the great skein of life. That is, they are the
ones who gently and carefully help people to die. The "little bald doctors," though, deny the two senior citizens the most obvious category,
the easiest vocabulary. "We're no angels, Ralph," one of them says.[70] They
are something else entirely, something for which other theologies, other
forms of god-talk, must be invoked. "Do you see and understand that
what we do, we do with love and respect?" they ask. "That we are, in fact,
the physicians of last resort?"[71]

For all our pretension to knowledge, we understand the process of
dying no more than we understand the nature of death or the afterlife.
By and large, we know when someone is alive, and when she is dead. We
know the difference between the states of being alive and being dead.
And, within what must seem to some extravagant, to others painfully
limited parameters, we can keep one state from becoming the other—at
least for a time. But, King prods his Constant Reader, what do we *really* know about it, and who decides when it's time? Perhaps, as the two
strange beings imply, were it not for their intervention, the "small, unimportant *snick!*" that marks the severing of one's life string, the kiss on
the forehead and the blessing, "Go in peace, friend," the process of dying
might stretch out endlessly. Taken thus, perhaps they are closer to angels
than they imagine.

"We don't have names," one of them tells Ralph and Lois, "not the way
Short-Timers do—but you may call us after the fates in the story this
man has already told you," that is, the three sisters of Fate, the *moirai*
of Greek mythology.[72] Clotho is the one who spins the thread of each
human life, while Lachesis measures the thread allotted to each of us.
Atropos, the one known as "inevitable," and a principal supernatural

antagonist in *Insomnia*, cuts the thread and releases each separate life into death. Aliens, angels, or the incarnation of destiny—whatever we call them, King suggests, they are only words, the cloak of language, the artifice of vocabulary. They can never be more than our pale attempt to render even marginally understandable the least comprehensible, but most undeniable experience of our existence.

In contrast to the information we're given about the good folks of Castle Rock or Chester's Mill, we learn nothing of Ralph or Lois's "religious" lives. The language they use initially to describe Clotho, Lachesis, and Atropos tells us they were raised at least nominally Christian, perhaps in the same Methodist church as Eddie Kasprak and his parents. Such religious upbringing as they have shows up in snatches of scripture and bits of hymns dimly remembered, theological Post-It notes that could come as easily from popular culture as from preparation for communion. We know little more than that. Some larger, vaguer vision of The Way Things Are may inform such snippets of god-talk, but we can only infer.

Whatever they *do* think, though, is turned on its head by their first real encounter with the "little bald doctors." All of existence, it seems, "exists" in multilevel, multidimensional forms, each part of the structure determined by its lifespan relative to all others.

"You and Lois and all the other Short-Time creatures," Clotho explains—meaning creatures with terrestrial lifespans, creatures like us—"live on the first two floors of this structure."[73] But this is only the beginning. Later, once the two strange beings have described the nature of death and the afterlife, Clotho urges them, in a passage worth quoting at length,

> Be content with this: beyond the Short-Time levels of existence and the Long-Time levels on which Lachesis, Atropos, and I exist, there are yet other levels. These are inhabited by creatures we could call All-Timers, beings which are either eternal or so close to it as to make no difference. Short-Timers and Long-Timers live in overlapping spheres of existence—or connected floors of the same building, if you like—ruled by the Random and the Purpose. Above these floors, inaccessible to us but very much a part of the same tower of existence live other beings. Some of them are marvelous and wonderful; others are hideous beyond *our* ability to comprehend, let alone yours.[74]

As much as anything, Ralph and Lois are given a sense of the *scale* of existence, a perspective on their place in the universe granted few other "Short-Timers." Our many and varied religious traditions, both the venerable and the venal, the dead gods and the living—all this takes us barely past the rim of the historical horizon, a fraction of the time human beings have been spiritually aware and have wondered about the unseen order. Throughout, as the gods rise and fall, as worshipers gather and cast sidelong glances at anyone else who claims to have the Truth, the relationship between the seen and the unseen is revealed less as a stable framework on which we can rely than an intricate cat's cradle of shifting perceptions, struggles for power, and the changing shape of what we think we know.

"I know you," said the elderly woman in the Sarasota supermarket. "You're Stephen King. You write those scary stories."[75]

It's no secret that we fear what we don't understand. It's a truism so closely bred in the bone that it's almost part of our DNA. Hundreds of thousands of years ago, and for all the millennia since, what we didn't understand could kill us. And it did. And it still can. We learned to fear those who are different from us—not infrequently with good reason. And we passed those fears on to our children, sometimes teaching them openly, other times through story. All the while, we watched to see that they learned. Because learning was survival, and we could drift off into endless sleep secure in the knowledge that we'd done our best to keep the next generation safe. Florida snowbirds "as darkly tanned as a cordovan shoe" may not appreciate the horror fiction of America's dark theologian, but the kinds of storyworlds he weaves matter. They matter immensely. Not because of what they say about him—and he'd likely be the first to admit it—but because of what they say about us, about visions of the unseen order that continue to resonate with us, and that we continue to probe in sacred myth and scary story. For Stephen King, they matter because of the questions we never stop asking, the ones that keep us up at night, staring into the dark, not because we are religious, but because we are human.

NOTES

PREFACE

1 King, *Bazaar of Bad Dreams*, 447.
2 King, *Bazaar of Bad Dreams*, 447.
3 Alastair Harper, "The Only Amazing Thing about Stephen King Is His Ego,"
   Guardian, August 21, 2017, www.theguardian.com.
4 Harold Bloom, "Dumbing Down American Readers," *Boston Globe*, September
   24, 2003, www.boston.com.
5 Bloom, "Dumbing Down American Readers."
6 Bloom, "Dumbing Down American Readers."
7 Bloom, *Stephen King*, 3.
8 See Bourdieu, *Distinction*.
9 King, *Nightmares and Dreamscapes*, 876.
10 Following current anthropological convention, "hominin" refers to modern
   humans, extinct human species, and our nearest evolutionary ancestors. This use-
   fully differentiates us from the more commonly used "hominid," which includes
   great apes in the evolutionary chain.
11 King, *Nightmares and Dreamscapes*, 7.
12 King, *Nightmares and Dreamscapes*, 7.

INTRODUCTION

1 See Boyd, *On the Origin of Stories*; Cron, *Wired for Story*; and Gottschall, *The
   Storytelling Animal*.
2 See George Ratliff, dir., *Hell House* (Cantina Pictures, 2001).
3 King, *Danse Macabre*, 193.
4 Ratliff, *Hell House*.
5 King, *Just after Sunset*, 538.
6 Heidegger, *Heidegger: Basic Writings*, 195.
7 King, *Bazaar of Bad Dreams*, 268.
8 Stephen King, "The Body," in *Different Seasons*, 399.
9 This same interpretive lens could easily be applied, for example, to such horror
   writers as Clive Barker, Algernon Blackwood, Angela Carter, Nick Cutter, James
   Herbert, Shirley Jackson, M. R. James, Edward Lee, H. P. Lovecraft, Arthur Machen,
   and numerous others. Each of these raises the same questions of ultimate meaning,
   and challenges in some way the received answers proffered by organized religion.

10 King, *Danse Macabre*, xiii.

11 See, for example, Atran, *In Gods We Trust*; Boyer, *Religion Explained*; Cowan, *Sacred Terror*; Malinowski, *Magic, Science and Religion*; and Otto, *The Idea of the Holy*.

12 See, for example, Asma, *On Monsters*; Beal, *Religion and Its Monsters*; and Campbell, *The Masks of God*.

13 King, "An Evening at the Billerica Library," in Underwood and Miller, *Bare Bones*, 19.

14 See, for example, Cowan, "Dealing a New Religion"; Steadman, *H. P. Lovecraft*; and Tyson, *Dream World of H. P. Lovecraft*.

15 For in-depth discussions of each, see Cowan, *Sacred Terror*; and Cowan, *Sacred Space*.

16 Cowan, *Sacred Terror*, 51.

17 Prothero, *Religious Literacy*, 1.

18 Pew Research Center, "U.S. Public Becoming Less Religious," November 3, 2015, 3.

19 Stephen King, quoted in Winter, *Faces of Fear*, 242.

20 This is not to suggest that other of King's works, most notably the *Dark Tower* series, would not reward a similar reading. Certainly they would. But, as King himself points out, these novels are solidly in the genre of epic fantasy. Since this book is concerned with his horror fiction, reading *The Dark Tower* as narrative theology must await another day.

21 King, *Just after Sunset*, 537.

22 Cowan, *Sacred Terror*, 17.

23 Stephen King, "N.," in *Just after Sunset*, 297.

24 King, *Just after Sunset*, 537.

25 King, *Danse Macabre*, 41.

CHAPTER 1. AMERICA'S DARK THEOLOGIAN

1 Ingebretsen's *Maps of Heaven and Hell* is something of an exception here. While Ingebretsen does discuss King's work in some detail, particularly *Carrie* and *'Salem's Lot*, his goal is to locate King in the larger sweep of religiously inspired fear that extends from Jonathan Edwards to the late modern horror-meisters.

2 Magistrale, *Landscape of Fear*, 38.

3 Magistrale, *Landscape of Fear*, 37, 40.

4 Magistrale, *Landscape of Fear*, 36.

5 Magistrale, *Landscape of Fear*, 36, 37.

6 King's *Dolores Claiborne*, which as an example of extended first-person narrative is a tour-de-force, is an obvious exception to this, as is his time travel romance, *11/22/63*.

7 King, *Cell*, 82.

8 See Prothero, *Religious Literacy*. For similar discussions in terms of cinema horror, see Cowan, *Sacred Terror*; and for science fiction, see Cowan, *Sacred Space*.

9 Magistrale, *Landscape of Fear*, 37.

10 See Cowan, "Pulp Evangelism"; Frykholm, *Rapture Culture*; Gribben, *Writing the Rapture*; and Shuck, *Marks of the Beast*.

11 In "Structural Characteristics of the Cinematic Christ-Figure," for example, Kozlovic lists more than two dozen ways to identify Christ-figures in film and television, including characters who offer "holy exclamations" such as "'My God!' or 'Oh, God'" or even "Gee!" For a rebuttal of Kozlovic, consider Deacy's "Reflections on the Uncritical Appropriation of Cinematic Christ-Figures."

12 Alber, "Unnatural Narratology," 449.

13 Alber, "Impossible Storyworlds," 80.

14 Boyd, *On the Origin of Stories*, 192.

15 Boyd, *On the Origin of Stories*, 204.

16 Boyd, *On the Origin of Stories*, 204.

17 King, *Girl Who Loved Tom Gordon*, 62.

18 King, *Girl Who Loved Tom Gordon*, 60.

19 King, *Girl Who Loved Tom Gordon*, 60.

20 King, "The Body," 388.

21 King, *Girl Who Loved Tom Gordon*, 68.

22 King, *Girl Who Loved Tom Gordon*, 68.

23 King, *Girl Who Loved Tom Gordon*, 68.

24 King, *Girl Who Loved Tom Gordon*, 69.

25 King, *Girl Who Loved Tom Gordon*, 71.

26 King, *Girl Who Loved Tom Gordon*, 71.

27 King, *Girl Who Loved Tom Gordon*, 72.

28 King, *Girl Who Loved Tom Gordon*, 72.

29 King, *Girl Who Loved Tom Gordon*, 79, 74. Unless otherwise noted, italics in quotations are in the original.

30 James G. Frazer, *The Golden Bough*, in Otto and Stausberg, *Defining Magic: A Reader*, 83.

31 King, *Girl Who Loved Tom Gordon*, 79.

32 King, *Girl Who Loved Tom Gordon*, 79.

33 King, *Girl Who Loved Tom Gordon*, 80.

34 King, *Girl Who Loved Tom Gordon*, 80.

35 King, *Girl Who Loved Tom Gordon*, 80.

36 Vyse, *Believing in Magic*, 4.

37 Vyse, *Believing in Magic*, 5.

38 King, *Girl Who Loved Tom Gordon*, 81.

39 King, *Girl Who Loved Tom Gordon*, 81.

40 King, *Girl Who Loved Tom Gordon*, 85.

41 King tells the story of receiving the news that *Carrie* would be published in paperback, but misreading the contract. His wife, Tabitha, helpfully pointed out that the advance on the paperback edition was not $40,000, but $400,000.

42 King, *Carrie*, 8.

43 King, *Carrie*, 66. N.b., the incorrect grammar in Margaret's explanation is from the original, and could be King signaling her lack of formal education.

44 Ingebretsen, *Maps of Heaven and Hell*, 62, 63.

45 King, *Carrie*, 5.

46 King, *Carrie*, 28.

47 Hogan, *Dark Romance*, 268. It's important to note that Hogan is discussing, however briefly, Brian De Palma's 1976 film adaptation of the novel.

48 Badley, "Sin-Eater," 104.

49 Badley, "Sin-Eater," 118.

50 Davis, *Stephen King's America*, 22.

51 Yarbro, "Cinderella's Revenge," 46–47.

52 Yarbro, "Cinderella's Revenge," 47.

53 Yarbro, "Cinderella's Revenge," 47.

54 On Cinderella and the various ways it has been interpreted, see the work of Jack Zipes, particularly *Breaking the Magic Spell* and *Why Fairy Tales Stick*. See also Cowan, *Magic, Monsters, and Make-Believe Heroes*.

55 King, *Danse Macabre*, 180.

56 See, for example, Lindsey, "Horror, Femininity, and Carrie's Monstrous Puberty"; and Paul, *Laughing Screaming*, esp. 353–80.

57 Gallagher, "Reading between the Lines," 38.

58 Despite the fact that belief has declined in recent years, and "nones" (those who hold to no belief) are growing demographically, according to the Pew Research Center's 2014 U.S. Religious Landscape Study, nearly 90 percent of Americans still hold to belief in God or some kind of universal governing spirit.

59 Stephen King, "That Feeling, You Can Only Say What It Is in French," in *Everything's Eventual*, 454–55.

60 Stephen King, "The Man in the Black Suit," in *Everything's Eventual*, 46, 47.

61 King, "Man in the Black Suit," 38.

62 King, "Man in the Black Suit," 38.

63 King, "Man in the Black Suit," 38.

64 King, "Man in the Black Suit," 38.

65 King, *Under the Dome*, 934.

66 King, "Man in the Black Suit," 36.

67 King, "Man in the Black Suit," 67.

68 King, *Just after Sunset*, 530.

69 See Winter, *Faces of Fear*.

70 King, "Man in the Black Suit," 47.

71 King, "Man in the Black Suit," 51.

72 King, "Man in the Black Suit," 50, 51.

73 King, "Man in the Black Suit," 52.

74 King, "Man in the Black Suit," 51.

75 King, "Man in the Black Suit," 53.

76 King, "Man in the Black Suit," 53.

77 King, "Man in the Black Suit," 63.

78 King, "Man in the Black Suit," 62.

79 King, "Man in the Black Suit," 64.

80 King, "Man in the Black Suit," 63.

81 King, "Man in the Black Suit," 65.

82 King, "Man in the Black Suit," 65.

83 Davies, *The Fifth Business*.

84 King, *Revival*, 1.

85 King, "Man in the Black Suit," 46.

CHAPTER 2. THIN SPOTS

1 King, *Nightmares and Dreamscapes*, 882.

2 Stephen King, "Children of the Corn," in *Night Shift*, 276.

3 Stephen King, quoted in Lehmann-Haupt and Rich, "The Art of Fiction," 469–70.

4 The metataxis of horror invokes a sudden shift in accepted or dominant categories of the sacred, something most often realized through the *inversion* of culturally dominant religious traditions, the *invasion* of other religions, and rendering accepted religious belief and practice *insignificant*. See Cowan, *Sacred Terror*, 61–92.

5 King, "Children of the Corn," 268.

6 King, "Children of the Corn," 256.

7 King, "Children of the Corn," 256.

8 King, "Children of the Corn," 263.

9 King, "Children of the Corn," 263.

10 King, "Children of the Corn," 265.

11 King, "Children of the Corn," 265.

12 King, "Children of the Corn," 267.

13 H. P. Lovecraft, "The Shadow over Innsmouth," in *The Call of Cthulhu*, 277.

14 King, "Children of the Corn," 266.

15 King, "Children of the Corn," 266.

16 King, *Nightmares and Dreamscapes*, 882.

17 King, "Children of the Corn," 276.

18 King, *Nightmares and Dreamscapes*, 4.

19 James, *Varieties of Religious Experience*, 61.

20 King, "Children of the Corn," 265.

21 Lovecraft, "Shadow over Innsmouth," 277.

22 Cowan, *Sacred Terror*, 15.

23 Smith, *Imagining Religion*, 110.

24 King, *Doctor Sleep*, 300.

25 Straub, "Meeting Stevie," 8.

26 Straub, "Meeting Stevie," 8.

27 Straub, "Meeting Stevie," 11.

28 Stephen King, "Crouch End," in *Nightmares and Dreamscapes*, 614–49.

29 King, "Crouch End," 617.

30 In his famous essay "Supernatural Horror in Literature," Lovecraft distinguishes "weird fiction" from straight-up ghost stories, and presages precisely the kind of "fifth-business" storytelling exemplified in the work of Stephen King. "Serious weird stories," Lovecraft writes, are "made realistically intense by close consistency and perfect fidelity to nature except in the one supernatural direction the author allows himself." Lovecraft, *Annotated Supernatural Horror in Literature*, 61.

31 King, *Just after Sunset*, 534.

32 King, *Just after Sunset*, 534.

33 Arthur Machen, "The Great God Pan," in *Three Imposters*, 16.

34 Machen, "Great God Pan," 16.

35 Machen, "Great God Pan," 16.

36 H. P. Lovecraft, "From Beyond," in *Dreams in the Witch House*, 23–29; King, "N.," 272–351.

37 Following Indian folklorist A. K. Ramanujan, a *telling* describes a story for which we have no identifiable *ur*-text, no original to which we can turn for comparison. *Variants*, on the other hand, or *versions* refer to storyworlds for which some identifiable original exists. "Cinderella," for example, in whatever form, is a telling; while there may be culturally canonical forms, the original is lost to us. The many imitators of *Peter Pan*, such as Joel Schumacher's film *The Lost Boys* and Steven Spielberg's *Hook*, are variants. See Ramanujan, "Three Hundred *Ramayanas*."

38 Machen, "Great God Pan," 2.

39 Machen, "Great God Pan," 2.

40 Lovecraft, "From Beyond," 23, 24.

41 Lovecraft, "From Beyond," 24.

42 Lovecraft, "From Beyond," 29.

43 Lovecraft, "From Beyond," 24.

44 In keeping with the intertextual nature of King's work, one of the ways he continually engages his Constant Reader and repays his loyal fans, this article is written by "Julia Shumway," the journalist who appears as a main character in *Under the Dome*.

45 King, "N.," 287.

46 King, "N.," 286, 287.

47 King, "N.," 289.

48 King, "N.," 289–90.

49 Machen, "Great God Pan," 7.

50 King, "N.," 290.

51 King, "N.," 291.

52 King, "N.," 297.

53 King, "N.," 298.

54 King, "N.," 298.

55 King, "N.," 299.

56 King, "N.," 300.

57 Stephen King, "Suffer the Little Children," in *Nightmares and Dreamscapes*, 115.

58 See Craig S. Smith, "A Casualty on Romania's Road Back from Atheism," *New York Times*, July 3, 2005, A3.

59 Cron, *Wired for Story*, 84.

60 King, "Suffer the Little Children," 115.

61 King, "Suffer the Little Children," 116.

62 King, "Suffer the Little Children," 118.

63 King, "Suffer the Little Children," 106.

64 King, "Suffer the Little Children," 108.

65 King, "Suffer the Little Children," 108.

66 Berton, *The Comfortable Pew*.

67 See Cowan, *Sacred Terror*, 167–99; and Laycock, *Dangerous Games*.

68 King, "Suffer the Little Children," 112.

69 King, "Suffer the Little Children," 113.

70 King, "Suffer the Little Children," 113.

71 King, *Nightmares and Dreamscapes*, 880.

72 Stephen King, "Mile 81," in *Bazaar of Bad Dreams*, 5–50.

73 King, "Mile 81," 19.

74 King, "Mile 81," 49.

75 Other novels based either implicitly or explicitly on extraterrestrial contact include *Dreamcatcher*, *From a Buick 8*, and *Under the Dome*.

76 King, *Tommyknockers*, 174.

77 King, *Tommyknockers*, 181.

78 King, *Tommyknockers*, 204.

79 King, *Tommyknockers*, 194.

80 King, *Tommyknockers*, 206.

81 King, *Tommyknockers*, 747.

82 King, *Danse Macabre*, 139.

83 King, *Tommyknockers*, 99.

84 King, *Tommyknockers*, 99.

85 See von Däniken, *Chariots of the Gods?*; and Sitchin's trilogy *12th Planet*; *Stairway to Heaven*; and *Wars of Gods and Men*.

86 Sitchin, *12th Planet*, viii.

87 Tiamat is one of the primordial gods of ancient Mesopotamia, whose story is recorded in the Babylonian creation myth, the *Enûma Elish*.

88 Clarke, "Hazards of Prophecy," 148.

89 Sitchin, *12th Planet*, 4.

90 King, *Tommyknockers*, 183.

91 See Brown, *Channeling Zone*; Gutierrez, *Handbook of Spiritualism and Channeling*; Hill, *Paranormal Media*; and Klimo, *Channeling*.

92 Few of King's fans will have difficulty seeing the connection between Stephen King/Richard Bachman and Thad Beaumont/George Stark.

93 King, *Dark Half*, 264.

94 King, *Dark Half*, 265.

95 King, *Dark Half*, 314.
96 Findley, *Headhunter*, 3.
97 Findley, *Headhunter*, 3.
98 Findley, *Headhunter*, 3.
99 See Funke, *Inkheart*; *Inkspell*; and *Inkdeath*.
100 King, *Nightmares and Dreamscapes*, 10.
101 King, *Dark Half*, 379.

CHAPTER 3. DEADFALL

1 King, *Pet Sematary*, 44.
2 King, *Under the Dome*, 115.
3 King, *Everything's Eventual*, 511.
4 Boyd, *On the Origin of Stories*, 201.
5 Stephen King, "Mister Yummy," in *Bazaar of Bad Dreams*, 354.
6 King, "Mister Yummy," 356.
7 King, "Mister Yummy," 356.
8 King, "Mister Yummy," 352.
9 King, "Mister Yummy," 359.
10 King, "Mister Yummy," 361.
11 King, "Mister Yummy," 361.
12 King, "Mister Yummy," 356.
13 King, *Doctor Sleep*, 139.
14 King, *Everything's Eventual*, 511. Aside from the life of a popular author, a subject to which he returns over and over, and an obvious ambivalence toward academics, this is one of the few times when King's own life maps obviously onto his fiction.
15 Stephen King, "Riding the Bullet," in *Everything's Eventual*, 531.
16 King, "Riding the Bullet," 527.
17 King, "Riding the Bullet," 530.
18 King, "Riding the Bullet," 530.
19 King, "Riding the Bullet," 531.
20 King, "Riding the Bullet," 530.
21 King, "Riding the Bullet," 539.
22 King, "Riding the Bullet," 539.
23 King, "Riding the Bullet," 539.
24 King, "Riding the Bullet," 540.
25 See Brunvard, *Vanishing Hitchhiker*.
26 King, *Everything's Eventual*, 511.
27 Linda Lyons, "Paranormal Beliefs Come (Super) Naturally to Some: More People Believe in Haunted Houses Than Other Mystical Ideas," Gallup poll, November 1, 2005.
28 Lyons, "Paranormal Beliefs."
29 Lyons, "Paranormal Beliefs."

30 Albert L. Winseman, "Eternal Destinations: Americans Believe in Heaven, Hell," *Gallup Poll News Service*, May 25, 2004.

31 Thomas, *Religion and the Decline of Magic*, 701.

32 Thomas, *Religion and the Decline of Magic*, 701.

33 Thomas, *Religion and the Decline of Magic*, 701–2.

34 Stephen King, "1408," in *Everything's Eventual*, 457–510.

35 King, "1408," 469.

36 King, *Just after Sunset*, 533. King was responding to criticism of his novella "Apt Pupil" (*Different Seasons*, 111–290), which concerned, in part, Nazi concentration camps. A Jewish reviewer objected to the story, saying, "It was wrong of me to write about the concentration camps . . . because I was not a Jew. I replied that made writing the story all the more important—because writing is an act of willed understanding."

37 King, *Bazaar of Bad Dreams*, 268.

38 Stephen King, "The Things They Left Behind," in *Just after Sunset*, 261.

39 King, "Things They Left Behind," 250.

40 One of them, though, chooses not to make the journey. Stanley Uris has matured into a successful businessman, but is so shaken by the thought of facing It again that he commits suicide, cutting his wrists lengthwise to ensure that he bleeds out as quickly as possible and with no hope of revival if he's discovered.

41 King, *It*, 175.

42 King, *It*, 243.

43 King, *It*, 244.

44 Cox and Gilberts, *Oxford Book of Ghost Stories*, ix.

45 King, *It*, 315.

46 King, *It*, 315.

47 King, *It*, 315.

48 See Barker, *Haunt of Fears*; and Wright, *Comic Book Nation*.

49 King, *It*, 316.

50 King, *It*, 316.

51 On the Japanese ritual of *mizuko kuyo*, for example, which is performed to placate the spirits of aborted fetuses, stillborn babies, and children who die in infancy, see Hardacre, *Marketing the Menacing Fetus*; and Wilson, *Mourning the Unborn Dead*. For a lighthearted look, see Yoda and Alt, *Yurei Attack!*

52 King, *Pet Sematary*, 305.

53 King, *Pet Sematary*, 175, 176.

54 King, *Pet Sematary*, 193.

55 King, *Pet Sematary*, 262.

56 King, *Pet Sematary*, 262.

57 King, *Pet Sematary*, 262.

58 King, *Pet Sematary*, 262.

59 King, *Pet Sematary*, 263.

60 Bellah et al., *Habits of the Heart*, 221.

61 King, *Pet Sematary*, 347.

62 King, *Pet Sematary*, 496.

63 King, *Tommyknockers*, 386.

64 King, *Dark Half*, 379.

65 If readers are interested in where many of the locations for King's stories are in Maine, King includes a map as a frontispiece to his novel *Dolores Claiborne*. While not every location is plotted, it does help orient readers to many of the King storyworlds.

66 King, *Duma Key*, 551.

67 King, *Bag of Bones*, 122.

68 King, *Bag of Bones*, 125.

69 King, *Bag of Bones*, 125.

70 King, *Bag of Bones*, 125.

71 King, *Bag of Bones*, 125.

72 King, *Bag of Bones*, 129.

73 King, *Bag of Bones*, 156.

74 King, *Bag of Bones*, 486.

75 King, *Bag of Bones*, 485.

76 King, *Bag of Bones*, 487.

77 King, *Bag of Bones*, 522. "The TR" is King's narrative shorthand for "Township Range," the zoning code used in Maine to identify an unincorporated residential area.

78 King, *Bag of Bones*, 488.

79 King, *Bag of Bones*, 490.

80 King, *Danse Macabre*, 4.

81 For discussions of the various sociological uses of these terms, see Cowan, *Bearing False Witness*; Cowan and Bromley, *Cults and New Religions*; and Stark and Bainbridge, *Future of Religion*.

82 King, *Bag of Bones*, 493.

83 King, *Pet Sematary*, 496.

84 On *tapophobia* and our often amusing attempts to manage it, see Bondeson, *Buried Alive*.

85 Stephen King, "Autopsy Room Four," in *Everything's Eventual*, 4.

86 King, "Autopsy Room Four," 4.

87 King, "Autopsy Room Four," 5.

88 Reizler, "Social Psychology of Fear," 490.

89 Stephen King, "Willa," in *Just after Sunset*, 26.

90 King, "Willa," 26.

91 Evans-Wentz, *Tibetan Book of the Dead*, 94.

92 Stephen King, "That Feeling, You Can Only Say What It Is in French," in *Everything's Eventual*, 454–55.

93 King, "That Feeling, You Can Only Say What It Is in French," 453.

94 King, *Everything's Eventual*, 456.

CHAPTER 4. A JUMBLE OF WHITES AND BLACKS

1 King, *Danse Macabre*, 41.
2 See Boyd, *On the Origin of Stories*, 137–38; and Heider and Simmel, "Experimental Study of Apparent Behavior."
3 King, "That Feeling, You Can Only Say What It Is in French," 454–55.
4 King, "That Feeling, You Can Only Say What It Is in French," 455; emphasis added.
5 King, "That Feeling, You Can Only Say What It Is in French," 455.
6 King, "That Feeling, You Can Only Say What It Is in French," 453.
7 Cowan, *Sacred Terror*, 229.
8 King, "That Feeling, You Can Only Say What It Is in French," 454–55.
9 Korzybski, *Science and Sanity*, 58.
10 King, "Willa," 23.
11 Katz, "Language, Epistemology, and Mysticism," 26.
12 King, *Shining*, 411.
13 King, *Shining*, 411.
14 Berger and Luckmann, *Social Construction of Reality*, 15.
15 King, *Shining*, 411–12.
16 Dawkins, *God Delusion*, 318.
17 King, *Shining*, 412.
18 King, *Shining*, 412.
19 King, *Shining*, 412.
20 King, *Shining*, 412.
21 King, *Shining*, 412.
22 King, *Shining*, 412.
23 King, *Shining*, 412.
24 King, *Shining*, 412–13.
25 King, *Shining*, 414.
26 King, *Shining*, 415.
27 M. R. James, "Some Remarks on Ghost Stories," in *Haunted Dolls' House*, 260.
28 King, *It*, 727.
29 King, *It*, 727.
30 For a fascinating (and near exhaustive) consideration of these films, see Bill Warren's two-volume work, *Keep Watching the Skies!*
31 King, *It*, 790.
32 King, *It*, 727.
33 King, *It*, 728.
34 King, *It*, 728.
35 See Cowan, *Remnant Spirit*, esp. 97–124.
36 King, *It*, 175.
37 King, *It*, 634.
38 King, *It*, 634.

39 King, *It*, 919.

40 King, *It*, 919.

41 King, *It*, 920.

42 King, *It*, 920.

43 King, *It*, 919.

44 King, *It*, 920.

45 See Prothero, *Religious Literacy*.

46 King, *It*, 920.

47 King, *It*, 920.

48 King, *It*, 920.

49 King, *It*, 921.

50 King, *It*, 921.

51 King, *It*, 921.

52 King, *Green Mile*, 419–20.

53 See Cowan, "Seeing the Saviour in the Stars."

54 See Kozlovic, "Structural Characteristics of the Cinematic Christ-Figure." For a more critical view, see Deacy, "Reflections on the Uncritical Appropriation of Cinematic Christ-Figures."

55 Christopher John Farley, "That Old Black Magic," *Time*, November 27, 2000, 4.

56 See, for example, Hicks, "Hoodoo Economics"; and Okorafor, "Stephen King's Super-Duper Magical Negroes." It's important to note, as does Heather Hicks, that the role of supporting magical character is not always assigned to persons of color; occasionally, white women are the vehicles for supernatural power, both benevolent and malevolent. Consider, for example, the change Martin Scorsese made in *The Last Temptation of Christ*: In Kazantzakis's novel, the Devil is represented by a small black boy, while the film casts the tempter as a small blonde girl (with an upper-class English accent).

57 Okorafor, "Stephen King's Super-Duper Magical Negroes."

58 Okorafor, "Stephen King's Super-Duper Magical Negroes."

59 Okorafor, "Stephen King's Super-Duper Magical Negroes."

60 On the hero's journey in Hollywood storyworld creation, see Vogler, *Writer's Journey*.

61 King, *Green Mile*, 93.

62 King, *Green Mile*, 190.

63 King, *Green Mile*, 191.

64 King, *Green Mile*, 190, 191.

65 King, *Green Mile*, 191.

66 King, *Green Mile*, 191.

67 King, *Needful Things*, 4.

68 King, *Needful Things*, 4.

69 King, *Needful Things*, 10.

70 Lehmann-Haupt and Rich, "Art of Fiction," 487.

71 King, *Needful Things*, 570.

72 Stone, "Sanctification of Fear," ¶2.

73 King, *Needful Things*, 101.

74 King, *Needful Things*, 107.

75 King, *Needful Things*, 108.

76 King, *Needful Things*, 639.

77 See Cowan, *Bearing False Witness*.

78 Hunt, *In Defense of the Faith*.

79 King, *Needful Things*, 639.

80 King, *Needful Things*, 639.

81 Chaplin [Hyla], *Convent and the Manse*; O'Gorman, *Convent Life Unveiled*; Monk, *Awful Disclosures of Maria Monk*; Dhu, *Stanhope Burleigh*.

82 Dhu, *Stanhope Burleigh*, v.

83 Rhodes, *Reasoning from the Scriptures with Catholics*; White, *Fatal Flaw*; Hunt, *Woman Rides the Beast*. See also Cowan, *Bearing False Witness*, 171–90.

84 Lockwood, "Evolution of Anti-Catholicism," 53; Baldwin, "Pious Prejudice," 55.

CHAPTER 5. RETURN TO ACKERMAN'S FIELD

1 Stephen King, "Rainy Season," in *Nightmares and Dreamscapes*, 460.

2 King, "Rainy Season," 467.

3 King, "Rainy Season," 474.

4 King, "Rainy Season," 476.

5 King, "Rainy Season," 457.

6 King, "Rainy Season," 458.

7 King, "Rainy Season," 460.

8 King, "Rainy Season," 477.

9 King, "Rainy Season," 477.

10 King, "Rainy Season," 478.

11 King, "Rainy Season," 479.

12 Luhrmann, *Persuasions of the Witch's Craft*, 12, 335–52.

13 King, "N.," 298.

14 King, "N.," 302.

15 King, "N.," 304.

16 King, *Shining*, 415.

17 King, "N.," 304.

18 For a variety of perspectives, see Bell, *Ritual*; Jahoda, *Psychology of Superstition*; Smith, *To Take Place*; and Vyse, *Believing in Magic*.

19 King, "N.," 316.

20 King, "N.," 317.

21 James, *Varieties of Religious Experience*, 61.

22 James, *Varieties of Religious Experience*, 36; emphasis in the original.

23 King, "N.," 292.

24 King, "N.," 317. On this, the classic statements are Freud, *Future of an Illusion*; and *Civilization and Its Discontents*.

25 King, "N.," 317.

26 Freud notes that "the analogy between religion and obsessional neurosis" is useful in that "devout believers are safeguarded in a high degree against the risk of certain neurotic illnesses; their acceptance of the universal neurosis spares them the task of constructing a personal one." Freud, *Future of an Illusion*, 56.

27 Freud, *Future of an Illusion*, 56.

28 King, "N.," 302.

29 King, "N.," 302.

30 King, "N.," 316.

31 King, "N.," 317.

32 King, "N.," 316.

33 King, "N.," 318.

34 King, "N.," 325.

35 Turner, *Forest of Symbols*, 97–111; see also Turner, *Ritual Process*, 94–165.

36 Turner, *Ritual Process*, 94.

37 Turner, *Ritual Process*, 94.

38 Turner, *Ritual Process*, 95.

39 King, *Pet Sematary*, 86.

40 King, *Pet Sematary*, 86.

41 King, *Pet Sematary*, 87.

42 King, *Pet Sematary*, 87.

43 King, *Pet Sematary*, 172.

44 King, *Pet Sematary*, 102.

45 King, *Pet Sematary*, 104.

46 King, *Pet Sematary*, 160.

47 King, *Pet Sematary*, 161.

48 King, *Pet Sematary*, 159.

49 King, *Pet Sematary*, 159.

50 King, *Pet Sematary*, 159.

51 King, *Pet Sematary*, 3, 10.

52 King, *Pet Sematary*, 159.

53 King, *Pet Sematary*, 159–60.

54 King, *Pet Sematary*, 161.

55 King, *Pet Sematary*, 162.

56 King, *Pet Sematary*, 163, 164.

57 King, *Pet Sematary*, 164.

58 Eliade, *Patterns in Comparative Religion*, 14.

59 King, *Pet Sematary*, 164.

60 Think, for example, of Carl Sagan's novel *Contact*. As far as astrophysicist Ellie Arroway knows, her journey in The Machine took her to the heart of the galaxy and back in eighteen hours. From the perspective of those in the control room, the entire trip occurs in the two or three seconds it took for The Machine's occupant pod to fall to the steel net strung below the launch gantry. Regardless, no one can

convince Ellie that she had not made the journey, that she has not experienced a different reality. See Sagan, *Contact*, 378–80; and Cowan, *Sacred Space*, 6–10.

61 King, *Pet Sematary*, 165.
62 King, *Pet Sematary*, 165.
63 King, *Pet Sematary*, 165.
64 King, *Pet Sematary*, 166.
65 King, *Pet Sematary*, 166.
66 King, *Pet Sematary*, 166.
67 Richard Matheson, in Winter, *Faces of Fear*, 32.
68 For the classic statements on this, see Durkheim, *Elementary Forms of Religious Life*; and Eliade, *Sacred and the Profane*.
69 King, *Pet Sematary*, 167.
70 King, *Pet Sematary*, 170.
71 Smith, *To Take Place*, 103.
72 Turner, *Ritual Process*, 94.
73 King, *Pet Sematary*, 170.
74 King, *Pet Sematary*, 175.
75 King, *Pet Sematary*, 175.
76 King, *Pet Sematary*, 177.
77 King, *Pet Sematary*, 177.
78 King, *Pet Sematary*, 163, 164.
79 King, *Pet Sematary*, 177.
80 King, *Pet Sematary*, 179.
81 King, *Pet Sematary*, 42, 44.
82 King, *Pet Sematary*, 184.
83 King, *Pet Sematary*, 192.
84 King, *Pet Sematary*, 191.
85 King, *Pet Sematary*, 191.
86 Turner, *Ritual Process*, 95. Here, in the full quote, Turner is distinguishing between ritual and ceremony; the former is "transformative," the latter "confirmatory."

CHAPTER 6. FORTY YEARS IN MAINE

1 King, *Carrie*, 12.
2 King, *Carrie*, 6–7.
3 King, *Carrie*, 16.
4 King, *Carrie*, 17.
5 King, *Carrie*, 24.
6 On pointing out the sins and shortcomings of others as an essential component of religious worldview maintenance, see Cowan, *Bearing False Witness?*; and Cowan, *Remnant Spirit*.
7 King, *Carrie*, 27.
8 King, *Carrie*, 38.

9 Augustine, *Concerning the City of God*, 580, 581. Lest readers think this understanding limited to the early Church, consider Duke University theologian Lauren Winner. "In the Christian grammar," she writes in *Real Sex*, which is subtitled *The Naked Truth about Chastity*, "we have no *right* to sex. The place where the church confers that privilege on you is the wedding; weddings grant us license to have sex with one person. . . . Any other kind of sex is embodied apostasy." *Real Sex*, 123, 124.

10 King, *Carrie*, 38.

11 On the question of suffering in the face of religious duty, see my discussion of the *Babylon 5* episode "Believers," in Cowan, *Sacred Space*, 208–11.

12 King, *Carrie*, 28.

13 King, *Carrie*, 29.

14 King, *Carrie*, 29.

15 King, *Carrie*, 33.

16 King, *Carrie*, 65.

17 In sociological terms, Margaret White's faith reflects what Rodney Stark and William Sims Bainbridge call a "subculture-evolution model" of new religious formation. That is, she has gradually pulled further and further back from the dominant forms of Christianity around her, and formed what they would consider "a novel religious culture," in this case consisting of only herself and her daughter. See Stark and Bainbridge, *Future of Religion*, 183–87.

18 King, *Carrie*, 46.

19 King, *Carrie*, 47.

20 Halle, *Inside Culture*, 171.

21 Halle, *Inside Culture*, 191.

22 King, *Carrie*, 48.

23 See Cowan, *Bearing False Witness?*, 173–78.

24 King, *Carrie*, 48.

25 King, *Carrie*, 48.

26 King, *Carrie*, 48.

27 King, *Carrie*, 29.

28 King, *Carrie*, 67.

29 King, *Carrie*, 70–71.

30 King, *Carrie*, 71.

31 King, *Carrie*, 66.

32 Tertullian, "On the Apparel of Women," book I, chapter 1.

33 King, *Carrie*, 66.

34 King, *Carrie*, 66.

35 King, *Carrie*, 52.

36 King, *Carrie*, 67.

37 King, *Carrie*, 99.

38 King, *Dead Zone*, 51.

39 King, *Dead Zone*, 51.

40 King, *Dead Zone*, 47.

41 King, *Dead Zone*, 47.

42 King, *Dead Zone*, 46.

43 King, *Dead Zone*, 46.

44 King, *Dead Zone*, 52.

45 King, *Dead Zone*, 53.

46 Stark, *What Americans Really Believe*, 77.

47 Stark, *What Americans Really Believe*, 78.

48 Consider, among other things, the ways fundamentalist Christians react to tragedy. Following the September 11 attacks, Jerry Falwell blamed feminists, gays, lesbians, and the American Civil Liberties Union as the reason God removed his protection from the United States. In the wake of Hurricane Katrina, Texas pastor John Hagee claimed that one of the largest natural disasters in American history was sent by God to prevent New Orleans's annual Gay Pride Parade. After the 2010 Haiti earthquake, which killed over 150,000 people and displaced nearly a million, fundamentalist mainstay Pat Robertson that it was God's punishment for a nineteenth-century pact with the Devil made by the Haitian government. Finally, in 2012, after a mass shooting at a Colorado movie theater, fundamentalist Christian Jerry Newcombe told fellow believers that "we're reaping what we've been sowing as a society." "Jerry Newcombe, Evangelical Leader, Says Only Christian Victims of Colorado Shooting Going to Heaven," *Huffington Post*, July 23, 2012.

49 King, *Dead Zone*, 53.

50 King, *Dead Zone*, 53.

51 King, *Dead Zone*, 53.

52 King, *Dead Zone*, 82.

53 King, *Dead Zone*, 103.

54 King, *Dead Zone*, 104.

55 King, *Dead Zone*, 143.

56 King, *Dead Zone*, 79.

57 For the classic discussion of this, see Festinger, Riecken, and Schachter, *When Prophecy Fails*.

58 King, *Dead Zone*, 79.

59 King, *Dead Zone*, 80.

60 King, *Dead Zone*, 80.

61 King, *Dead Zone*, 80.

62 See Stephen King, "The Mist," in *Skeleton Crew*, 24–154. In this story, a dense fog descends on the small town of Bridgeton, Maine, trapping a group of people in a supermarket. Those who try to leave are quickly attacked by horrific flying monsters that seem to have appeared out of nowhere. At one point, Mrs. Carmody, a notorious local fundamentalist, insists that their only path to salvation lies in blood sacrifice.

63 King, *Under the Dome*, 47.

64 King, *Under the Dome*, 48.

65 King, *Under the Dome*, 48, 49.

66 See Cowan, *Sacred Terror*, 61–92.

67 King, *Danse Macabre*, 41.

68 King, *Under the Dome*, 157.

69 See King, "Things They Left Behind," 218–61; King, *Stand*, 918; and King, *Desperation*, 167.

70 King, *Under the Dome*, 157.

71 King, *Under the Dome*, 898.

72 King, *Under the Dome*, 898.

73 King, *Under the Dome*, 934.

74 King, *Under the Dome*, 935.

75 Gottschall, *The Storytelling Animal*, 67.

76 King, *Revival*, 70.

77 King, *Revival*, 68.

78 King, *Revival*, 69.

79 King, *Revival*, 69.

80 King, *Revival*, 69.

81 King, *Revival*, 69.

82 King, *Revival*, 70.

83 King, *Revival*, 70.

84 King, *Revival*, 71.

85 King, *Revival*, 71.

86 King, *Revival*, 71.

87 See Dawkins, *God Delusion*; and Hitchens, *God Is Not Great*. Dawkins is unequivocal on this point. "I am persuaded," he writes in *The God Delusion*, "that the phrase 'child abuse' is no exaggeration when used to describe what teachers and priests are doing to children whom they encourage to believe in something like the punishment of unshriven mortal sins in an eternal hell" (318).

88 King, *Revival*, 72–73.

89 King, *Revival*, 73.

90 King, *Revival*, 168.

CHAPTER 7. IF IT BE YOUR WILL

1 Another significant publishing milestone for King occurred in 1987. That year he released *Misery*, *The Tommyknockers*, *The Drawing of the Three* (the second in his *Dark Tower* series), and the mass market edition of his 1984 fantasy novel *The Eyes of the Dragon*.

2 King, *Desperation*, 182.

3 King, *Desperation*, 158.

4 King, *Desperation*, 172–73.

5 King, *Desperation*, 173.

6 King, *Desperation*, 174.

7 King, *Desperation*, 174.

8 King, *Desperation*, 174.

9 King, *Desperation*, 176.

10 King, *Desperation*, 180.

11 King, *Desperation*, 43.

12 King, *Desperation*, 385.

13 See De Waal, *Bonobo and the Atheist*.

14 King, *Desperation*, 387.

15 King, *Desperation*, 387.

16 King, *Desperation*, 385; emphasis added.

17 King, *Desperation*, 385.

18 King, *Desperation*, 647.

19 King, *Desperation*, 651.

20 King, *Desperation*, 653.

21 King, *Desperation*, 657.

22 King, *Desperation*, 657.

23 King, *Desperation*, 658.

24 Berger, *Sacred Canopy*, 58.

25 King, *Danse Macabre*, 41.

26 King, *Just after Sunset*, 537.

27 King, *Green Mile*, 191.

28 King, *Green Mile*, 529, 530.

29 King, *Green Mile*, 531.

30 King, *Green Mile*, 532.

31 King, *Green Mile*, 532, 533.

32 King, *Green Mile*, 533.

33 King, *Green Mile*, 535.

34 King, "Things They Left Behind," 255.

35 King, "Things They Left Behind," 257.

36 Stephen King, "My Pretty Pony," in *Nightmares and Dreamscapes*, 493.

37 King, "My Pretty Pony," 496.

38 King, "My Pretty Pony," 497.

39 King, "My Pretty Pony," 497.

40 Stone, "Sanctification of Fear," ¶3.

41 Barker, *Hellbound Heart*, 4.

42 Richard Feynman, quoted in Weinberg, *Facing Up*, 233.

43 Stone, "Sanctification of Fear," ¶2.

44 Weinberg, *Facing Up*, 242.

45 King, *Tommyknockers*, 520.

46 King, *Tommyknockers*, 520.

47 King, *Needful Things*, 644.

48 King, *Misery*, 9.

49 King, *Tommyknockers*, 539.

50 King, *Needful Things*, 570.

51 King, *Under the Dome*, 898.

52 King, *Under the Dome*, 898.

53 King, *Under the Dome*, 898.

54 Bonting, "Theological Implications of Possible Extraterrestrial Life," 587; emphases added.

55 Consider astrophysicist Ellie Arroway's response to the Machine Consortium in Robert Zemeckis's film adaptation of Carl Sagan's *Contact*. If she were permitted only one question to ask the extraterrestrials who have made first contact, "I suppose it would be, 'How did you do it?' 'How did you evolve?' 'How did you survive this technological adolescence without destroying yourselves?'"

56 Sagan, *Pale Blue Dot*; King, *Under the Dome*, 914.

57 King, *Under the Dome*, 914.

58 King, *Under the Dome*, 1033.

59 King, *Green Mile*, 535.

60 King, *Desperation*, 617.

61 King, *Desperation*, 618.

62 King, *Desperation*, 621.

63 King, *Desperation*, 621.

64 King, *Desperation*, 621.

65 King, *Desperation*, 458.

66 King, *Revival*, 403.

CHAPTER 8. THE LAND BEYOND

1 King, *From a Buick 8*, 176.

2 See H. P. Lovecraft, "The Colour Out of Space," in *Call of Cthulhu*, 170–99. S. T. Joshi notes that "The Colour Out of Space," published in 1927 in *Amazing Stories* (the first true science fiction pulp), is the first of Lovecraft's stories "to effect that union of horror and science fiction which would become the hallmark of his later work." Lovecraft, *Call of Cthulhu*, 399.

3 King, *From a Buick 8*, 443.

4 King, *From a Buick 8*, 16–17.

5 King, *From a Buick 8*, 140.

6 King, *From a Buick 8*, 216.

7 Carroll, *The Annotated Alice*, 67.

8 King, *Duma Key*, 4.

9 King, *Duma Key*, 4.

10 King, *Duma Key*, 481.

11 King, *Duma Key*, 490.

12 King, *Duma Key*, 538.

13 Haldane, *Possible Worlds*, 286. A similar remark is attributed to astronomer, physicist, and cosmologist Sir Arthur Eddington.

14 King, *Just after Sunset*, 538.

15 Rushdie, "Imagine There's No Heaven," 380.

16 Rushdie, "Imagine There's No Heaven," 381.

17 Hitchens, *God Is Not Great*, 4.

18 King, *It*, 965.

19 King, *It*, 965.

20 King, *It*, 966.

21 Hecht, *Doubt: A History*, xii.

22 From the mid-1920s through the late 1930s, sociologists Robert Staughton Lynd and Helen Merrell Lynd conducted a famous, in-depth case study of Muncie, Indiana, which they renamed in their books "Middletown." They wanted to describe and explain the ways what they considered an "average" American community had responded to the rapid economic, technological, and political changes of recent decades. See Lynd and Lynd, *Middletown*; and *Middletown in Transition*.

23 King (writing as Richard Bachman), *Regulators*, 377.

24 King, *Duma Key*, 544.

25 King, *Duma Key*, 550.

26 King, *Duma Key*, 550.

27 King, *Duma Key*, 551.

28 King, *Duma Key*, 573.

29 King, *Duma Key*, 554.

30 King, *Duma Key*, 554.

31 King, *Duma Key*, 555.

32 King, *Duma Key*, 552.

33 King, *Duma Key*, 572.

34 King, *Duma Key*, 569.

35 King, *Duma Key*, 591.

36 King, *Duma Key*, 591.

37 On this, see H. L. Mencken's famous essay "Memorial Service," originally published in the March 1922 issue of *Smart Set*. Having listed literally dozens of gods, he concludes, "They were gods of the highest standing and dignity—gods of civilized peoples—worshiped and believed in by millions. All were theoretically omnipotent, omniscient and immortal. And all are dead." In *H. L. Mencken on Religion*, 296–97.

38 King, *Duma Key*, 591.

39 Homer, *Odyssey* 11: 628–30.

40 Homer, *Odyssey* 11: 632–33.

41 Homer, *Odyssey* 11: 634–35.

42 King, *Duma Key*, 623.

43 See Cowan, *Sacred Terror*, 109–12.

44 King, *Duma Key*, 627.

45 King, *Duma Key*, 766.

46 For two of the classic statements on this problem, see Berger, *Sacred Canopy*; and Berger and Luckmann, *Social Construction of Reality*.

47 Cowan, *Sacred Terror*, 89.

48 King, *Revival*, 315.

49 King, *Revival*, 168.

50 King, *Revival*, 320.

51 King, *Revival*, 361.

52 King, *Revival*, 73.

53 King, *Revival*, 368.

54 King, *Revival*, 367.

55 King, *Revival*, 373.

56 King, *Revival*, 378.

57 King, *Revival*, 380.

58 King, *Revival*, 382.

59 King, *Revival*, 380.

60 King, *Revival*, 381.

61 King, *Revival*, 394.

62 King, *Revival*, 403.

63 King, "Evening at the Billerica Library," 19.

64 Although secularization theory still clings to life in the academy, for one of the most trenchant critiques, see Jeffrey K. Hadden, "Desacralizing Secularization Theory," in Hadden and Shupe, *Secularization and Fundamentalism Reconsidered*, 3–26.

65 King, "Evening at the Billerica Library," 19.

66 King, "Evening at the Billerica Library," 18.

67 King, *Insomnia*, 282.

68 See Strieber, *Communion*; *Solving the Communion Enigma*; and *Transformation*.

69 King, *Insomnia*, 286.

70 King, *Insomnia*, 521.

71 King, *Insomnia*, 523.

72 King, *Insomnia*, 516.

73 King, *Insomnia*, 519.

74 King, *Insomnia*, 546.

75 King, *Bazaar of Bad Dreams*, 447.

WORKS CITED

Alber, Jan. "Impossible Storyworlds—and What to Do with Them." *Storyworlds: A Journal of Narrative Studies* 1, no. 1 (2009): 79–96.

———. "Unnatural Narratology: The Systematic Study of Anti-Mimeticism." *Literature Compass* 10, no. 5 (2013): 449–60.

Asma, Stephen T. *On Monsters: An Unnatural History of Our Worst Fears*. New York: Oxford University Press, 2009.

Atran, Scott. *In Gods We Trust: The Evolutionary Landscape of Religion*. New York: Oxford University Press, 2002.

Augustine. *Concerning the City of God against the Pagans*. Translated by Henry Bettenson. Harmondsworth, UK: Penguin, 1972.

Badley, Linda. "The Sin-Eater: Orality, Postliteracy, and Early Stephen King." In *Stephen King*, edited by Harold Bloom, 95–124. New York: Chelsea House, 2007.

Baldwin, Lou. "Pious Prejudice: Catholicism and the American Press over Three Centuries." In *Anti-Catholicism in American Culture*, edited by Robert P. Lockwood, 55–88. Huntingdon, IN: Our Sunday Visitor, 2000.

Barker, Clive. *The Hellbound Heart*. New York: HarperPaperbacks, 1986.

Barker, Martin. *A Haunt of Fears: The Strange History of the British Horror Comics Campaign*. London: Pluto, 1984.

Beal, Timothy. *Religion and Its Monsters*. New York: Routledge, 2002.

Bell, Catherine. *Ritual: Perspectives and Dimensions*. New York: Oxford University Press, 1997.

Bellah, Robert N., et al. *Habits of the Heart: Individualism and Commitment in American Life*. Rev. ed. Berkeley: University of California Press, 1996.

Berger, Peter L. *The Sacred Canopy: Elements of a Sociological Theory of Religion*. New York: Anchor, 1967.

Berger, Peter L., and Thomas Luckmann. *The Social Construction of Reality: A Treatise on the Sociology of Knowledge*. Harmondsworth, UK: Penguin, 1966.

Berton, Pierre. *The Comfortable Pew: A Critical Look at Christianity and the Religious Establishment in the New Age*. Toronto: McLelland and Stewart, 1965.

Bloom, Harold, ed. *Stephen King*. Updated ed. Bloom's Modern Critical Views. New York: Chelsea House, 2007.

Bondeson, Jan. *Buried Alive: The Terrifying History of Our Most Primal Fear*. New York: Norton, 2001.

Bonting, Sjoerd L. "Theological Implications of Possible Extraterrestrial Life." *Zygon* 38, no. 3 (2003): 587–602.

Bourdieu, Pierre. *Distinction: A Social Critique of the Judgment of Taste*. Translated by Richard Nice. Cambridge: Harvard University Press, 1984.

Boyd, Brian. *On the Origin of Stories: Evolution, Cognition, and Fiction*. Cambridge, MA: Belknap, 2009.

Boyer, Pascal. *Religion Explained: The Evolutionary Origins of Religious Thought*. New York: Basic Books, 2001.

Brown, Michael F. *The Channeling Zone: American Spirituality in an Anxious Age*. Cambridge: Harvard University Press, 1997.

Brunvard, Jan Harold. *The Vanishing Hitchhiker: American Urban Legends and Their Meanings*. New York: Norton, 1981.

Campbell, Joseph. *The Masks of God*. 4 vols. New York: Penguin, 1959–68.

Carroll, Lewis. *The Annotated Alice: Alice's Adventures in Wonderland and Through the Looking-Glass*. Edited and annotated by Martin Gardner. New York: Norton, 2000.

Chaplin, Jane Dunbar [Hyla]. *The Convent and the Manse*. Boston: Jewett, 1853.

Clarke, Arthur C. "Hazards of Prophecy." In *The Futurists*, edited by Alvin Toffler, 133–50. New York: Random House, 1972.

Cowan, Douglas E. *Bearing False Witness: An Introduction to the Christian Countercult*. Westport, CT: Praeger, 2003.

———. "Dealing a New Religion: Material Culture, Divination, and Hyper-Religious Innovation." In *The Brill Handbook of Hyper-Real Religion*, edited by Adam Possamai, 247–65. Leiden: Brill, 2012.

———. *Magic, Monsters, and Make-Believe Heroes: Fantasy Culture and the Mythic Imagination*. Berkeley: University of California Press, forthcoming.

———. "Pulp Evangelism and Narrative Structure in Evangelical Fiction." In *Border Crossings: Explorations of an Interdisciplinary Historian*, edited by Ulrich van der Heyden and Andreas Feldtkeller, 31–41. Munich: Franz Steiner Verlag.

———. *The Remnant Spirit: Conservative Reform in Mainline Protestantism*. Westport, CT: Praeger, 2003.

———. *Sacred Space: The Quest for Transcendence in Science Fiction Film and Television*. Waco, TX: Baylor University Press, 2010.

———. *Sacred Terror: Religion and Horror on the Silver Screen*. Waco, TX: Baylor University Press, 2008.

———. "Seeing the Saviour in the Stars: Religion, Conformity, and *The Day the Earth Stood Still*." *Journal of Religion and Popular Culture* 21, no. 1. www.usask.ca.

Cowan, Douglas E., and David G. Bromley. *Cults and New Religions: A Brief History*. 2nd ed. Oxford: Wiley Blackwell, 2015.

Cox, Michael, and R. A. Gilberts, eds. *The Oxford Book of Ghost Stories*. New York: Oxford University Press, 1986.

Cron, Lisa. *Wired for Story: The Writer's Guide for Using Brain Science to Hook Readers from the Very First Sentence*. Berkeley: Ten Speed, 2012.

Davies, Robertson. *The Fifth Business*. Toronto: Penguin Canada, 1970.

Davis, Jonathan P. *Stephen King's America*. Bowling Green, OH: Bowling Green State University Popular Press, 1994.

Dawkins, Richard. *The God Delusion*. Boston: Houghton Mifflin, 2006.

Deacy, Christopher. "Reflections on the Uncritical Appropriation of Cinematic Christ-Figures: Holy Other or Wholly Inadequate?" *Journal of Religion and Popular Culture* 13 (2006). www.utpjournals.press/doi/abs/10.3138/jrpc.13.1.001.

De Waal, Frans. *The Bonobo and the Atheist: In Search of Humanism among the Primates*. New York: Norton, 2013.

Dhu, Helen. *Stanhope Burleigh: The Jesuits in Our Homes*. New York: Stringer and Townsend, 1855.

Durkheim, Emile. *The Elementary Forms of Religious Life*. 1912. Translated by Karen E. Fields. New York: Free Press, 1995.

Eliade, Mircea. *Patterns in Comparative Religion*. 1958. Translated by Rosemary Sheed. Lincoln: University of Nebraska Press, 1996.

———. *The Sacred and the Profane: The Nature of Religion*. Translated by Willard R. Trask. San Diego: Harcourt Brace Jovanovich, 1959.

Evans-Wentz, W. Y., ed. *The Tibetan Book of the Dead, or The After-Death Experiences on the* Bardo *Plane, according to Lāma Kazi Dawa-Sandup's English Rendering*. 3rd ed. London: Oxford University Press, 1957.

Festinger, Leon, Henry W. Riecken, and Stanley Schachter. *When Prophecy Fails: A Social and Psychological Study of a Modern Group That Predicted the Destruction of the World*. New York: Harper Torchbooks, 1956.

Findley, Timothy. *Headhunter*. Toronto: HarperCollins, 1993.

Freud, Sigmund. *Civilization and Its Discontents*. 1930. Translated and edited by James Strachey. New York: Norton, 1961.

———. *The Future of an Illusion*. 1927. Translated and edited by James Strachey. New York: Norton, 1961.

Frykholm, Amy Johnson. *Rapture Culture: "Left Behind" in Evangelical America*. New York: Oxford University Press, 2004.

Funke, Cornelia. *Inkdeath*. Translated by Anthea Bell. New York: Scholastic, 2008.

———. *Inkheart*. Translated by Anthea Bell. New York: Scholastic, 2003.

———. *Inkspell*. Translated by Anthea Bell. New York: Scholastic, 2005.

Gallagher, Bernard J. "Reading between the Lines: Stephen King and Allegory." In *The Gothic World of Stephen King: Landscape of Nightmares*, edited by Gary Hoppenstand and Ray B. Brown, 37–48. Bowling Green, OH: Bowling Green State University Popular Press, 1987.

Gottschall, Jonathan. *The Storytelling Animal: How Stories Make Us Human*. New York: Mariner, 2012.

Gribben, Crawford. *Writing the Rapture: Prophecy Fiction in Evangelical America*. New York: Oxford University Press, 2009.

Gutierrez, Cathy, ed. *Handbook of Spiritualism and Channeling*. Leiden: Brill, 2015.

Hadden, Jeffrey K., and Anson Shupe, eds. *Secularization and Fundamentalism Reconsidered*. New York: Paragon House, 1988.

Haldane, J. B. S. *Possible Worlds*. 1927. Reprint. New Brunswick, NJ: Transaction, 2002.

Halle, David. *Inside Culture: Art and Class in the American Home.* Chicago: University of Chicago Press, 1993.

Hardacre, Helen. *Marketing the Menacing Fetus in Japan.* Berkeley: University of California Press, 1997.

Hecht, Jennifer Michael. *Doubt: A History: The Great Doubters and Their Legacy of Innovation from Socrates and Jesus to Thomas Jefferson and Emily Dickinson.* New York: HarperSanFrancisco, 2003.

Heidegger, Martin. *Heidegger: Basic Writings from "Being and Time" (1927) to "The Task of Thinking" (1964).* Edited by David Farrell Krell. Rev. ed. New York: HarperSanFrancisco, 1993.

Heider, Fritz, and Marianne Simmel. "An Experimental Study of Apparent Behavior." *American Journal of Psychology* 57, no. 2 (1944): 243–59.

Hicks, Heather J. "Hoodoo Economics: White Men's Work and Black Men's Magic in Contemporary American Film." *Camera Obscura* 18, no. 2 (2003): 27–55.

Hill, Annette. *Paranormal Media: Audiences, Spirits and Magic in Popular Culture.* New York: Routledge, 2011.

Hitchens, Christopher. *God Is Not Great: How Religion Poisons Everything.* Toronto: McLelland and Stewart, 2007.

Hogan, David J. *Dark Romance: Sexuality in the Horror Film.* Jefferson, NC: McFarland, 1986.

Hunt, Dave. *In Defense of the Faith: Biblical Answers to Challenging Questions.* Eugene, OR: Harvest House, 1996.

———. *A Woman Rides the Beast: The Catholic Church and the Last Days.* Eugene, OR: Harvest House, 1994.

Ingebretsen, Edward J. *Maps of Heaven and Hell: Religious Terror as Memory from the Puritans to Stephen King.* Armonk, NY: M. E. Sharpe, 1996.

Jahoda, Gustav. *The Psychology of Superstition.* Harmondsworth, UK: Penguin, 1969.

James, M. R. *The Haunted Dolls' House and Other Ghost Stories.* Edited by S. T. Joshi. New York: Penguin Classics, 2006.

James, William. *The Varieties of Religious Experience.* 1902. Reprint. New York: Modern Library, 1999.

Katz, Steven T. "Language, Epistemology, and Mysticism." In *Mysticism and Philosophical Analysis,* edited by Steven T. Katz, 22–74. New York: Oxford University Press, 1978.

King, Stephen. *Bag of Bones.* New York: Gallery, 1998.

———. *The Bazaar of Bad Dreams.* New York: Scribner, 2015.

———. *Carrie.* 1974. Reprint. New York: Anchor, 2002.

———. *Cell.* New York: Pocket Star, 2006.

———. *Danse Macabre.* Rev. ed. New York: Gallery, 2010.

———. *The Dark Half.* New York: Signet, 1989.

———. *The Dead Zone.* New York: Signet, 1979.

———. *Desperation.* New York: Viking, 1996.

———. *Different Seasons.* New York: Signet, 1982.

——. *Doctor Sleep*. New York: Scribner, 2013.

——. *Dolores Claiborne*. New York: Viking, 1992.

——. *Dreamcatcher*. New York: Scribner, 2001.

——. *Duma Key*. New York: Pocket Books, 2008.

——. *11/22/63*. New York: Gallery, 2012.

——. *Everything's Eventual*. New York: Pocket Books, 2002.

——. *From a Buick 8*. New York: Pocket Books, 2002.

——. *The Girl Who Loved Tom Gordon*. New York: Pocket Books, 1999.

——. *The Green Mile*. New York: Pocket Books, 1996.

——. *Insomnia*. New York: Gallery, 1994.

——. *It*. New York: Signet, 1980.

——. *Just after Sunset: Stories*. New York: Pocket Books, 2008.

——. *Misery*. New York: Signet, 1987.

——. *Needful Things*. New York: Signet, 1991.

——. *Nightmares and Dreamscapes*. New York: Pocket Books, 1993.

——. *Night Shift*. New York: Doubleday, 1978.

——. *Pet Sematary*. New York: Pocket Books, 1983.

——. *The Regulators* (as Richard Bachman). New York: Gallery, 1996.

——. *Revival*. New York: Gallery, 2014.

——. *The Shining*. 1977. Reprint. New York: Anchor, 2013.

——. *Skeleton Crew*. New York: Signet, 1985.

——. *The Stand*. New York: Anchor, 1990.

——. *The Tommyknockers*. New York: Signet, 1987.

——. *Under the Dome*. New York: Gallery, 2009.

Klimo, Jon. *Channeling: Investigations on Receiving Information from Paranormal Sources*. Rev. ed. Berkeley, CA: North Atlantic Books, 1998.

Korzybski, Alfred. *Science and Sanity: An Introduction to Non-Aristotelian Systems and General Semantics*. 5th ed. Englewood, NJ: Institute of General Semantics, 1958.

Kozlovic, Anton Karl. "The Structural Characteristics of the Cinematic Christ-Figure." *Journal of Religion and Popular Culture* 8 (2004). www.utpjournals.press/doi/abs/10.3138/jrpc.8.1.005.

Laycock, Joseph P. *Dangerous Games: What the Moral Panic over Role-Playing Games Says about Play, Religion, and Imagined Worlds*. Berkeley: University of California Press, 2015.

Lehmann-Haupt, Christopher, and Nathaniel Rich. "The Art of Fiction: Interview with Stephen King." In *The Paris Review Interviews*, 462–500. New York: Picador, 2007.

Lindsey, Shelley Stamp. "Horror, Femininity, and Carrie's Monstrous Puberty." *Journal of Film and Video* 43, no. 4 (1991): 33–44.

Lockwood, Robert P. "The Evolution of Anti-Catholicism in the United States." In *Anti-Catholicism in American Culture*, edited by Robert P. Lockwood, 15–54. Huntingdon, IN: Our Sunday Visitor, 2000.

Lovecraft, H. P. *The Annotated Supernatural Horror in Literature*. Edited by S. T. Joshi. New York: Hippocampus, 2000.

——. *The Call of Cthulhu and Other Weird Stories*. Edited by S. T. Joshi. New York: Penguin, 1999.

——. *The Dreams in the Witch House and Other Weird Stories*. Edited by S. T. Joshi. New York: Penguin, 2004.

Luhrmann, Tanya. *Persuasions of the Witch's Craft: Ritual Magic in Contemporary England*. London: Picador, 1989.

Lynd, Robert S., and Helen M. Lynd. *Middletown: A Study in Modern American Culture*. New York: Harcourt, Brace, 1929.

——. *Middletown in Transition: A Study in Cultural Conflicts*. New York: Harcourt, Brace, 1937.

Machen, Arthur. *The Three Imposters and Other Stories*. Edited by S. T. Joshi. Hayward, CA: Chaosium, 2007.

Magistrale, Tony. *Landscape of Fear: Stephen King's American Gothic*. Madison, WI: Popular Press, 1988.

Malinowski, Bronislaw. *Magic, Science and Religion, and Other Essays*. Garden City, NY: Anchor, 1954.

Mencken, H. L. *H. L. Mencken on Religion*. Edited by S. T. Joshi. Amherst, NY: Prometheus, 2002.

Monk, Maria. *Awful Disclosures of Maria Monk, as Exhibited in Her Sufferings during Her Residence of Five Years as a Novice and Two Years as a Black Nun in the Hotel Dieu Nunnery, at Montreal, Ont*. Rev. ed. New York: Truth Seeker, 1876.

O'Gorman, Edith. *Convent Life Unveiled: Trials and Persecutions of Miss Edith O'Gorman, Otherwise Sister Teresa de Chantal, of St. Joseph's Convent, Hudson City, N.J.* Hartford: Connecticut Publishing Company, 1871.

Okorafor, Nnedi. "Stephen King's Super-Duper Magical Negroes." *Strange Horizons*, October 2004. www.strangehorizons.com.

Otto, Bernd-Christian, and Michael Stausberg, eds. *Defining Magic: A Reader*. Bristol, CT: Equinox, 2013.

Otto, Rudolf. *The Idea of the Holy*. 1923. Translated by John W. Harvey. Reprint. London: Oxford University Press, 1950.

Paul, William. *Laughing Screaming: Hollywood Horror and Comedy*. New York: Columbia University Press, 1994.

Possamai, Adam, ed. *Handbook of Hyper-Real Religions*. Leiden: Brill, 2012.

Prothero, Stephen. *Religious Literacy: What Every American Needs to Know—and Doesn't*. New York: HarperSanFrancisco, 2007.

Ramanujan, A. K. "Three Hundred *Ramayanas*: Five Examples and Three Thoughts on Translation." In *Many "Ramayanas": The Diversity of a Narrative Tradition in South Asia*, edited by Paula Richman, 22–49. Berkeley: University of California Press, 1991.

Reizler, Kurt. "The Social Psychology of Fear." *American Journal of Sociology* 49, no. 6 (1944): 489–98.

Rhodes, Ron. *Reasoning from the Scriptures with Catholics*. Eugene, OR: Harvest House, 2000.

Rushdie, Salman. "Imagine There's No Heaven: A Letter to the Six Billionth World Citizen." In *The Portable Atheist: Essential Readings for the Non-Believer*, edited by Christopher Hitchens, 380–83. Philadelphia: Da Capo, 2007.

Sagan, Carl. *Contact*. New York: Pocket Books, 1985.

———. *Pale Blue Dot: A Vision of the Human Future in Space*. New York: Ballantine, 1994.

Shuck, Glenn W. *Marks of the Beast: The "Left Behind" Novels and the Struggle for Evangelical Identity*. New York: New York University Press, 2005.

Sitchin, Zecharia. *The Stairway to Heaven: Book II of the Earth Chronicles*. New York: Avon, 1980.

———. *The 12th Planet*. New York: Avon, 1976.

———. *The Wars of Gods and Men: Book III of the Earth Chronicles*. New York: Avon, 1985.

Smith, Jonathan Z. *Imagining Religion: From Babylon to Jonestown*. Chicago: University of Chicago Press, 1982.

———. *To Take Place: Toward Theory in Ritual*. Chicago: University of Chicago Press, 1987.

Stark, Rodney. *What Americans Really Believe*. Waco, TX: Baylor University Press, 2008.

Stark, Rodney, and William Sims Bainbridge. *The Future of Religion: Secularization, Revival, and Cult Formation*. Berkeley: University of California Press, 1985.

Steadman, John L. *H. P. Lovecraft and the Black Magickal Tradition*. San Francisco: Weiser, 2015.

Stone, Bryan P. "The Sanctification of Fear: Images of the Religious in Horror Films." *Journal of Religion and Film* 5, no. 2 (2001). www.unomaha.edu.

Straub, Peter. "Meeting Stevie." In *Fear Itself: The Horror Fiction of Stephen King, 1976–1982*, edited by Tim Underwood and Chuck Miller, 7–13. London: Pan Books, 1982.

Strieber, Whitley. *Communion*. New York: Avon, 1987.

———. *Solving the Communion Enigma: What Is to Come*. New York: Tarcher/Penguin, 2011.

———. *Transformation: The Breakthrough*. New York: Beech Tree, 1988.

Thomas, Keith. *Religion and the Decline of Magic: Studies in Popular Beliefs in Sixteenth- and Seventeenth-Century England*. Harmondsworth, UK: Penguin, 1971.

Turner, Victor. *The Forest of Symbols: Aspects of Ndembu Ritual*. Ithaca: Cornell University Press, 1967.

———. *The Ritual Process: Structure and Anti-Structure*. Ithaca: Cornell University Press, 1969.

Tyson, Donald. *The Dream World of H. P. Lovecraft: His Life, His Demons, His Universe*. Woodbury, MN: Llewellyn, 2010.

Underwood, Tim, and Chuck Miller, eds. *Bare Bones: Conversations on Terror with Stephen King*. London: New English Library, 1988.

Vogler, Christopher. *The Writer's Journey: Mythic Structure for Writers*. 3rd ed. Studio City, CA: Michael Wiese Productions, 2007.

von Däniken, Erich. *Chariots of the Gods? Unsolved Mysteries of the Past.* Translated by Michael Heron. London: Corgi, 1968.

Vyse, Stuart A. *Believing in Magic: The Psychology of Superstition.* New York: Oxford University Press, 1997.

Warren, Bill. *Keep Watching the Skies! American Science Fiction Movies of the Fifties.* Jefferson, NC: McFarland, 1982, 1986.

Weinberg, Steven. *Facing Up: Science and Its Cultural Adversaries.* Cambridge: Harvard University Press, 2001.

White, James R. *The Fatal Flaw: Do the Teachings of Roman Catholicism Deny the Gospel.* Southbridge, MA: Crowne, 1990.

Wilson, Jeff. *Mourning the Unborn Dead: A Buddhist Ritual Comes to America.* New York: Oxford University Press, 2009.

Winner, Lauren. *Real Sex: The Naked Truth about Chastity.* Grand Rapids, MI: Brazos, 2005.

Winter, Douglas E. *Faces of Fear: Encounters with the Creators of Modern Horror.* New York: Berkley, 1985.

Wright, Bradford W. *Comic Book Nation: The Transformation of Youth Culture in America.* Baltimore: Johns Hopkins University Press, 2001.

Yarbro, Chelsea Quinn. "Cinderella's Revenge: Twists on Fairy Tale and Mythic Themes in the Work of Stephen King." In *Fear Itself: The Horror Fiction of Stephen King, 1976–1982,* edited by Tim Underwood and Chuck Miller, 45–55. London: Pan Books, 1982.

Yoda, Hiroko, and Matt Alt. *Yurei Attack! The Japanese Ghost Survival Guide.* North Clarendon, VT: Tuttle, 2012.

Zipes, Jack. *Breaking the Magic Spell: Radical Theories of Folk and Fairy Tales.* Rev. ed. Lexington: University of Kentucky Press, 2002.

———. *Why Fairy Tales Stick: The Evolution and Relevance of a Genre.* New York: Routledge, 2006.

INDEX

afterlife, 10, 61, 64–68, 82, 86, 89–90, 206–7; belief in, 68–70. *See also* death; ghosts

agnosticism, 19, 20

Alber, Jan, 16

Alien, 99

Aliens, 181–82

allegory, 14–15, 37, 40, 57, 105, 110, 116, 199

Andrews, V. C., 31, 70

apocalyptic literature, 14–15, 24, 171, 172

arachnophobia, 23

atheism, 158–59, 162

Augustine, 142, 166, 224n9

"Autopsy Room Four," 84–85, 86, 90

availability heuristic, 68

Bag of Bones, 77–84, 106, 195

Bakker, Jim, 110

Baptist Church, 37–39, 41–42, 80, 82–83, 100, 107–8, 109–14, 142–43, 152, 161, 179, 200

Barker, Clive, 178

Berger, Peter, 172

Berton, Pierre, 52

Bible, 4, 14, 33, 38, 54, 74, 99, 152, 170; as talisman, 33, 35

Bloom, Harold, xi

"Body, The," 5, 18

Bonting, Sjoerd, 182–83

Book of the Dead, The, Egyptian, 90; Tibetan, 85–86

Boston Red Sox, ix, 21–22, 120

Bourdieu, Pierre, 11

Boyd, Brian, 16–17, 64

Buddhism, 8, 11, 28, 42, 44, 52, 74, 76, 91, 92, 172; Tibetan (Yogacara), 85–87, 88–89, 90

Carrie, x, xiv, 5, 6, 13, 23–27, 35, 103, 139–48, 193, 194, 210n1, 211n41, 212n43; and religious experience, 139–48; as Cinderella tale, 25–26; DePalma film, x

Carroll, Lewis, 188

Chernobyl, 57

children, 18, 37; and religious socialization, 11, 34, 38, 83, 92–94, 98–104, 114, 161–62, 208; as monsters, 36–39, 50–53; as victims, 42–43, 50–53, 73–75, 81, 161, 200

"Children of the Corn," 4, 27, 36–39, 41, 54

Christianity, 13–14, 29–30, 42, 52, 105, 207; and *Carrie*, 139–48; and Christ-figures, 104–105, 165, 193, 211n11; and *The Dead Zone*, 148–56; and death, 64, 70, 74, 82; conflict within, 109–114; fundamentalist, 3–4, 6, 14–15, 37, 42, 54, 107–9, 172, 195, 224n9; and *Revival*, 159–64; and *Under the Dome*, 156–59, 182, 183

Christine, 136

Clarke, Arthur C., 58

Congregationalist Church, 142, 156–57

cosmology, 19, 28, 38, 82, 83, 118, 156–57, 158; and *Duma Key*, 189–90, 195–201; and *Insomnia*, 204–8; and *It*, 191–92; and *The Regulators*, 192–95; and *Revival*, 201–204

coulrophobia, 23

"Crouch End," 49

Cujo, 109

Däniken, Erich von, 57, 68

Danse Macabre, 5, 11, 26, 56, 88, 157, 173

Dark Half, The, 60–62, 78, 109

ABOUT THE AUTHOR

Douglas E. Cowan is Professor of Religious Studies and Social Development Studies at Renison University College. He is the author of *Sacred Terror: Religion and Horror on the Silver Screen* and *Sacred Space: The Quest for Transcendence in Science Fiction Film and Television*. He lives in Waterloo, Ontario, Canada.